Liberal realism

MANCHESTER
1824

Manchester University Press

Liberal realism

A realist theory of liberal politics

Matt Sleat

Manchester University Press

Published by Manchester University Press
Altrincham Street, Manchester M1 7JA, UK
www.manchesteruniversitypress.co.uk

British Library Cataloguing-in-Publication Data is available

ISBN 978 0 7190 8890 2 hardback

ISBN 978 1 5261 2281 0 paperback

First published by Manchester University Press in hardback 2013

This edition first published 2017

The publisher has no responsibility for the persistence or accuracy of URLs for any external or third-party internet websites referred to in this book, and does not guarantee that any content on such websites is, or will remain, accurate or appropriate.

Printed by Lightning Source

Liberalism – it is well to recall this to-day – is the supreme form of generosity; it is the right which the majority concedes to minorities and hence it is the noblest cry that has ever resounded in this planet. It announces the determination to share existence with the enemy; more than that, with an enemy that is weak. It was incredible that the human species should have arrived at so noble an attitude, so paradoxical, so refined, so acrobatic, so anti-natural. Hence, it is not to be wondered at that this same humanity should soon appear anxious to get rid of it. It is a discipline too difficult and complex to take firm root on earth.

José Ortega y Gasset, *The Revolt of the Masses*

Contents

Acknowledgements

This book has taken me a couple of years to write and I have benefited from the generous assistance and help of several people along the way, all of whom I would like to take this opportunity to thank. I am fortunate enough to be part of a Department where collegiality and a collaborative research culture are not embellishments for our REF submissions but accurately reflect my experience since joining the University of Sheffield in 2007. My colleagues, past and present, including Garrett Brown, Alasdair Cochrane, Inanna Hamati-Ataya, Graham Harrison, Mike Kenny, and Andrew Vincent, are all scholars in the truest and best sense of the term. All of them have had to tolerate, some more willingly than others, numerous papers, draft chapters, or general discussions about realism, and I am indebted to each and every one of them. Some of this material has also been presented at several conferences or workshops over the years, and I would like to thank those who attended and offered comments, in particular Alex Bavister-Gould, John Dunn, Derek Edyvane, Elizabeth Frazer, Ed Hall, John Horton, Glen Newey, Jon Parkin, Janosch Prinz, Enzo Rossi, Steve Smith, and Tim Stanton. Special thanks are owed to Rob Lamb who very kindly organised a symposium on the manuscript for this book at the University of Exeter in December 2012. I am very grateful to all those who participated in the symposium for their comments and feedback, and especially to Richard Bellamy from whose observations I benefited enormously.

While this manuscript bears little relation to my PhD thesis, nevertheless one of the central ideas here – that liberalism is unable to fully comprehend its own contested and partisan nature, and hence of politics properly understood – is one that I was struggling to both understand and express during my time as a research student at the University of York. The Morrell Centre of Toleration at the University of York remains one of the most vibrant and active hubs of research in political theory in the UK, and it was a truly wonderful and privileged place to undertake a PhD. I would like to thank my PhD supervisors Susan Mendus and Matt Matravers for their generosity in terms of time, advice and, in particular, patience.

The writing of this monograph has also coincided with several changes in my personal life, the most important and happiest of which was my marriage to Nicola in November 2010. She has had to live and breathe this book with me, and her tolerance and support have been invaluable. I cannot thank her enough.

But I want to dedicate this book to my parents, Ian and Edwina Sleat. My previous attempt at a dedication to express my appreciation for their support was woefully inadequate, for which I apologise profusely. So this time I will simply say, though from the bottom of my heart: thank you.

Introduction
The resurgence of realist political theory

For more than a hundred years, the reality of conflict had been spirited out of sight by political thinkers of Western civilisation. The men of the nineteen-thirties returned shocked and bewildered to the world of nature.
E. H. Carr[1]

Events at the beginning the twenty-first century, in particular the terrorist atrocities in New York, Madrid, and London, have forced us to recognise the presence of radical political disagreement. In the context of the international sphere, and especially during the Cold War, no one could deny the existence of outsiders who rejected liberalism in favour of anti-liberal forms of political association such as communism, theocracy, or some variation of totalitarianism. Yet it is only recently that we have become more sensitive to the fact of radical political disagreement and conflict, the presence of often not insignificant minorities who endorse non- or anti-liberal political ideals, *within* liberal states. Correspondingly, whereas much recent contemporary liberal political theory has hitherto taken place against the assumed social backdrop of peace, stability, and widespread consensus around liberal values, increased awareness of dissent from liberalism within liberal societies has cast significant doubt on the validity of these assumptions. It is in this political context that a burgeoning interest in realist political theory has arisen.

As the term suggests, there is a sense in which realism claims to stand in a close relationship to, or is sensitive to the facts of, political reality. Other theories, liberalism included, fail to take into account important truths about politics and, in doing so, provide either an incomplete account of the political or one that cannot be suitably normative and action-guiding for us when considering how to act. The reality of political life is simply very different from what liberal political theory has taken it to be.[2] Where liberals have assumed peace, stability, and a consensus on liberal values, at the heart of realism is a vision of the political in which disagreement and conflict over all political questions, including the most important and fundamental such as the terms that govern our shared political association, is an essential, inevitable, and ineradicable feature of politics. While realism accepts Max Weber's notion that politics is a struggle for power, or for influence over how power is distributed, between those who disagree about values, ends, and meanings, it also recognises that politics is about finding ways of living together with those with whom we have such differences.[3] Politics is an activity that takes place in circumstances of radical disagreement, discord, and disharmony yet which enables or facilitates stability and order. And it is this account of politics that makes realism a political theory for our time.

In the intellectual context of a growing dissatisfaction with the so-called 'high liberal theory' exemplified by the work of Anglo-American theorists such as John Rawls and Ronald Dworkin that has dominated the discipline for several decades, it has been the work of Bernard Williams and Raymond Geuss that has probably done the most to thrust realist political thought back into the academic spotlight.[4] Well-known review articles by William Galston and Marc Stears have also been crucial in interpreting a body of contemporary work that shares several similar themes, characteristics or assumptions that can plausibly be thought of as realist. These have included several contemporary theorists beyond Williams and Geuss who have never conceived of themselves as realists (and possibly never will).[5] While realism is an umbrella term which brings together the work of a diverse range of political theorists, it is not an umbrella that many have chosen to walk under.[6] They might be other things, agonists for instance, critical theorists, republicans, or even liberals (albeit somewhat disillusioned ones), but few use the term realist to describe their theories.[7] Neither do these theorists always recognise each other as fellow travellers under the same (realist) umbrella. Like any category, realism is one that has been constructed, that stands in need of interpretation and hides a plethora of different and sometimes contradictory voices. Nevertheless, realists do share a similar set of concerns and theoretical assumptions.[8] Furthermore, they almost all appeal to or engage with one or more of the key theorists in the realist canon, Thucydides, Machiavelli, Hobbes, Hume, Nietzsche, Weber, and Schmitt most notably.[9] So while in the face of this body of disparate and often disconnected work it would be wrong to pretend that there is anything resembling a single theory of political realism, it is still possible to speak meaningfully of this contemporary literature as realist.

Politics looks fundamentally different if viewed through this realist rather than a liberal lens. As I hope to demonstrate in this monograph, realism represents a profoundly different vision of the political from contemporary liberalism. At the most fundamental level, realism emphasises political conflict, disagreement, and discord where liberalism highlights political consensus, agreement, and harmony. Though these theoretical differences have not led contemporary realists to reject liberal political practices and institutions (Carl Schmitt and his admirers the notable exception), there is a strong recurring theme which insists that liberal theory is ill-suited to our current social and political context, and of radical political, not just moral and religious, disagreement in particular. The focus of much realism has therefore been to provide a theory of the political that allows us to properly understand and hence defend the conditions necessary for liberal politics, and possibly even the flourishing of liberal states. To paraphrase Duncan Bell, it strives to balance liberal politics on realist foundations.[10] This monograph is intended to make a contribution very much in this spirit. Its primary objective is to present an outline of a theory of politics that is realistic yet still recognisably liberal; hence it is a theory of liberal realism.

Looking at politics through the realist lens allows us to focus on those aspects of politics that help us better understand the nature of political disagreement, how we should understand liberalism in light of this context of political conflict rather than consensus, and the mechanisms and institutions through which liberal politics can best respond to it.[11] In other words, a more realist liberalism will hopefully put liberal politics on a firmer, more appropriate, set of theoretical foundations for the twenty-first century. But there might be one prima facie reason for doubting the plausibility of such an account. As Stephen Holmes has argued, several of the most profound thinkers of modernity who made claims to be more realistic about the nature of politics have been thoroughly anti-liberal.[12] Indeed, many of the main figures in the realist canon, such as Machiavelli, Hobbes, Nietzsche, and Schmitt were profoundly critical of liberalism and continue to influence numerous contemporary critics of both liberal theory and politics. We might think, therefore, that realism is intrinsically opposed to liberalism and that, as such, the sort of realistic account of liberal theory that I seek to develop here is doomed to fail from the start.

This would be premature, if not a mistake. It is probably going too far to say, with Michael C. Williams, that 'Realism is not opposed to liberalism: it is a form of liberalism' but it is nevertheless true that many realists, classical and contemporary, have sought to pursue realist avenues of inquiry precisely because they want to better shore up and provide intellectual and practical defence for liberal politics.[13] They are, to adopt Williams' term, 'wilful' realists in that they seek to 'construct a viable, principled understanding of modern politics, and to use this understanding to avoid its perils and achieve its promise', more often than not specifically in relation to a recognisably liberal form of politics.[14] What I present here might be thought of as a form of this 'wilful realism': I want to use some of the insights of realist political thought, especially the recognition of the conflictual dimensions of politics and the ramifications of this for how we should think about the normative foundations of political associations, the role of power, and the conditions of legitimacy, so as to provide a more realistic account of liberal theory. I am not one of those theorists who think that the fate of liberal politics will be decided on the battlefield of academia. But I do believe that the way we think about politics matters in the sense that the theoretical and normative assumptions and framework that we adopt both illuminate and obscure, emphasise and minimise, particular aspects and facets of the political world. And, in a context in which political, economic, social, and technological developments move more rapidly than ever before, the capacity for politics to be able to respond to these is, at least in some part, determined by the ability of political theory to help us re-think politics in a manner befitting the needs of the day.

In this sense I endorse also E. H. Carr's understanding of the impact of realism. It is not that realism is necessarily an alternative to the aspirations of utopianism, in this case of liberal ideals, but is rather the realisation of the forces and realities with which we must struggle in order to realise those ideals in the twenty-first century: 'The impact of thinking upon wishing which … follows the breakdown of its first visionary projects, and marks the end of its specifically utopian period, is commonly called realism'.[15] Both utopianism and realism have their place in political thinking. But just as Carr argued that the international order had to accept the role of conflict and power in order both to understand the failings of the utopian projects of the inter-war period and to put those aspirations on a sounder foundation in the future, so liberalism has to re-think the nature of its own foundations so as to make it better able to survive, flourish, and meet the challenges of radical political disagreement. In this sense, realism is best understood as a critical tool of the present but not one that is antithetical to normative or utopian aspirations.[16] Indeed, as I shall argue, and again taking my lead from Carr, it would be an incomplete, unattractive, and unrealistic realism that ignored the role of such idealism in our political lives.

Building on this, if the primary objective of this monograph is to present what I take to be the most plausible and attractive account of a more realistic theory of liberal politics, then the secondary aim is to demonstrate that realism represents a complete and compelling vision of politics in its own right, and hence is not merely a critical theory that seeks to act as a corrective to other political theories, as some have claimed. As Galston states, 'it isn't yet clear whether realism is essentially critical and cautionary, a warning against liberal utopianism, as opposed to a coherent affirmative alternative'.[17] In a sense what

I want to suggest throughout is a middle-ground understanding of the status of realism: realism is an alternative and more plausible vision of the political upon which many substantive accounts, liberalism being but one of them, can be built. It is therefore critical in the sense of challenging liberalism but affirmative in the sense that it offers the foundations for developing a more plausible liberal theory in the context of radical political disagreement. Or so I hope to demonstrate. Furthermore, I want to convince the reader, if he or she is not already so inclined to think, that realism does indeed represent an urgent and pressing challenge to liberal theory that pushes it on several of its most fundamental assumptions. As such, whether or not readers agree with the direction in which I travel here, the aim is to assure them that there is a real problem, or maybe set of problems, that liberals need to pay more attention to than they hitherto have.

Before setting out, it would be useful to briefly discuss three aspects of the way I understand and employ realist theory in this monograph, which will hopefully explain in a little more detail what I take realism to be (or not to be) as well as why my line of inquiry takes the particular form it does: the relationship between realism and normative political theory, realism and the ideal/non-ideal theory debate, and realism and international political realism.

Realism as political understanding

Realism is often regarded as being an essentially descriptive theory that aims to accurately reflect the true nature of politics, focusing particularly on the realities of power, conflict, and coercion in political life. In such a theory, it is unclear what place, if any, there can be for the sort of normative theorising that characterises other political theories, including liberalism. As Mark Philp put it, 'People worry about realism that what it gains from focusing on the realities of political power tends to be outweighed by the loss of critical distance involved in jettisoning the standard normative commitments of liberalism'.[18] This ambiguity has allowed realism to be interpreted and dismissed by hostile liberals as solely engaged in a descriptive enterprise, and hence the challenge that realism poses is deemed to be irrelevant to liberalism's normative tasks of setting out a framework for how our political world *should* be rather than how it actually *is*. Realists are, on this account, guilty of getting their ises and oughts mixed up.

It is worth noting that there are several realists who do seek to make some quite substantive normative political recommendations, the agonists (such as Chantal Mouffe, James Tully, and William Connolly) and international realists most obviously. Realists themselves rarely think they are merely doing descriptive work. Moreover, to ask whether realism is descriptive or normative is, from the perspective of many realists, a false dichotomy, one which attempts to impose upon realist political thought a distinction which it does not recognise to be particularly useful.[19] The attempt to get our understanding of politics right serves an important normative function. This is emphasised most strongly in the work of John Dunn and Glen Newey. As they understand it, the attempt to put political theory in touch with the realities of political life is not simply an end in itself, but is seen as a necessary step in order to help us think more clearly and in ways more attuned to the specificity of politics, a necessary precondition, one would think, for doing any political theory whatsoever, including of the normative variety. Dunn writes, and in a passage worth quoting in its entirety:

> If the key to politics really is how human beings see their world and how they try to bend this to their wills, it is vital to judge how far they see that world accurately and how far the ways in which they wish to alter it are ways in which it can in practice be altered. Insofar as they fail to see it accurately, they can scarcely hope to understand what they are doing; and they are exceedingly unlikely to alter it even broadly as they wish. Today we are pretty confident that the line between true and false beliefs about politics is not a clear and bright one, and that there is no single authoritative site, no privileged human or supra-human but humanly accessible, vantage point from which it can be identified decisively or once and for all ... Only utter confusion, however, could possibly lead us to believe that there is no distinction between true and false beliefs about politics, or that false beliefs about politics will not, in most instances and over enough time, do great harm to their human believers or others whom they affect ... This is discouraging, since the most casual inspection of politics in action, or the most desultory attention to most people's political beliefs, shows at once that a very large proportion of political beliefs are predominantly false. Dispiriting or not, however, one thing which they could not reasonably discourage is the attempt to understand politics better.[20]

Newey, whose work is highly critical of contemporary normative theorising and has been frequently disparaged for lacking its own prescriptive recommendations, explicitly attacks and attempts to rectify what he calls the 'explanatory insufficiency' of contemporary liberal theory which, he believes, leaves it unable to properly understand actual political practice.[21] Yet the point of this debunking exercise is not simply for the sake of obtaining a more accurate description of politics but to equip us with an appropriate understanding of politics which can then provide the basis for our thinking about a variety of different political problems. Indeed, he believes that once political theory is better grounded in a more appropriate understanding of politics itself, it will allow us to fruitfully apply our theoretical tools to a much wider set of political issues than our current conception allows for.[22]

One way to characterise realist political theory is as an exercise in political understanding. Such understanding does not preclude the possibility of making normative political prescriptions, but does require that any such recommendations be grounded in as descriptively and explanatorily accurate a vision of politics as we can muster. To give but a few examples of the sort of political truths that realists believe must be taken more seriously: they urge us to start our theorising not from people's motivations as they should be in a morally ideal world, but as they actually are, capturing the plethora of reasons, self-interested and moral, that prompt people to action or obedience.[23] We must avoid falling into the trap of speaking about legislation as if it arises from the will of a single person, when all legislative bodies are made up of many people representing a plurality of different and conflicting interests and views.[24] Likewise, we need to recognise that the legislative process is a somewhat murkier business than one enlightened sovereign coming to a decision after following the correct rational procedure, and that legislation (in democracies at least) is passed on the basis of voting and majority-decisions, with all the arbitrariness that this allows for.[25] Importantly, we need to be attentive to the fact that there is a big gap between developing a theory and putting it into practice, a gap which, even with the best will in the world, inevitably distorts political ambitions 'into standardised, hegemonic, bureaucratic nightmares through the machinery of a modern state controlled by particular groups who interpret ideals through the lens of their own particular interests even when they are attempting to serve the common good'.[26] More basic than that, theory needs to remember that political ambitions need to be implemented and can only be so via already existing political processes. This means that there are limits to what it is politically possible to enact at any given time, maybe even limits to what can ever be enacted. In our case, this means that theory needs to be more sensitive to the possibility of its normative recommendations successfully making it through the rigors of our democratic processes, internalising the recognition that all policies inevitably undergo amendments as a result of the sort of compromise and concessions democratic politics necessitates.

As Dunn has forewarned, it is very likely that the pursuit of this sort of political understanding is liable to diminish political optimism.[27] Once such facts are fully recognised it is to be expected that it will have an effect on what one thinks it is realistic to hope for politically.[28] But the realist intention is not to undermine political hope and the possibility of a better political future completely, only to direct such aspirations into more realistic goals. The high premium realism places on, as Dunn would put it, ensuring we have true beliefs about politics, and hence on the ambition of descriptive and explanatory accuracy, inevitably means that the sort of normative theorising consistent with it is relatively modest. But this is not the same as saying that realism cannot make any normative prescriptions at all. So while the normative ambitions of political theory might be reined in somewhat by realism's concern for descriptive accuracy and the realities of our political experience, we should not mistake this as undermining the prospects of normative political theorising per se but as an attempt to replant it in an understanding of politics likely to bear more pertinent fruit.

Of course, one might respond to all this by saying that realists are simply barking up the wrong tree and that the question of whether, for example, the true conception of justice could be implemented here and now is simply irrelevant to the theorist's task of addressing the age-old question 'What is justice?'. I do not want to make the strong claim that political theorists should essentially give up such grand normative undertakings completely. I do not think realism needs to be committed to this position and indeed I think one of realism's most distinctive characteristics can be identified in a more nuanced response to this criticism which returns to the centrality of conflict in its account of the political. Relying on a distinction made by Jeremy Waldron, we can say that there are two tasks for political philosophy: i) theorising about justice (or rights, the common good, etc.), and ii) theorising about politics.[29] Those who are engaged in the first task are attempting to set out what they take to be the most theoretically consistent, compelling, and persuasive account of justice. Such theorists will inevitably spend most of their time perfecting and presenting the arguments in favour of the principles of this conception of justice, answering the objections of critics, and criticising the arguments underpinning alternative accounts. While I think such theorists would still do well to recognise and attend to some of the discrepancies realists identify between several of their most fundamental theoretical assumptions and the reality of political life, realists need not disparage the aims and purposes of this first normative task. Indeed, those who are engaged in it can make, and often have made, important contributions to both academic and public political debates. What they do not address, and need not given the nature of their set task, is how we are to proceed politically in the face of the disagreement that exists within our society about what justice is, and in which the theorist's voice is but one amongst a multitude of others all advocating different positions.[30] This is, however, the question that preoccupies those who engage in the second task of political philosophy, the theorisation of politics itself, understood as an activity which is generated by and responds to the fact of political disagreement. What I want to emphasise here is not only the division of labour that this realist account provides, one which appreciates the value of the normative inquiry into the nature and content of justice (and other political concepts), but the theoretical distinction between politics and justice that it opens up as well. There is, on this account, 'logical space' between the substantive conception of justice one advocates and the political arena such that, while I do not stop advocating and promoting my own particular convictions, I nevertheless recognise that they are but one set of convictions amongst many others, and that politics is therefore required in order to help us reach a common decision.

It follows from this way of thinking about realism as an exercise in political understanding that it does not have a distinct political programme in the way that is true of liberalism, socialism, Marxism, anarchism, fascism, etc. Realism is not a political ideology with a recognisably distinct set of recommendations for the political design of a society's institutional structure, practices, or values. We do not have realist states, realist democracies, or realist political parties. Rather realism asks us to take seriously a particular way of thinking about politics, though it leaves the question of how to respond to political disagreement theoretically underdetermined. But then, in a sense, that illustrates one of the central ideas of realism, that even the most fundamental political decisions, such as the basic normative framework of a society (e.g. liberal democratic or social democratic), are *political* issues which have to be addressed by us, together, despite the fact that we hold different and conflicting views, in some cases radically so.

Realism and non-ideal theory

William Galston's 'Realism in political theory' was available for some time in draft form prior to its publication in a special edition of the *European Journal of Political Theory* on realism in 2010, and has played an important role in reigniting interest in realism and setting the agenda for further study.[31] Galston explicitly portrays realism as synonymous with non-ideal theory, or, as he puts it, 'an alternative to ideal theory'. The target of the realists' ire is those who he calls the idealists, those who engage in *ideal* political theorising.[32] So on Galston's account, realism is an attempt to provide a non-ideal alternative to the idealised theorising exemplified in the work of 'high liberals' such as Rawls and Dworkin. Realism is the non-ideal reflection of ideal theory.

The ideal/non-ideal theory debate has moved to the forefront of academic debates in recent years, and many scholars have been exploring the manner in which a non-ideal liberal theory could be developed.[33] While the exact contours of this debate have yet to really settle, nevertheless the crucial sites of engagement do in many ways overlap with some of the interests of realist thought. So, for instance, non-ideal theory examines the relevance and pertinence of issues surrounding the feasibility of implementing normative recommendations to theorising itself, the appropriate level of abstraction that a theory should engage in, and the suitability of including assumptions about human nature or our social world that deviate significantly from or altogether ignore salient empirical facts that render those assumptions highly unconvincing (Rawls' assumption regarding full compliance with principles of justice being the non-ideal theorist's favourite example). All of these concerns are essentially connected by a worry that ideal theory is either unable to function as a plausible guide to action, or that by ignoring relevant aspects of the real world it could be damaging or destructive if we tried to implement its recommendations in practice.[34] There is also the very strong sense in which a thoroughly non-ideal theory needs to re-engage with the day-to-day and familiar materials of politics that it has largely forgotten, to re-introduce parties, personalities, contingency, institutions, patronage, leadership, power, elections, and so on back into theorising.

There are evidently parallel interests that connect realism and non-ideal theory. But I want to resist Galston's thought that realism is synonymous with non-ideal theory and insist that realism is a distinct form of political theorising.[35] And I want to do so for two reasons. Non-ideal theory is parasitic on ideal theory. In order for a theory to be non-ideal, we need to know what the ideal is. Ideal theory clearly has conceptual primacy in the sense that it provides the constructive goals towards which non-ideal theory works.[36] This is why many of the questions that non-ideal theory addresses centre on how the ideal can be achieved, or the manner in which the ideal needs to be compromised, in non-ideal conditions. So non-ideal theory can only exist in relation to an ideal theory. As Rawls said, 'ideal theory, which defines a perfectly just basic structure, is a necessary complement to nonideal theory without which the desire for change lacks an aim'.[37] It is essentially a move, or maybe series of moves, *within* liberal theory, a non-ideal variation on an ideal liberal theme. If realism were non-ideal theory then it would simply be that part of liberal thought that looks at how ideal normative recommendations can be put into political practice. But this misses the extent to which realism is a fundamentally different way of conceiving politics to liberalism, grounded in a very different set of assumptions about politics, the circumstances in which politics arises, the questions that it takes politics to address, and the most salient features of any plausible political theory. It is, in short, a radically different vision of politics. This is most evident if we think about the realist canon: Thucydides, Machiavelli, Hobbes, and then more recently Nietzsche, Weber and Schmitt, were not thinkers who thought long and hard about how political ideals should be implemented in practice (though some of them did), but theorists who had very different visions of what politics is from liberalism. The same is true of contemporary realists also.

Furthermore, one of the central debates of non-ideal theory has been the role or suitability of the more abstract theorising, often very disconnected from the real world of political life, that (it is accused) has often characterised ideal liberalism. Non-ideal theory therefore has to be less abstract and more attentive to the concrete political issues and contexts of the day. While realism needs to be sensitive to the realities of politics, most importantly the presence and inevitability of political disagreement and conflict, this does not, and should not, necessarily equate with an aversion to the sort of abstract theorising that non-ideal theorists seek to avoid. For realists, abstraction is not too much of a problem in and of itself; what matters is that you abstract from the correct theoretical starting point (which links to the issue of political understanding discussed above). So political realism does not advocate abandoning theorising at a high level of abstraction, nor does it demand exclusive concern with the everyday notion of politics and its content at the expense of the very theoretical questions surrounding politics (most obviously, what is politics?) that have very little salience to questions about implementation, feasibility, or practicalities that concern non-ideal theorists. Hence I disagree with the sentiment expressed by John Dunn when he derides Bonnie Honig's *Political Theory and the Displacement of Politics*, despite its obvious intention of re-engaging theory with politics, for having 'no detectable concern with what most people today mean by politics: the outcome and consequences of elections; the making of war or peace within or across borders; the public modulation of life chances by taxation; and the provision or denial of health, education and physical security to women or men or children; or the formulation of public policy over domestic production or international trade.'[38] To think that a realistic account of politics must be exclusively or overwhelmingly concerned with such day-to-day political questions, and not engage with the more abstract yet still politically important issues of identity, difference, and recognition that occupy Honig is unnecessarily constrictive.[39] Realism can and rightly does deal with the most abstract theoretical questions of politics.

Political realism and realism in international political theory

Throughout my discussion of realism and its vision of the political I shall not only draw upon the literature on realism in international relations (let me call it IR realism) but do so in a way that recognises little distinction between it and political realism. This attempt to integrate the two literatures is novel and something that I think contemporary political realism would benefit from doing more of.[40] Yet this raises the question of the relationship between the much more developed tradition and larger body of work on IR realism and contemporary political realism. Though neither Williams nor Geuss explicitly relate their theories to IR realism, they would obviously both have been very aware of the connection and inferences that they were making, with all its connotations, when they used the term realist. In other words, they chose this term purposefully and one can only assume that they saw at least some connection to IR realism. But this connection was never explored and little has been done so far to examine it in any great detail.

It is obviously the case that political realism and IR realism share some canonical figures, maybe Thucydides and Hobbes most notably, though the work of Weber has influenced scholars on both sides also (Hans J. Morgenthau and Bernard Williams in particular).[41] But contemporary political realists have said very little about their connection to the historical tradition of realism and it is still an open but interesting question how this is to be understood.[42] It would be misleading to think that these common historical figures loom large in all political realists' thought; indeed because contemporary political realism is made up by an assortment of very different theorists, coming at the same issues from very different philosophical and political traditions, we unsurprisingly find that many realists take their lead from theorists who are either realists but not canonical members of the IR realist tradition, such as Schmitt (Mouffe) and Nietzsche (Honig, Williams, Geuss), or theorists who cannot meaningfully be thought of as realists at all, such as Derrida (Honig), Lenin (Geuss), and Arendt (Tully). In other words, the traditions informing IR and political realism, while they might share certain key figures, could actually be quite different.

Nevertheless, there are clear similarities between IR and political realism in terms of the concerns that they address, their starting assumptions for thinking about politics, and the manner in which they understand the role, place, and interpretation of particular concepts such as power and legitimacy. That politics takes place against the background of deep and permanent disagreement, including political disagreement, and is at least in the first instance required to provide a framework that creates order and stability is, for instance, a common way of thinking about the nature of the political. They likewise share a common scepticism about the possibility of universal consensus on fundamental normative principles and values, as well as the contingency and fragility of any political order, and stress the indispensable role of power and coercion to create and maintain stability where none naturally exists. While political realists have not explicitly drawn these connections, IR realists have been thinking about the same or similar topics for many years and it would be foolish to think that they have nothing interesting or important to add to our understanding of political realism or its critique of liberalism.

Furthermore, while IR realists do not take politics at the domestic and the international level to be totally analogous, nevertheless they do take politics at both levels to be responding to essentially the same question. While they might, for example, appreciate the differences between the moral and social behaviour of individuals and social groups (including nations), nevertheless the general political question of how to bring order where there is naturally no consensus or agreement, and hence always the possibility of conflict and violence, remains the same. At the level of the state, we (at least those in stable states) have developed a set of institutions and norms that have proven to be very successful in providing such order while we have yet to find similarly effective and mutually acceptable institutions at the international level. While political realists have focused almost exclusively on the relationship between those who are members of the same political association rather than between states, nevertheless this notion that the two levels are not fully analogous yet address the same problem is something that I think they could, and probably should, accept.

Because of the theoretical similarities of IR and political realism, as well as the former's unwillingness to draw a sharp divide between the domestic and the international, I see little reason not to draw upon the rich and sophisticated theoretical discussions that the key texts of IR realism offer. While I would not go as far as to say that any of the key texts of IR realism, Morgenthau's *Politics among Nations* or Carr's *The Twenty Years' Crisis* for instance, deserve a place amongst the great tomes of political theory in the twentieth century, they do offer theories of realism that are nuanced and sophisticated in a manner far beyond the crude caricature of realism that dominates both contemporary international political theory and most undergraduate studies of IR realism.[43] In drawing upon their work I hope to at least indirectly encourage other political realists to see IR realism as a fruitful resource for thinking and developing their ideas. And insofar as one of the key challenges for developing political realism is demonstrating that it is a compelling and systematic account of politics in its own right, it strikes me that appealing to international political theory, where realism is one of the most diverse, complex, and well-developed theories, might prove beneficial.

Structure of the argument

The nature of the realist challenge to liberal politics has yet to be developed into anything like a definitive statement. Nor has the organisation of the numerous facets of realist political thought been sorted into its more essential and peripheral components. As such, the first three chapters are dedicated to setting out what I take to be the central thrust of the challenge that realism poses to liberalism, focusing specifically on its account of politics and political legitimacy. The first two chapters set out the liberal and realist 'visions of the political'. In relation to the former, I argue that contemporary liberalism has, albeit often implicitly rather than explicitly, adopted a 'consensus vision of the political' in the sense that politics takes place in the context of and with reference to a set of fundamental political principles which we can understand as enjoying the endorsement of those subject to them. Crucially, this is not a contingent feature of the liberal vision but is generated by the fundamental normative commitment to respecting the freedom and equality of all citizens, which is then reflected in its account of the conditions of political legitimacy. The second chapter then presents the realist vision of the political, emphasising how politics takes place in circumstances of radical disagreement, including on fundamental political principles, and is best seen as a response to such conflict. In the absence of a pre-political consensus that can provide the terms of the political association, coercion, and power become much more central to the question of how political unity is both created and maintained. Chapter 3 then tries to show both the manner in which realism's conflictual vision of the political represents a challenge to liberalism and the main theoretical difficulty that lies ahead for the rest of the monograph in developing a theory of liberal realism: recognising that liberalism's reliance on a consensus vision of the political is employed as a means to respect the freedom and equality of all persons, how is this normative commitment to be realised if we drop this vision in favour of realism's more conflictual account of politics, especially in relation to those that reject liberalism?

The fourth chapter then turns to look at two accounts of liberal politics that are more realist in orientation yet rely on a much less substantive notion of political consensus, Judith Shklar's liberalism of fear and the modus vivendi liberalism advocated by, amongst others, John Gray and more recently David McCabe. Prima facie one might think that in having a less substantive and hence demanding account of political consensus, in the sense of what it is citizens have to mutually accept in order to justify a liberal regime, both or either of these accounts might provide the resources to develop a more realistic account of liberalism without completely abandoning the consensus vision of politics. In other words, these might represent the easiest way forward in developing a theory of liberal realism. However, in both cases I argue that neither is fully compelling in this regard largely because though they do rely on a less substantive notion of political consensus they are still nonetheless vulnerable to political realism's critique of universal agreement. As such, the only basis on which to develop a theory of liberal realism is therefore by abandoning the hankering for consensus and start from realism's recognition of the fact of radical and permanent political disagreement.

Developing the structure of such an account is the aim of the final three chapters of the monograph. To establish the foundations for this, I further develop realism's account of politics in chapter 5 by engaging with the hugely influential and best developed account of political realism (despite the fact that it was published posthumously and incomplete) provided by Bernard Williams. Unfortunately, however, and for reasons I set out in chapter 5, I disagree with Williams on several crucial points. But these disagreements help establish what I take to be necessary elements of the realist account of politics that the theory of liberal realism which follows develops: that politics necessarily involves successful domination, but that this cannot be all that politics consists of, and that the first question of politics is the provision of a political framework, not the avoidance of tyranny. The final two chapters then seek to identify the main contours of liberal realism in light of these features. Chapter 6 explores the ramifications of politics-as-a-struggle-for-power in relation to liberalism's own self-understanding, especially in relation to the reasonableness of radical political disagreement (including the reasonableness of rejecting liberalism), the necessarily partisan nature of its normative foundations, and how, once these are accepted, liberal realism should understand the relationships between citizens in conditions of political conflict. In the final chapter, chapter 7, I return to the question identified in chapter 3 as central to the development of a realistic yet recognisably *liberal* theory of politics, i.e. how we can ensure that *all* persons are respected as free and equal in a liberal state once we abandon the consensus vision of the political. Once we accept the conflictual vision of politics, and the notion that politics necessarily involves domination in relation to those that reject liberalism, then it becomes clear that any realistic yet still adequately liberal understanding of legitimacy must speak to two different audiences, liberals themselves (including those who hold competing liberal accounts of the political ideal) and those that reject liberalism. In chapter 7 I outline what I take to be a plausible and compelling outline of what such a dual account could look like, emphasising the extent to which though liberalism must accept that it is a form of domination vis-à-vis those that reject it, and hence is a form of hegemony, it is nevertheless what Stephen Macedo calls a 'moderate hegemony'. I build on this idea by discussing some of the ways in which liberals act as what I call 'restrained masters' by placing a series of institutional and normative constraints on their use of power, and it is through this restraint that those that reject liberalism are nevertheless still respected as free and equal citizens despite the fact that they are living according to a will other than their own.

Finally, I should say that I make no claim to present here the definitive realistic theory of liberalism, or that the direction in which I travel is necessarily that which all similar attempts must follow. I present this project very much in the spirit of offering a first attempt to sketch out the rationale for developing a theory of liberal realism and what such a theory might look like. Because I think the overall enterprise is an important and urgent one, even if this monograph serves only as a guide to others for how not to proceed (though I obviously hope this is not the case), then both my own and the readers' efforts will hopefully not be completely in vain.

Notes

1   E. H. Carr, *The Twenty Years' Crisis* (Basingstoke: Palgrave, 2001), p. 207
2   While liberal political theory has undoubtedly been the exclusive subject of contemporary realists' attention, there is good reason to think that several of their critiques would apply, to greater or lesser degrees, to other forms of political thought

too. Certainly earlier realists of the twentieth century often criticised Marxism or socialism on the same or similar grounds as liberalism. See, for instance, R. Niebuhr, *The Children of Light and the Children of Darkness* (London: University of Chicago Press, 2011)

3   M. Weber, 'The profession and vocation of politics', in M. Weber, *Political Writings*, ed. Peter Lassman and Ronal Speirs (Cambridge: Cambridge University Press, 1994), 309–69, p. 311

4   R. Geuss, *Philosophy and Real Politics* (Oxford: Princeton University Press, 2008); B. Williams, *In the Beginning was the Deed* (Oxford: Princeton University Press, 2005). The key texts of this 'high liberalism' include R. Dworkin, *Sovereign Virtue – The Theory and Practice of Equality* (London: Harvard University Press, 2002); J. Rawls, *A Theory of Justice – Revised Edition* (Oxford: Oxford University Press, 1999); J. Rawls, *Political Liberalism* (New York: Columbia University Press, 1996)

5   W. Galston, 'Realism in political theory', *European Journal of Political Theory*, 9:4 (2010), 385–411; M. Stears, 'Liberalism and the politics of compulsion', *British Journal of Political Science*, 37 (2007), 533–53

6   Apart from those texts already mentioned, the other notable texts of this recent resurgence of interest in political realism include: R. Bellamy, *Political Constitutionalism – A Republican Defence of the Constitutionality of Democracy* (Cambridge: Cambridge University Press, 2007); C. A. J. Coady, *Messy Morality – The Challenge of Politics* (Oxford: Oxford University Press, 2008); J. Dunn, *The Cunning of Unreason* (London: HarperCollins, 2000); R. Geuss, *Politics and the Imagination* (Oxford: Princeton University Press, 2010); R. Geuss, *History and Illusion in Politics* (Cambridge: Cambridge University Press, 2001); J. Gray, *Two Faces of Liberalism* (New York: New Press, 2000); B. Honig, *Political Theory and the Displacement of Politics* (New York: Cornell University Press, 1993); C. Mouffe, *On the Political* (London: Routledge, 2005); G. Newey, *After Politics – The Rejection of Politics in Contemporary Liberal Philosophy* (Basingstoke: Palgrave, 2001); M. Philp, *Political Conduct* (London: Harvard University Press, 2007); J. Tully, *Public Philosophy in a New Key – Volume I: Democracy and Civic Freedom* (Cambridge: Cambridge University Press, 2008); J. Tully, *Public Philosophy in a New Key – Volume II: Imperialism and Civic Freedom* (Cambridge: Cambridge University Press, 2008); J. Waldron, *Law and Disagreement* (Oxford: Oxford University Press, 1999). Collections of note include a special edition of the *European Journal of Political Theory* on 'Realism and political theory' that was published in 2010 (*European Journal of Political Theory*, 9:4, 379–512); J. Floyd and M. Stears (eds), *Political Philosophy versus History? Contextualism and Real Politics in Contemporary Political Thought* (Cambridge: Cambridge University Press, 2011). Matthew Humphrey has recently argued that the work of Michael Freeden can also meaningfully be thought of as sharing many realist concerns (M. Humphrey, 'Getting 'real' about political ideas: Conceptual morphology and the realist critique of Anglo-American political philosophy', in B. Jackson and M. Stears (eds), *Liberalism as Ideology: Essays in Honour of Michael Freeden* (Oxford: Oxford University Press, 2012), pp. 241–58)

7   None, as far as I am aware, have distanced themselves from the term, however

8   I therefore reject Duncan Bell's assertion that 'Realism is perhaps best understood negatively – in terms of what realists fear, what they seek to avoid, and what they criticise as dangerous or misguided'. I think there is much more to be said of the unity of realist thought than a set of shared common fears, as I hope to show here (D. Bell, 'Political realism and the limits of ethics', in D. Bell (ed.), *Ethics and World Politics* (Oxford: Oxford University Press, 2010), p. 109)

9   While it is fairly uncontroversial to call most of the theorists on this list realists, Hume and Nietzsche's place in this tradition is still being debated. For realist interpretations of Hume and Nietzsche see, for instance F. G. Whelan, *Hume and Machiavelli: Political Realism and Liberal Thought* (Oxford: Lexington Books, 2004); P. E. Kirkland, 'Nietzsche's tragic realism', *The Review of Politics*, 72:1 (2010), 55–78

10   D. Bell, 'Under an empty sky: Realism and political theory', in D. Bell (ed.), *Political Thought and International Relations – Variations on a Realist Theme* (Oxford: Oxford University Press, 2009), p. 16

11   As Geuss notes, 'a focus on conflict and discord has, at least, distinct methodological advantages, given the centrality of disagreement in politics' (*History and Illusion in Politics*, p. 6)

12   S. Holmes, *The Anatomy of Anti-Liberalism* (London: Harvard University Press, 1996)

13   M. C. Williams, *The Realist Tradition and the Limits of International Relations* (Cambridge: Cambridge University Press, 2005), p. 10

14   *Ibid.*, p. 9

15   Carr, *The Twenty Years' Crisis*, pp. 9–10

16   Raymond Geuss makes a similar point in his 'Realismus, Wunschdenken, Utopie', *Deutsche Zeitschrift für Philosophie*, 58:3 (2010), 419–29

17   Galston, 'Realism in political theory', p. 408

18   M. Philp, 'What is to be done? Political theory and political realism', *European Journal of Political Theory*, 9:4 (2010), 466–84, p. 467

19   Geuss, *Philosophy and Real Politics*, pp. 16–17

20   Dunn, *The Cunning of Unreason*, p. 7

21   Newey, *After Politics*, p. 4

22   *Ibid.*, p. 34

23   Geuss, *Philosophy and Real Politics*, p. 59

24   J. Waldron, *The Dignity of Legislation* (Cambridge: Cambridge University Press, 1999)

25   Waldron, *Law and Disagreement*, pp. 88–91

26   Stears, 'Liberalism and the politics of compulsion', p. 543

27   Dunn, *The Cunning of Unreason*, pp. 330–1

28   Hence Dunn describes *The Cunning of Unreason* not as a book about the inevitability of political disappointment but 'as a book about how (and how not) to hope' (p. xi)

29   Waldron, *Law and Disagreement*, p. 3

30   Indeed realists tend to be somewhat sceptical about the authority of the theorist's voice in the democratic conversation, doubting that it has any special authority above and beyond the contribution of any other equal citizen. Waldron states, for instance, 'It is our [political philosophers] task to think these things [political questions] through as carefully as it is possible to think them. But it is a mistake, I believe, to

regard our thought as different in kind from that of a citizen-participant in politics. Political philosophy – at least in the normative philosophy-and-public-affairs mode – is simply conscientious civic discussion without a deadline' (*Law and Disagreement*, p. 229)

31   Galston, 'Realism in political theory'. Much of this article was also recast as part of a reflection by Galston on the legacy of John Rawls (W. Galston, 'Realism and moralism in political theory: The legacies of John Rawls', in S. P. Young (ed.), *Reflections on Rawls – An Assessment of his Legacy* (Surrey: Ashgate, 2009), pp. 111–30)

32   Galston, 'Realism in political theory', p. 400

33   For the ideal/non-ideal theory debate, see, for example, G. A. Cohen, 'Facts and principles', *Philosophy and Public Affairs*, 31:3 (2003), 211–45; C. Farrelly, 'Justice in ideal theory: A refutation', *Political Studies*, 55 (2007), 844–64; A. Mason, 'Just constraints', *British Journal of Political Science*, 34:2 (2004), 251–68; D. Miller, 'Political philosophy for earthlings', in D. Leopold and M. Stears (eds), *Political Theory – Methods and Approaches* (Oxford: Oxford University Press, 2008), 29–48; A. J. Simmons, 'Ideal and nonideal theory', *Philosophy and Public Affairs*, 38:1 (2010), 3–36; Z. Stemplowska, 'What's ideal and ideal theory?', *Social Theory and Practice*, 34 (2008), 331–40; A. Swift, 'The value of philosophy in non-ideal circumstances', *Social Theory and Practice*, 34 (2008), 363–87; L. Valentini, 'On the apparent paradox of ideal theory', *Journal of Political Philosophy*, 17:3 (2009), 332–55

34   Galston, 'Realism in political theory', p. 407

35   This understanding of realist political theory as consisting primarily of non-ideal concerns, in particular the recognition of the difficulty of applying ideas in practice, can also be found in D. Runciman, 'What is realistic political philosophy?', *Metaphilosophy*, 43:1-2 (2012), 58–70; Humphrey, 'Getting 'real' about political ideas: Conceptual morphology and the realist critique of Anglo-American political philosophy'; and A. Sangiovanni, 'Normative political theory? A flight from reality', in Bell (ed.), *Political Thought and International Relations – Variations on a Realist Theme*

36   David Leopold, 'A cautious embrace: Reflections on (left) liberalism and utopia' in Jackson and Stears (eds), *Liberalism as Ideology*, 9–33, p. 27

37   Rawls, *Political Liberalism*, p. 285

38   J. Dunn, 'Review of *Political Theory and the Displacement of Politics* by Bonnie Honig', *International Affairs*, 70:2 (1994), 321. This statement is of course made more interesting given Dunn's own status as a realist thinker

39   It is certainly wrong to insinuate that questions of identity are not as much a part of the 'external world' as the issues Dunn lists: 'But for those who happen to be principally interested in politics as more demotically understood there is still a great deal too much about identity and distressingly little about the external world', *ibid*

40   See Bell (ed.), *Political Thought and International Relations – Variations on a Realist Theme*

41   See Williams, *The Realist Tradition and the Limits of International Relations*

42   There have been some attempts to draw these connections, however. Though it is not explicit, Glen Newey's introduction to Hobbes' *Leviathan* clearly tries to associate Hobbes' intellectual motivations and assumptions with several of the concerns of contemporary political realists (G. Newey, *Hobbes and Leviathan* (Oxon: Routledge,

2007)). See also R. Geuss, 'Thucydides, Nietzsche, and Williams', in his *Outside Ethics* (Oxford: Princeton University Press, 2005), pp. 219–33

43 See Bell (ed.), *Political Thought and International Relations – Variations on a Realist Theme*; Williams, *The Realist Tradition and the Limits of International Relations*; M. C. Williams (ed.), *Realism Reconsidered: The Legacy of Hans J. Morgenthau* (Oxford: Oxford University Press, 2007)

1

The liberal vision of the political

Consensus, freedom, and legitimacy

It could quite plausibly be thought that liberalism has little to say about politics itself. Certainly liberal theorists in the latter part of the twentieth century were more occupied with questions regarding the demands of distributive justice or the requirements of citizenship in multicultural societies, for instance, than abstract reflection upon the nature of the political or politics as a human activity. But liberalism is a *political* theory and hence must employ some notion of politics, even if it is more often than not implicit or assumed. What I want to do in this chapter is try to bring what is actually a rather distinctive and substantive vision of the political at the heart of contemporary liberal theory to the surface, and in doing so set out its fundamental features.

One of the most familiar characteristics of liberalism is its commitment to placing normative and practical constraints on political power, and moral limits on permissible political action. It is a theory of politics in which political power is controlled and directed in a manner that ensures the ruled are not oppressed or tyrannised at the hands of those who rule over them. The state, and the officers of the state who control its coercive mechanisms, are often viewed in liberal theory as a threat to individual freedom and therefore political power stands in need of restraint. Central to its strategy of restraining power is a particular vision of politics, the normative ends that it should pursue and its rightful limits. This vision, which I call a 'consensus' vision of the political, views political activity and political relationships as taking place within and with reference to a set of principles that are universally endorsed by those subject to them, or can be represented as such. By making such consensus a condition of politics, liberal theory's vision of politics ensures that political associations are regulated by principles and employ their power in ways that respect the freedom and moral equality of *each and every* person over whom they rule. This requires, as we shall see, a particular theorisation of the relationship between human freedom and law or authority that reconciles what have often been seen as two irreconcilable concepts. And legitimacy is reconceived as a criterion that ensures that such reconciliation holds for all members of the political association, not merely some subset of them, and hence is in an important sense the test for whether liberalism's foundational normative concern of respecting the freedom and moral equality of all persons is met. In short, liberalism imagines a non-oppressive or non-tyrannical form of politics, a politics that allows each and every person to live according to principles that can meaningfully be said to represent their own will rather than the coercive imposition of someone else's. Liberalism is therefore nothing short of a magnificent achievement of human imagination.

Legitimacy and autonomy

All liberals share a commitment to individual freedom of some sort. An important question for liberals will therefore always be how we reconcile this individual freedom with our evident need to live together under a single political authority with the necessary capacity to enforce, when required, compliance with its laws through the threat or actual use of physical coercive power. This problem is further complicated by the fact that, at least in modern societies, people hold and seek to pursue a variety of different and often conflicting moral and religious life plans. The question then becomes one of how people can remain free to follow their diverse range of conceptions of the good yet be subject to the laws of the same political authority.

This is far from a question of merely theoretical interest. Early liberals were gravely concerned by the development of the centralised modern state (as we now call it) and the fact that it possessed an unprecedented and immensely unequal degree of power compared to not only the individual but also the local barons and landowners who had up to the seventeenth century represented the main source of security for the majority of subjects against a potentially tyrannical monarch. On numerous occasions during the sixteenth and seventeenth centuries, European monarchs proved to be both willing and able to impose their own particular set of religious beliefs upon their subjects, even if these were not widely shared, and often with horrific and bloody consequences. There was therefore felt to be a pressing need for an effective defence of the individual against those agents of the state who had the means to employ overwhelming and irresistible coercive power to force them to live according to moral and religious principles that they rejected. And insofar as the power of the state has only exponentially grown since this period, with developments in technology, bureaucracy, military and surveillance capability, etc., this general concern about how we protect the individual from the potential oppressive use of state power is one that remains with us today.

So liberals are adamant that political order cannot simply be based on the successful rule of one group of people over another via force. That would make politics no more than tyranny, right no more than might. They strive, rather, to provide an account of political community in which its members must be able to recognise its fundamental political principles as expressions of their own will rather than the forceful imposition of someone else's.[1] Political rule and law are reconceived as coercively enforceable but nevertheless voluntarily and freely imposed bonds. As Jeremy Waldron summarises their approach, liberals 'concede that the enforcement of social rules involves actions which characteristically and in familiar circumstances threaten freedom and threaten it seriously. But since it is possible for an individual to *choose* to live under a social order, to *agree* to abide by its restraints, and therefore to use his powers as a free agent to commit himself for the future, the enforcement of such an order does not necessarily mean that freedom as a value is being violated'.[2] This influential response, one which drew upon theoretical innovations introduced by Jean-Jacques Rousseau, hinged on the development of a novel normative view of the relationship between human freedom and law such that persons are only free if they obey laws, moral or political, that they made for themselves. As Rousseau famously put it, 'obedience to a law one prescribes for oneself is freedom'.[3] But it is in the work of Immanuel Kant that we get the most developed and influential articulation of this idea of moral and political laws as self-imposed bonds.

Freedom, as Kant understood it, is 'independence from being constrained by another's choice' and is 'the only original right belonging to every man by virtue of his humanity'.[4] Freedom is the right that everyone possesses to be independent from coercion by another's will. In the *Groundwork of a Metaphysics of Morals* Kant argued that man is not a means for the arbitrary use of others' wills, but rather 'must in all his actions ... be regarded *at the same time as an end*'.[5] From this postulate follows Kant's (second) formulation of the categorical imperative: '*So act that you use humanity, whether in your person or in the person of any other, always at the same time as an end, never merely as a means*'.[6] It is a unique capacity of free agents, Kant believed, that they are able to set goals for themselves and decide how best to pursue them.[7] Insofar as people are free in this sense, they will inevitably have different views on what the end of happiness will consist of. As such, 'No-one can compel me to be happy in accordance with his conception of the welfare of others, for each may seek his happiness in whatever way he sees fit, so long as he does not infringe upon the freedom of others to pursue a similar end which can be reconciled with the freedom of everyone else within a workable general law – i.e. he must accord to others the same rights as he enjoys himself'.[8] Each must have the freedom to pursue their own ideas of the good consistent with others having an equal degree of freedom to do so also.

This is the role that public law, or principles of right as Kant called them, must play in a political community: they must be directed towards restricting those actions which would violate the freedom of others. 'Right is', as Kant put it, 'the restriction of each individual's freedom so that it harmonises with the freedom of everyone else'.[9] In effect, right makes explicit the normative conditions which must obtain between two or more people's wills if their freedom is to be respected.[10] And the universal principle of right states that 'Any action is *right* if it can co-exist with everyone's freedom in accordance with a universal law, or if on its maxim the freedom of choice of each can co-exist with everyone's freedom in accordance with a universal law'.[11] Kant was thus adamant that a political community is a relationship between individuals who are free and retain their freedom even though they are subject to coercive laws.[12]

This reconciliation between law and individual freedom is made possible by defining freedom, at least in the political sphere, as 'the attribute of obeying no other law than that to which he [the individual] has given his consent'.[13] An important ramification of this is that the legislative will of the political association must somehow represent the will of all. If it does not, then the law, and the coercive enforcement of that law, will effectively signify the imposition of the will of one particular individual or group of individuals on all others. Individuals must be their own lawgivers. As Kant wrote, 'the will of another person cannot decide anything for someone without injustice ... Thus an individual will cannot legislate for a commonwealth. For this requires freedom, equality, and *unity* of the will of *all* the members'.[14] And this will must be based on an end that all necessarily share: 'a unilateral will (and a bilateral but still *particular* will is also unilateral) cannot put everyone under an obligation that is in itself contingent; this requires a will that is *omnilateral*, that is united not contingently but a priori and therefore necessarily, and because of this is the only will that is lawgiving. For only in accordance with this principle of the will is it possible for the free choice of each to accord with the freedom of all'.[15] The legislative authority can therefore only belong to the united will of the people.[16]

At the empirical level, it might look initially very difficult to identify ends that all are committed to in conditions where people endorse a variety of different and often conflicting moral and religious views. Indeed, Kant's recognition of this deep pluralism might seem to undercut the grounds for thinking that such a united will is plausible. But for Kant, what distinguishes political unions from any other form of community is that the former is directed towards ends that all persons *ought to share* and which is thus an absolute and primary duty in all external relationships whatsoever among human beings' rather than towards contingent ends to which they happen to be jointly committed.[17] This end which unites the will of all turns out to be the right of persons to live together under coercive law yet with the liberty to pursue their own conception of the good life free from (illegitimate) infringements from others. In other words, all persons ought to be committed to individual freedom and it is this end, which might not be shared by all but ought to be, that provides the normative foundation for civic unions.

Though Kant believed that the dignity of human freedom as expressed in the universal principle of right does impose an obligation upon us, it is not one that he expects us to naturally or voluntarily act in accordance with. Rather, because it is morally necessary, indeed an absolute and primary duty, for us to realise human freedom, we can be compelled by others to carry out our duty of entering civil society and living according to the principles of right which maintain it if we do not voluntarily do so ourselves.[18] It was on these grounds that Kant justified the legitimacy of using coercive power over those that violate principles of right. As he put it,

> Resistance that counteracts the hindering of an effect promotes this effect and is consistent with it ... But coercion is a hindrance or resistance to freedom. Therefore, if a certain use of freedom is itself a hindrance to freedom in accordance with universal laws (i.e. wrong), coercion that is opposed to this (as a hindering of a hindrance to freedom) is consistent with freedom in accordance with universal laws, that is, it is right. Hence there is connected with right by the principle of contradiction an authorisation to coerce someone who infringes upon it.[19]

Stated differently, freedom is freedom from any constraint other than coercion by law consistent with the universal principle of right, which is a freedom that allows all individuals to pursue their own ends provided that this pursuit leaves the same freedom available to all others.[20] And so on these grounds Kant believed it is legitimate to coerce people in order to prevent them from reducing the freedom of others via their own (illegitimate) coercive actions.

All of this might seem to obscure the role that consent plays in Kant's theory. After all, Kant is on the one hand saying that we must consent to the law in order for it to be consistent with our freedom, while on the other hand arguing that it is legitimate to coerce us to obey laws that we have a moral obligation to follow *even if* we as a matter of fact fail to recognise the presence or force of that obligation. But this connection between consent, freedom, and right is only fully brought together in Kant's notion of the 'original contract'. The original contract is essentially a hypothetical test which we can apply to all laws in order to assess their legitimacy: the original contract 'can oblige every legislator to frame his laws in such a way that they could have been produced by the united will of a whole nation, and to regard each subject, in so far as he can claim citizenship, as if he had consented within the general will. This is the test of the rightfulness of every public law'.[21] Thus 'if the law is such that a whole people could not possibly agree to it (for example, if it stated that a certain class of subjects must be privileged as a hereditary ruling class), it is unjust; but if it is at least possible that a people could agree to it, it is our duty to consider the law as just, even if the people is at present in such a position or attitude of mind that it would probably refuse its consent if it were consulted'.[22] But Kant was clear that 'we need by no means assume that this contract ... based on a coalition of the wills of all private individuals in a nation to form a common, public will for the purposes of rightful legislation, actually exists as a *fact*, for it cannot possibly be so'.[23] Rather, Kant said that the original contract is 'an *idea* of reason', where an idea is understood to be 'a concept of reason, whose object can be met with nowhere in experience'.[24] Nevertheless, he believed that such ideas 'serve to guide the understanding through reason in respect of experience' and, as such, ideas can play a crucial role in providing a standard for assessing the adequacy of a state and its legislation.

The original contract is a standard of political judgement, a criterion for assessing whether a law is consistent with the freedom of those subject to it. It requires individuals to submit their own personal wills to a universal will and, in doing so, every subject becomes a fellow-legislator. They therefore remain free in the sense that they are independent from coercion by the will of another. But crucially this does not require individuals' actual agreement, indeed even that persons be actually consulted as to whether they would consent to the legislation or not, only that the present legislation can be represented as something which people could conceivably consent to given that it is not inconsistent with their freedom. Kant's guidance to the monarchs of his day was therefore that they govern 'in accordance with principles akin in spirit to the laws of freedom which a people of mature rational powers would prescribe for itself, even if the people is not literally asked for its consent'.[25] Political or legal principles that are inconsistent with individual freedom, either my own or that of others, are not principles that a free being could consent to and remain free. So by appealing to hypothetical consent, Kant is able to restrict the range of legislation that citizens could accept to that subset of principles which is consistent with human freedom. Those laws are legitimate which could be consented to, or, put differently, are worthy of being consented to, by free rational beings.

In reconciling freedom and law in this manner, Kant provided a theoretical framework that allows us to bypass existing social and political structures and set normative criteria for the appropriate use of coercive force and standards against which the employment of state power can be assessed. And by restricting (via philosophical argument) the legitimate use of power to that which respects the autonomy and equality of persons, he was able to reconcile the tension between the dignity of human freedom and the practical need to live together under a common political and coercive authority. The vision of the political which underpins all this takes politics to be directed towards a particular moral end, the respect for individuals' equal freedom, to which all citizens of the political community are or ought to be committed. The legitimate use of coercive power is then restricted to being employed only on terms that are consistent with public right, those that are consistent with the freedom and equality of others. To use the power of the state outside of this remit, to restrict freedom on any basis other than right, is to necessarily employ it illegitimately.

Legitimacy and freedom in conditions of reasonable pluralism

Liberalism, like any complex moral and political tradition, consists of several different and not always compatible theoretical strands, all of which conceive of the key concepts of liberal thought, such as legitimacy and freedom, in related but different ways. That the Kantian framework for thinking about liberal politics is currently dominant should not lead us to ignore the importance or insights of the other strands, such as the utilitarianism of Jeremy Bentham, James and John Stuart Mill, or the British idealism of T. H. Green and Bernard Bosanquet. And the alternative and more voluntarist accounts of contract theory, such as that offered by John Locke, retain their advocates also.[26] But it is nevertheless the case that the vision of the political, including the normative goals of politics and the account of political legitimacy, which dominates contemporary liberal theory clearly bears the marks of its specifically Kantian heritage.[27] And though, as we shall see, contemporary liberalism, especially in its 'political' guise, seeks to abscond reliance upon any so-called 'comprehensive moral doctrine', including Kantianism, the way it conceptualises politics is still framed in a way that (not contingently) speaks to the same normative concerns as Kant's political theory.

In his influential article 'Theoretical foundations of liberalism', Waldron claimed that the 'fundamentally liberal thesis', that which distinguishes it from all other accounts of politics, is its account of legitimacy. This states that 'a social and political order is illegitimate unless it is rooted in the consent of all those who have to live under it; the consent or agreement of these people is a condition of its being morally permissible to enforce that order against them'.[28] Examples of contemporary liberals theorising legitimacy in this manner are legion. To give but a flavour: Thomas Nagel stated in his *Equality and Partiality* that 'the task of discovering the conditions of legitimacy is traditionally conceived as that of finding a way to justify a political system to everyone who is required to live under it ... the search for legitimacy is a search for unanimity'.[29] Jean Hampton wrote that liberals are committed to the tenet that 'Any political society must be justified to the individuals who live within it, if that society is to be legitimate'.[30] And John Rawls insisted that 'the basic structure and its public policies are to be justifiable to all citizens, as the principle of political legitimacy requires'.[31] Indeed, 'A legitimate regime is such that its political and social institutions are justifiable to all citizens – to each and every one – by addressing their reason, theoretical and practical. Again: a justification of the institutions of the social world must be, in principle, available to everyone, and so justifiable to all who live under them. The legitimacy of a liberal regime depends on such a justification'.[32] In probably his most succinct and influential statement of what he called 'the liberal principle of legitimacy' in *Political Liberalism*, Rawls wrote that 'Our exercise of political power is fully proper only when it is exercised in accordance with a constitution the essentials of which all citizens as free and equal may reasonably be expected to endorse in the light of principles and ideals acceptable to their common human reason'.[33] In the work of these contemporary liberal theorists, and many others, we find time and time again the thought that the question of legitimacy is addressed by determining whether that which we are seeking to legitimate is acceptable to the constituency of persons subject to it.[34]

Stephen Macedo dubbed this commitment to the public justification of the political system to those subject to it the 'moral lodestar' of liberal thought.[35] 'Public justification', he states, 'embodies a complex form of respect for persons'.[36] This has been iterated by several other liberal theorists. Jonathan Quong, for instance, writes that 'Liberal philosophy's *foundational* commitment is to the *moral claim* that persons (or citizens) are free and equal, and thus the exercise of political power is legitimate only when it can be publicly justified'.[37] Nagel and Charles Larmore draw the Kantian link most explicitly however. In his 'Moral conflict and political legitimacy', Nagel explains the normative underpinning of the project of public justification thus: 'when we force people to serve an end that they cannot share, and that we cannot justify to them in objective terms, it is a particularly serious violation of the Kantian requirement that we treat humanity not merely as a means, but also as an end. The justification of coercion must meet especially stringent standards'.[38] The notion that 'basic political principles should be acceptable to those whom they are to bind', Larmore writes, 'reflects the abiding moral heart of liberal thought'.[39] In particular, the source of this conviction is the Kantian principle of respect for persons: 'If we try to bring about conformity to a rule of conduct solely by threat of force, we will be treating persons merely as means, as objects of coercion, and not also as ends, engaging directly their distinctive capacity as persons ... Thus, to respect others as persons in their own right when coercion is at stake is to require that political principles be as justifiable to them as they presumably are to us'.[40]

There might be a whole host of reasons for thinking that the legitimacy of a political regime depends upon the consent of those over whom it rules. In a more Lockean vein, for instance, Manin suggests that the basing of political legitimacy on unanimity

> seems to derive from the fundamental principle of modern individualism. By nature, every individual is free and equal to every other individual. There is no essential difference or natural hierarchy among individuals to justify the domination of some over others. Political power and the rules it promulgates can have no other legitimate basis than the will of these equal members. The rules can, therefore, be legitimate only as long as they arise from the will of all and represent the will of all.[41]

If there is no such thing as natural political authority, and all persons are naturally free and morally equal, then it would seem to follow that political rule can only be legitimate if it has been consented to. But the language of treating people as ends not means, as well as the general notion that we respect the freedom of others by ensuring that political principles are acceptable to them, is intentionally and familiarly Kantian.

Yet recent years have seen a marked attempt to try to divorce the justification of liberalism from Kantian, or indeed any, comprehensive moral doctrines.[42] This has largely taken place as part of the 'political' turn which Rawls' work undertook in the 1980s, culminating in the publication of *Political Liberalism* in 1993 (with some important revisions and clarifications taking place in the paperback edition of 1996 and the 1999 article 'The idea of public reason revisited'), and which remains the dominant version of liberal theory today.[43] Though it became a subject of some controversy, Rawls believed that his earlier book, *A Theory of Justice*, wrongly assumed that an essential feature of a well-ordered society would be that individuals would endorse the same conception of justice (justice as fairness) on the grounds that it is justified with reference to a comprehensive moral doctrine that they all share.[44] The difficulty with this position, Rawls believed, was that it ran counter to a central characteristic of modern liberal democratic societies, the fact of reasonable pluralism. In conditions of freedom, such as in liberal democratic states where fundamental liberties such as to speech and association are protected, it is reasonable for persons to reach different and conflicting conclusions regarding the most fundamental of moral and religious questions. Even when we reason conscientiously, doing our best to avoid the temptations and natural human tendencies towards bias, prejudice, self-interest, irrationality, etc., persons will nevertheless disagree; and, Rawls insisted, reasonably so. This is because such disagreement is the result of what he called the burdens of judgement. These are 'the many hazards involved in the correct (and conscientious) exercise of our powers of reason and judgement in the ordinary course of political life'.[45] These hazards include the difficulty of assessing and evaluating empirical and scientific evidence; disagreements about the kinds of considerations that are relevant in particular cases, and their relative weight; the need to rely on subjective judgement and interpretation in the face of vague concepts or hard cases; the way in which our judgement is shaped by 'our total experience, our whole course of life up to now', which will obviously differ (often wildly) from person to person; that there can be normative considerations that can be mustered for all sides of an argument; and finally, because no social and political world can possibly realise all values, we are forced to make hard decisions as to which values take priority, how we trade off different values, and so on.[46] As citizens in liberal democratic states, our moral and religious judgements are made in conditions in which it is reasonable to expect that persons will reach, even after employing their reason conscientiously, differing conclusions, which is to say that their disagreement is reasonable.[47] So, as Rawls came to accept that persons can reasonably be expected to hold a plurality of different and incompatible comprehensive moral doctrines, he realised that 'as used in [A] *Theory* [*of Justice*], the idea of a well-ordered society of justice as fairness is unrealistic. This is because it is inconsistent with realising its own principles under the best of foreseeable conditions'.[48] In essence, it is no longer viable to justify the fundamental principles of the political association on the grounds of the truth of any comprehensive moral doctrine, be it Kantian, utilitarian, Thomist, etc., due to the fact that citizens in Western liberal democratic societies reasonably disagree about the truth of such moral worldviews.

This has an obvious consequence for the liberal principle of legitimacy insofar as it severely constrains the reasons that can be employed in justification of the political order. Because we can reasonably disagree about moral and religious matters, attempts to justify political principles with reasons that draw upon, make reference to, or are grounded in comprehensive moral doctrines cannot provide the sort of commonly acceptable public justification that liberal legitimacy demands. As Bruce Ackerman sums up the difficulties that this poses, 'If we cannot find a way to talk to one another neutrally, we do not seem to have much choice but to … return to the age-old effort to base political life on the truth, the whole truth, and nothing but the truth about moral life'.[49] In conditions of reasonable pluralism, this would effectively also mean abandoning the hope of a non-oppressive politics.

Nevertheless, Rawls still believed that citizens could identify reasonable terms of co-operation by which they could live together. In order for principles to count as reasonable they have to be consistent with the demands of reciprocity, the desire for its own sake to co-operate with others on terms that all can accept, that are captured in the liberal principle of legitimacy.[50] Any reasonable conception of justice could, by definition, legitimately regulate the basic structure of society (its main economic, social, and political institutions) because, by virtue of being reasonable, it is a conception that we could reasonably expect others to accept. Yet Rawls believed that persons would disagree which particular set of political principles are the most reasonable. Or, put differently, reasonableness is not a standard of assessment that enables citizens to converge upon a single set of political principles as that which has the strongest claim to rightfully regulate the basic structure; reasonableness underdetermines legitimacy. Even justice as fairness, Rawls came to accept, was but one reasonable conception of justice amongst several others, with no intrinsic or special claim to legitimacy against its competitors.[51]

The question then arises why it is that any (reasonable) conception of justice can regulate the basic structure when it, like conceptions of the good, is the subject of reasonable disagreement.[52] Political liberals' answer to this has been

to insist that though we can indeed reasonably disagree as to which conception
of justice is the most reasonable, unlike moral or religious disagreements we
can still engage with each other in a justificatory dialogue that employs reasons
that we can reasonably expect others to accept, so-called 'public reasons'.[53]
These reasons are those which all reasonable citizens will share, some by
virtue of their status as reasonable (such as the criterion of reciprocity) and
others as members of a community with certain implicit beliefs and values
(such as, at least in modern liberal democratic states, the impermissibility of
slavery, the equality of genders, and so on). As Rawls put it, a citizen engages
in public reason 'when he or she deliberates within a framework of what he or
she sincerely regards as the most reasonable political conception of justice, a
conception that expresses political values that others, as free and equal citizens
might also reasonably be expected reasonably to endorse'.[54] By justifying
our favoured conception with reference only to reasons that citizens share,
we ensure that the basic structure of our shared political association can be
explained and justified to our fellow citizens in ways that do not draw upon
controversial moral or religious claims upon which we disagree. Assuming that
this is the case, it would then be reasonable for us to expect others to accept the
principles regulating the basic structure, even if, and this is crucial, they do not
actually endorse them as the most justified or reasonable principles. 'Citizens
will of course differ as to which conceptions of political justice they think are
the most reasonable', Rawls said, 'but they will agree that all are reasonable [i.e.
meet the criterion of reciprocity], even if barely so'.[55]

Likewise, when engaging in debates about the reform or modification
of these principles, we must be sure to couch our debates in terms of public
reason. Public reason therefore acts as a common language of justification
for citizens, the appropriate discourse in which our political discussions and
conflicts are to be couched in order to ensure that we are always respecting
others as free and equal despite our disagreements. But such deliberation
obviously cannot go on forever and so Rawls writes that at a certain point
citizens or their representatives must vote and

> when, on a constitutional essential or matter of basic justice, all appropriate
> government officials act from and follow public reason, and when all reasonable
> citizens think of themselves ideally as if they were legislators following public
> reason, the legal enactment expressing the opinion of the majority is legitimate
> law. It may not be thought the most reasonable, or the most appropriate, by
> each, but it is politically (morally) binding on him or her as a citizen and is to be
> accepted as such. Each thinks that all have spoken and voted at least reasonably,

and therefore all have followed public reason and honoured their duty of civility.[56]

A state is therefore legitimately structured if the justifications for its constitutional essentials can be cast in terms of public reasons that all citizens can reasonably be expected to share.

The role that public reason plays within political liberalism is essentially to provide the language of justification which is appropriate for the task of reaching agreement on a conception of justice in conditions of reasonable pluralism. Because citizens will, by definition, share public reasons then we can reasonably expect them to accept the conception of justice for which those reasons are being offered as a justification. We cannot reasonably expect citizens to accept reasons in favour of a particular conception which are drawn from any particular comprehensive moral doctrine as these are the subject of reasonable disagreement. But we can reasonably expect them to accept political principles which are justified with reference to public reasons. And so the requirement that the fundamental political principles of the political association be acceptable to all those subject to them is made compatible with the fact of reasonable moral and religious disagreement by restricting the justification that can be offered for them to only those public reasons that we can reasonably expect citizens to accept.[57]

But though moral and religious reasons are now deemed inappropriate political justifications this does not mean that the liberal principle of legitimacy itself needs to be, or indeed can be, completely divorced from its moral basis. David Estlund has pressed this point strongly, arguing that political liberalism has to assert the truth rather than the acceptability, of the liberal principle of legitimacy. If it does not, then there is no way of 'penetrating', as he puts it, the plurality of groups who hold different principles of legitimacy. Political liberalism needs 'a mooring – a single point of contact with the moral truth that permits political liberalism to float freely at all other points'.[58] Larmore develops this a little further when he writes

we would be wrong to suppose that the moral principle of respect for persons has the political significance it does because reasonable people share a commitment to it. On the contrary, the idea of respect is what directs us to seek the principles of our political life in the area of reasonable agreement. Respect for persons lies at the heart of political liberalism, not because looking for common ground we find it there, but because it is what impels us to look for common ground at all.[59]

But this commitment of respect for persons, Larmore considers, expresses a minimum moral conception that circumscribes the role of the state. Though it is less comprehensive than a fully developed account of the good life, over which people reasonably disagree, it is nevertheless a commitment that Larmore believes people can affirm despite such differences.[60] In other words, though the commitment to the public justification of political principles is not grounded in any specific comprehensive moral doctrine, that we do others a moral wrong if we force them to abide by laws that are not acceptable to them is nevertheless a moral commitment which liberals believe should determine which principles can rightfully specify the fundamental terms of the political association.

So while political liberalism avoids grounding itself in a Kantian comprehensive moral doctrine, nevertheless the liberal principle of legitimacy takes a form that is clearly deeply informed by that developed by Kant, insofar as it requires that political principles can be represented as acceptable to those subject to them, and retains the conceptualisation of human freedom as self-legislation that enables this strategy of reconciling liberty and law backed by coercive force. This continuity is, and despite the 'political turn', justified because political liberalism shares the same normative concern regarding how we respect the freedom and moral equality of all persons living under a shared political authority. Much of the vast detail and content of the Kantian edifice has indeed been abandoned; but the general structure and foundational commitments remain substantially intact. This is true of two further features of contemporary liberal theory which also deserve highlighting.

The original contract, as it features in Kant's practical philosophy, is, as we saw, conceived essentially as a hypothetical test which allows us to make judgements as to the legitimacy of particular political principles or pieces of legislation. It is hypothetical in the sense that it is sufficient for the purposes of legitimacy that political principles can be represented as terms that all individuals could accept insofar as they are consistent with their moral status as free and equal moral beings. The unrealistic criterion of the actual consent of a political association's members is not a requirement of legitimacy. Consent features in the same manner in contemporary liberal theory. The emphasis in Rawls' account of liberal legitimacy, for instance, is on what persons can *reasonably* be expected to accept, where the political principles that are the possible subject of reasonable affirmation are that subset which can be presented in terms of public reasons that respect others as free and equal. This normative criterion of reasonable expectation of acceptance is shared by most political liberals. Brian Barry puts the emphasis slightly differently, on what people cannot reasonably reject rather than what they can reasonably accept.[61] But while this has an important effect in changing the subset of principles that are potentially legitimate, as that group of principles that are reasonably rejectable is naturally going to be larger than that which are reasonably acceptable, it is still the case that the actual rejection of particular principles by citizens is not sufficient for the purposes of judging them illegitimate. Though the weight of the argument falls on rejection rather than acceptance, it is still the case that the relevant criterion for legitimacy is the reasonableness of the rejection rather than rejection itself. The reliance on hypothetical consent, especially in conditions in which universal acceptance is unrealistic, enables liberalism to distinguish between those cases in which an absence of actual endorsement does and does not mean that the criterion of legitimacy has not been met. Or, put differently, it ensures that liberal theory can operationalise the notion of a political consensus, and the normative role that it plays in determining legitimacy, even when such universal acceptance is unrealistic.

This does beg a crucial question however: given that not all people do, as a matter of fact, accept the underlying moral justification of the liberal principle of legitimacy, i.e. that *all* others are free and equal and/or that we respect this status by ensuring that we can reasonably expect them to endorse the principles that regulate the political association, where do such individuals feature in liberal philosophy? Crucially, does the fact of their rejection of this fundamental moral principle in any way affect the legitimacy of the liberal state or of its right to use coercive force over them? This is particularly important because liberalism understands itself to be a non-oppressive form of politics in which each and every individual is respected as a free and morally equal person. Contemporary liberals therefore insist that persons' actual rejection of liberalism has no bearing on the question of the legitimacy of the state to impose its principles upon them, and, where necessary, use coercive force to ensure their obedience. 'The terms of political association', Larmore writes, 'are to be judged by reference to what citizens *would* accept, *were they reasonable and committed to the principle of equal respect for persons*'.[62] Elsewhere he states that 'political principles should be justifiable to these people as well, though with the justification premised on the (*counterfactual*) supposition that they do prize the norms of rational dialogue and equal respect'.[63] Barry took a similar position. To quote a relevant section of *Justice as Impartiality* in full, Barry stated:

> my pretensions fall short of universality. This arises because my argument
> presupposes the existence of a certain desire: the desire to live in a society

whose members all freely accept its rules of justice and its major institutions [the
agreement motive]. Given the existence of that desire, the reason for observing
the constraints of impartial justice is that it sets out the terms upon which there
is any hope of reaching agreement. To the extent that the major institutions
conform to the demands of justice as impartiality they are legitimate. This means
that the members of the society can justifiably demand the cooperation of others
in maintaining those institutions.[64]

Again the idea is that the legitimacy of the political order is related to the
question of whether it is consistent with the demands of the desire to live with
others on terms that they cannot reasonably reject, the agreement motive,
rather than whether it is a political order which all people do not actually reject.

In *A Theory of Justice* Rawls is also clear that the basic structure of society
is to be evaluated according to principles presented as those that would be
chosen by persons coming together in a position of initial equality to settle the
terms of their association. But this does not mean that the legitimacy of those
principles requires the actual consent of citizens. After agreeing that no society
is actually a scheme of co-operation which persons literally voluntarily enter,
he went on to say, 'Yet a society satisfying the principles of justice as fairness
comes as close as a society can to being a voluntary scheme, for it meets the
principles which free and equal persons would assent to under circumstances
that are fair. In this sense its members are autonomous and the obligations they
recognise self-imposed'.[65] The move to political liberalism would require Rawls
to say that this is true in relation to a society whose regulative conception of
justice, which can be any reasonable conception rather than justice as fairness
exclusively, is consistent with the liberal principle of legitimacy as then it meets
the criterion of being a conception that free and equal persons could accept.
But it is still the case that the test of legitimacy is not whether the individuals
who live in it have agreed to its terms, but whether it can be represented as a
reasonable object of an agreement between them.[66]

Political liberalism has adapted the liberal principles of legitimacy so that
it is consistent with the deep and seemingly intractable moral and religious
disagreement that characterises modern liberal democratic societies.
Kantianism has become but one of several competing and controversial
comprehensive moral doctrines and, as such, is no longer a suitable basis upon
which to justify the fundamental terms of our shared political association. But
despite the novel emphasis on public reason, the general consensual account
of politics, and of the conditions of legitimacy, have remained. This is because
contemporary liberalism speaks to exactly the same normative concerns. This

is why the political principles regulating the political association must be reasonably acceptable by all those subject to them. To violate such principles, or to rule according to some that do not meet this condition of legitimacy, would be to create a society not of equal citizens in which they legitimately coerce one another according to principles shared in common, but a system in which some are oppressed by others.[67] The vocabulary of public justification has shifted so as to be appropriate to conditions of reasonable pluralism, but the normative commitments that generate the need for public justification have remained constant.

The consensus view of politics

The notion of consensus is given its most explicit role in Rawls' theory through the idea of what he called an 'overlapping consensus': 'In such a consensus, the reasonable [moral] doctrines endorse the political conception [of justice], each from its own point of view. Social unity is based on a consensus on the political conception.'[68] By 'each from its own point of view', Rawls meant that each person who holds a reasonable moral doctrine is able to find within it moral reasons to endorse the political conception of justice. These reasons will necessarily be private, or non-public, by virtue of the fact that they are drawn from comprehensive moral doctrines and hence are not reasons we can reasonably expect others to accept. But when such a consensus has been achieved, and liberal principles effectively regulate the basic structure, then these 'meet the urgent political requirement to fix, once and for all, the content of certain political basic rights and liberties, and to assign them special priority.' Furthermore, 'Doing this takes those guarantees off the political agenda and puts them beyond the calculus of social interests, thereby establishing clearly and firmly the rules of political contest', which, if we refuse to do, would have the effect of 'greatly raising the stakes of political controversy, [and] dangerously increas[ing] the insecurity and hostility of public life.'[69] By fixing the fundamental liberties in this manner, Rawls hoped to secure the moral basis for a liberal society – ensuring that the principles that regulate the shared political association are those that treat each and every citizen as free and equal when making collective decisions.

The requirement that the fundamental terms of the political association are representable as the subject of an overlapping consensus is, as I have been pressing, neither a contingent nor a peripheral aspect of Rawls' theory, or of much contemporary liberal political philosophy more generally. It is in many ways its central feature, founded in a distinct commitment of liberal morality and the concern, practical and theoretical, political and moral, for imagining a political society which is not the rule of one group over another but in which all can recognise in it principles they themselves have prescribed (and hence is not a form of tyranny or domination). And it is this that underpins liberalism's consensual vision of the political.

'In a constitutional regime', Rawls wrote, 'the special feature of the political relation is that political power is ultimately the power of the public, that is, the power of free and equal citizens as a collective body'.[70] Political relationships are, for liberals, those in which coercive force is employed according to principles which both the coercer and the coerced, the rulers and the ruled, can reasonably be expected to accept. It is not enough either that the rulers present legitimations for their authority which are sincerely accepted by themselves but rejected by those subject to their power, such as claims to class, racial, or ethnic superiority, or that reasons are offered that might be acceptable to the ruled though are known as false, and hence as deceptive, by those wielding the power. And while citizens are not expected to converge upon a single conception of justice as the most reasonable, their commitment to reciprocity and hence public reason ensures that they can all reasonably be expected to accept any reasonable conception that regulates the basic structure. Hence public reason is the context in which 'the political relation is to be understood'.[71]

By defining political relationships as those that are consistent with reciprocity, and hence the liberal principle of legitimacy, this distinguishes politics both from other forms of coercive relations, those that are not subject to the same legitimating conditions and are therefore not political such as the relationship between a parent and a child, a master and a slave, an employer and an employee, or from acts of simple violence performed by one person or group of persons over another. What this draws our attention to is the fact that *the liberal principle of legitimacy does not just determine the limits of rightful political action but of politics itself.* This is achieved by taking the boundaries of the political to map neatly onto those areas and activities in which the use of state power can be legitimately employed, those matters on which human reason converges and hence we can reasonably expect persons to agree. So the liberal view of politics requires us to distinguish between those acts of coercion that are in keeping with principles that all can reasonably be expected to accept, which are therefore political, and illegitimate ones, which are subject to the burdens of judgement and therefore outside of the political (though the question of whether they are legitimate or not needs to be determined by the criteria of legitimacy specific to that sphere of activity).[72] Gerald Gaus offers a similar interpretation of the relationship between politics, legitimacy and disagreement when he writes, 'the non-political is, by definition, those matters on which our use of reason leads us to different, reasonable conclusions. It is, by its very nature, the realm of reasonable pluralism. In contrast, we can, at least in part, *define* the political as those matters on which human reason converges, and so necessarily generates constitutional principles that satisfy the Principle of Liberal Legitimacy'.[73] If state power cannot be used according to principles consistent with liberal legitimacy then, by definition, it does not fall within the political sphere. The perimeters of the political are determined by legitimacy.

Politics, at least in constitutional liberal democratic regimes, therefore takes place within the parameters established by the commitment to reciprocity. It is the sphere of activity in which citizens employ coercive power according to principles that can be represented as shared in common ('Only a political conception of justice that all citizens might be reasonably expected to endorse can serve as a basis of public reason and justification').[74] As such, politics must take place against the backdrop of, or with reference to, a commonly shared set of political principles that set the terms of the political association and regulate the public relations between its members. So while liberalism accepts that individuals will continue to have significant moral and religious disagreements, it addresses the question of how such people can nevertheless live together as free and equal by assuming the possibility of universal agreement (even if only hypothetical) on the political principles that regulate their shared association.

This means that liberal theory, strictly speaking, assumes that the regulating principles of a liberal association can be arrived at prior to, or independently of, the processes and procedures of politics itself. We do not have a political realm, cannot do politics, *until* we have a set of principles in place that are consistent with liberal legitimacy. The consensus that is a precondition of politics must be, therefore, in an important sense non-political. But it is important to distinguish between two different forms of consensus that might satisfy this condition. The first works up from a commonly binding normative commitment or considerations that are deemed foundational for the political association, and which provide some guidance as to the way in which the institutions and practices of that association should be designed, or the procedures that allow persons to reach commonly binding and authoritative decisions. As Larmore insists, for instance, 'We must consider respect for persons as a norm binding on us independent of our will as citizens, enjoying a moral authority that we have not fashioned ourselves. For only so can we make sense of why we are moved to give our political life the consensual shape it has'.[75] On this account, it is because we take the respect for persons as pre-politically morally binding, or in Rawls' case the criterion of reciprocity, that we seek to engage with each other in terms of public reason when coming to make political decisions. The second consensus might be more substantive politically speaking and require agreement on specific principles of distributive justice, forms of institutional design or political practices, constitutional essentials, and so on. But in either case, the consensus to which politics as an activity refers must precede politics; it is a precondition of it.

To examine this from another direction, liberalism *must* be a politics of consensus because it is only if all people accept the political principles that regulate the authority that rules over them that they will be able to live on terms that respect them *all* as free and equal. In the absence of a consensus on political principles, even if only hypothetical, our shared association will represent a form of coercively imposed alien will in relation to many members, one in which they are forced to live according to fundamental principles of co-existence that they cannot be said to self- or co-legislate. Such a relationship is one of tyranny, oppression, and domination. As such, whenever coercion is used by the state or its officers beyond principles consistent with reciprocity, it is both illegitimate and, importantly, non-political. Illegitimate coercion is thus the antithesis of both freedom, insofar as people are being forced to obey wills other than their own, and politics. So consensus must be the precondition of politics because otherwise it is unable to ensure that liberal political orders respect rather than violate the freedom and equality of those over whom they rule.

Placing severe limits on the political is a key way in which early liberals attempted to defend individuals from the domination of those with their hands on the levers of state power. It enabled them to identify certain areas of human life, most usefully that of religious persuasion, as lying outside of the remit of the political and hence something that politicians could not legitimately interfere in. This understanding of politics as an activity which takes place against the backdrop of consensus on political fundamentals, such as the principles of justice which should regulate the basic structure of society or the purposes to which state power should be put, remains implicit in contemporary liberal theory. The importance of tolerating a plurality of religious beliefs remains but, as we have come to appreciate the numerous other areas of human life that are subject to reasonable disagreement, such as sexual orientations and practices, the ideals of familial and friendship relationships, the permissibility of pornography, gambling, or alcohol use, and so on, so liberals have determined that these too are not areas in which the state can legitimately employ its power to enforce one particular view over any other. These are issues that lie outside of politics and it would be illegitimate for the state to interfere in them. Indeed much of what many take to be desirable and attractive about liberal politics, especially the divide between the public and private spheres of our lives, stems from the assumption that the political stretches only as far as agreement upon fundamental principles can reasonably be expected.[76] This view of the political relies upon the idea that its perimeters can again be identified independently of the practices and processes of politics themselves.

That Rawls believed reciprocity is a condition of the political only in constitutional democratic regimes should not mislead us to thinking that this is the only form that liberals think politics can take. Liberals do not deny that there are other visions of the political on offer; they need only assert that theirs is normatively preferable to what has preceded it insofar as it provides the reconciliation between law and freedom, as well as the moral constraints to political power, necessary to respect the freedom and equality of all citizens. And liberalism's consensus vision of the political is generated by this noble and worthy normative objective.

Notes

1 For a good account of this concern, see T. Nagel, 'Moral conflict and political legitimacy', *Philosophy and Public Affairs*, 16:3 (1987), 215–40

2 J. Waldron, 'Theoretical foundations of liberalism', *The Philosophical Quarterly*, 37 (1987), 127–50, p. 134

3 J. J. Rousseau, 'Of the social contract', in J. J. Rousseau, *The Social Contract and Other Later Political Writings*, ed. Victor Gourevitch (Cambridge: Cambridge University Press, 1997), 39–152, p. 54

4 I. Kant, *The Metaphysics of Morals*, ed. Mary Gregor (Cambridge: Cambridge University Press, 1996), p. 30

5 I. Kant, *Groundwork of the Metaphysics of Morals*, ed. Mary Gregor (Cambridge: Cambridge University Press, 1997), p. 37. Emphasis in the original

6 *Ibid.*, p. 38. Emphasis in the original

7 Kant, *The Metaphysics of Morals*, p. 146

8 I. Kant, 'On the common saying: This may be true in theory, but it does not apply in practice', in I. Kant, *Political Writings*, ed. Hans Reiss (Cambridge: Cambridge University Press, 1997), 61–92, p. 74

9 *Ibid.*, p. 73. 'All right consists solely in the restriction of the freedom of others', *ibid.*, p. 75

10 P. Benson, 'External freedom according to Kant', *Columbia Law Review*, 87:3 (1987), 559–79, p. 574

11 Kant, *The Metaphysics of Morals*, p. 24

12 Kant, 'On the common saying: This may be true in theory, but it does not apply in practice', p. 73

13   Kant, *The Metaphysics of Morals*, p. 91

14   Kant, 'On the common saying: This may be true in theory, but it does not apply in practice', p. 77

15   Kant, *The Metaphysics of Morals*, p. 51

16   *Ibid.*, p. 91

17   Kant, 'On the common saying: This may be true in theory, but it does not apply in practice', p. 73

18   H. Reiss, 'Introduction', in Kant, *Political Writings*, 1–40, p. 23

19   Kant, *The Metaphysics of Morals*, p. 25

20   Reiss, 'Introduction', p. 22

21   Kant, 'On the common saying: This may be true in theory, but it does not apply in practice', p. 79

22   *Ibid.*, p. 79

23   *Ibid.*, p. 79

24   I. Kant, *Logic* (New York: Dover Publications, 1974), p. 97

25   I. Kant, 'The contest of faculties', in Kant, *Political Writings*, 176–90, p. 187

26   See, for example, A. J. Simmons, 'Justification and legitimacy', *Ethics*, 109:4 (1999), 739–71

27   There is a genuine and interesting question, asked in different ways by Raymond Geuss and Michael Freeden, as to how far Rawls and the form of political theory he inspired is truly congruous with the liberal tradition or whether it has successfully entrenched a recast, and possibly myopic, account of that tradition in which Kant is the key figure and Kantian philosophical concerns and assumptions given primacy, pushing to the margins the utilitarian, idealist, and other threads of this tradition that are more central than this account recognises. Though this is a fascinating question, for our purposes I am going to assume the dominance of Rawlsian 'political' liberalism and hence the centrality of Kant in the liberal tradition. See Geuss, 'Liberalism and its discontents', in his *Outside Ethics*, pp. 11–28; M. Freeden, *Ideologies and Political Theory: A Conceptual Approach* (Oxford: Oxford University Press, 1996). See also D. Weinstein, 'Liberalism and analytical political philosophy', in Jackson and Stears (eds), *Liberalism as Ideology*, pp. 140–58

28   Waldron, 'Theoretical foundations of liberalism', p. 140

29   T. Nagel, *Equality and Partiality* (Oxford: Oxford University Press, 1991), p. 33

30   J. Hampton, *Political Philosophy* (USA: Westview Press, 1998), p. 180

31   Rawls, *Political Liberalism*, p. 224

32   J. Rawls 'Remarks on political philosophy' in J. Rawls, *Lectures on the History of Political Philosophy*, ed. S. Freeman (London: Harvard University Press, 2007), 1–22, p. 12

33   Rawls, *Political Liberalism*, p. 137

34   Bernard Manin writes that 'in the political sphere, it is unanimity that provides the principle of legitimacy' ('On legitimacy and political deliberation', *Political Theory*, 15 (1987), 338–69, p. 341)

35   S. Macedo, *Liberal Virtues: Citizenship, Virtue and Community in Liberal Constitutionalism* (Oxford: Clarendon Press, 1991), p. 78

36   S. Macedo, 'The politics of justification', *Political Theory*, 18:2 (1990), 280–304, p. 282

37   J. Quong, *Liberalism without Perfection* (Oxford: Oxford University Press, 2010), pp. 2–3. Emphasis added

38   Nagel, 'Moral conflict and political legitimacy', p. 238

39   C. Larmore, 'The moral basis of political liberalism', *The Journal of Philosophy*, 96:12 (1999), 599–625, 605–6

40   I bid., pp. 607–8. Martha Nussbaum has also recently highlighted the specifically Kantian derivation of this notion of respect and the demands of public justification that it generates (M. C. Nussbaum, 'Perfectionist liberalism and political liberalism', *Philosophy and Public Affairs*, 39:1 (2011), 3–45, p. 18)

41   Manin, 'On legitimacy and political deliberation', p. 340

42   Rawls defines a moral doctrine as comprehensive 'when it includes conceptions of what is of value in human life, and ideals of personal character, as well as ideals of friendship and familial and associational relationships, and much else that is to inform our conduct, and in the limit to our lives as a whole' (*Political Liberalism*, p. 13)

43   J. Rawls, 'The idea of public reason revisited', in J. Rawls, *Collected Papers*, ed. S. Freeman (London: Harvard University Press, 1999), 573–615

44   Rawls, *Political Liberalism*, p. xiii. For the most strident refutation of Rawls' own account of what motivated the move from *A Theory of Justice* to *Political Liberalism* see B. Barry, 'John Rawls and the search for stability', *Ethics*, 105:4 (1995), 874–915

45   Rawls, *Political Liberalism*, p. 56

46   *Ibid.*, pp. 56–7

47   This account of the origins and nature of pluralism in liberal democratic societies has been widely endorsed by other political liberals. See, for example, Charles Larmore, 'Pluralism and reasonable disagreement', *Social Philosophy and Policy*, 11:1 (1994), 61–79

48   Rawls, *Political Liberalism*, p. xix

49   B. Ackerman, 'Why dialogue?', *The Journal of Philosophy*, 86:1 (1989), 5–22, p. 13

50   Rawls, *Political Liberalism*, p. 50

51   Rawls, 'The idea of public reason revisited' in *Collected Papers*, p. 581

52   This has come to be called the 'asymmetry objection' to political liberalism. See J. Quong, 'Disagreement, asymmetry, and liberal legitimacy', *Politics, Philosophy & Economics*, 4:3 (2005), 301–30

53   See, for example, Ackerman, 'Why dialogue?'; G. F. Gaus, *Justificatory Liberalism: An Essay on Epistemology and Political Theory* (Oxford: Oxford University Press, 1996); Gerald F. Gaus, 'Reasonable pluralism and the domain of the political: How the weaknesses of John Rawls's political liberalism can be overcome by a justificatory liberalism', *Inquiry*, 42:2 (1999), 259–84; C. Larmore, 'Political liberalism', *Political Theory*, 18 (1990), 339–60; Macedo, 'The politics of justification'; Nagel, 'Moral conflict and political legitimacy'

54   Rawls, 'The idea of public reason revisited' in *Collected Papers*, p. 581

55   *Ibid.*, p. 578

56   *Ibid.*, p. 578. See also p. 605

57   Sheldon Wolin is therefore right when he says, albeit a little disparagingly, that 'Public reason, we might say, is the general will in the age of academic liberalism' (S. Wolin,

'The liberal/democratic divide. On Rawls' political liberalism', *Political Theory*, 24:1 (1996), 97–119, p. 103)

58   D. Estlund, 'The insularity of the reasonable: Why political liberalism must admit the truth', *Ethics*, 108:2 (1998), 252–75, p. 254

59   Larmore, 'The moral basis of political liberalism', p. 609

60   Larmore, 'Political liberalism', pp. 340–1

61   B. Barry, *Justice as Impartiality* (Oxford: Oxford University Press, 1995)

62   Larmore, 'The moral basis of political liberalism', p. 615. Emphasis added

63   Larmore, 'Political liberalism', p. 352. Emphasis added

64   Barry, *Justice as Impartiality*, p. 164

65   Rawls, *A Theory of Justice*, p. 12

66   Waldron, 'Theoretical foundations of liberalism', p. 142

67   'When such principles are violated, instead of a society of equals who legitimately coerce one another through participating in common institutions, we have a political system when some are oppressed by others', Valentini, 'On the apparent paradox of ideal theory', p. 336

68   Rawls, *Political Liberalism*, p. 134

69   *Ibid.*, p. 161

70   *Ibid.*, p. 136. See also, pp. li, 68, 216

71   Rawls, 'The idea of public reason revisited' in *Collected Papers*, p. 766

72   As Marc Stears has noted ('Liberalism and the politics of compulsion', p. 536, n. 8), there is something of a discrepancy in liberal thought here, with some assuming that coercion cannot truly be thought of as coercion if it is being used according to liberal principles, so liberalism is a politics without coercion, and others accepting that liberal politics can be coercive but seeks to ensure that such use of state power is always restrained by the limits of legitimacy. Unlike Stears, and largely because the issue of legitimacy is more central to my study than it was to his article, I will adopt the second usage (though believe that my argument could be easily recast in terms of the first)

73   G. F. Gaus, *Contemporary Theories of Liberalism* (London: Sage, 2003), p. 190

74   Rawls, *Political Liberalism*, p. 137

75   Larmore, 'The moral basis of political liberalism', p. 609. See also p. 610 where Larmore again explicitly claims that the commitment to respecting the freedom and equality of all persons is a 'requirement whose validity is external to their collective will … Political liberalism makes sense only in the light of an acknowledgement of such a higher moral authority'

76   As Nagel points out, however, the fact that liberals put a high premium on individual freedom means that they would likely be against restrictions in these areas even if they did believe that it was the state's business to enforce personal morality, or, in the context of our discussion here, if the political did extend to such personal issues. This means that even with the justification for the public/private divide I'm presenting here, many will still suspect that liberalism is really just a disguise for 'a secular, individualistic and libertine morality – against religion and in favour of sex, roughly' (Nagel, 'Moral conflict and political legitimacy', p. 217)

2

The realist vision of the political

Conflict, coercion, and the circumstances of politics

Realism is, like liberalism, a rich and complex tradition and it would be impossible to do full justice to its numerous features and contours in the course of a single chapter. Fortunately the aim here is necessarily more modest. As with the presentation of liberalism in the previous chapter, what I want to do here is develop and present what I take to be the most plausible, consistent, and persuasive account of realism's vision of the political. This obviously requires me to be somewhat selective and exclusionary in relation to what facets of realism I discuss. But, as was mentioned in the introduction, in setting out this vision I also want to try to integrate the recent literature on realist political theory into a more general discussion of realism that draws upon earlier twentieth century exponents as well as exemplars of the realist tradition in international relations. In casting my net a little wider than most contemporary overviews of political realism I hope to be able to develop a fuller account of the central tenets of a realist vision of the political, one that will then form the basis for setting out the realist challenge to liberalism in the following chapter.

Conflict, politics, and legitimacy

Politics is a universal and ineradicable feature of human life. This is because the circumstances in which politics arises and is required are themselves perennial conditions of human existence. Put at its simplest, politics arises in human life because we have to live and act alongside those with whom we disagree, about religion, about morality, about politics, indeed about very many things. This is what Waldron has called the circumstances of politics: 'We may say', he writes, 'that the felt need among the members of a certain group for a common framework or decision or course of action on some matter, even in the face of disagreement about what that framework, decision, or action should be, are *the circumstances of politics*.[1] Politics arises because we disagree with those with whom we have to co-exist. If we agreed on all the matters on which we needed a commonly binding decision, decisions which all have to abide by, then there would be no need for politics. We would all agree what we should do and just get on and do it. But politics is also a response to political disagreement. This is necessarily the case because, as Bellamy points out,

> unlike natural science, there is no agreed epistemology or method for selecting between these views [as to what decision should be taken] other than the process of politics itself. Conservatives, Liberals and Socialists, Utilitarians, Kantians, Aristotelians and Nietzscheans, largely operate with different and incommensurable justifications for their core beliefs that lead them to focus on different features of a given policy and look to different sets of public reasoning to support their views. There is no entirely 'public' way of resolving such disputes, no Archimedean position that unequivocally pays equal concern and respect to all relevant, reasonable views in an uncontentious way.[2]

Of course, if no commonly binding decision is actually required, if we accept that individuals or groups should be free to make up their own minds and act on a particular issue as they please without the political association enforcing or pursuing any one position, then the need for which politics is the response does not arise. But, assuming this is not the case, then the circumstances of politics will pertain, and the need for politics will be generated.

What counts as a political question, a matter on which we need a common decision, is itself the subject of widespread disagreement. The very disagreement about whether something is a matter of public concern or not is itself one of the most hotly contested questions that politics must address.[3] It itself is a political question.[4] This ensures that the political is an undetermined realm. Though any political association will always need to determine the limits of politics for itself, and state what is and is not an appropriate realm of human activity on which a common decision can or should be reached, these limits are contestable and contested.[5] The sphere of the political is therefore potentially limitless in the sense that any question can come to be political if it becomes a subject on which a commonly binding decision is deemed necessary. As Schmitt put it, 'everything is at least potentially political'.[6] So while not all disagreements between persons will generate the circumstances of politics, they all have the potential to do so if they become a matter on which a commonly binding decision is deemed necessary.

Disagreement in politics is the rule rather than the exception. The persistence of disagreement is one of the fundamental and 'stubborn facts' of political life which ensures that there is rarely any natural harmony or order in human affairs.[7] The most basic political question, what I shall call '*the* political question', is how we are to live together in the face of such deep and persistent disagreement. The primary objective of politics must therefore be to provide a framework that creates order and stability by establishing the terms on which we are to co-exist and also the means for making future commonly binding decisions in conditions of disagreement (including the procedures for altering the terms of co-existence). Any successful answer to the political question will therefore require a structure of institutions and practices that provides the basis for persons to live together under a common political authority. Of course, the terms of our political association are themselves matters over which we disagree, because we disagree about the values that should guide our shared lives, the principles that we should adhere to, or the ends that political power should serve. Any political framework will, by its very nature, be *an* answer to many of the most fundamental and contested political questions, such as who rules, where sovereignty lies, and the procedures through which decisions are to be made. It is a settlement that enables co-existence and action-in-concert. As such, answering the political question is the 'basic' task of any political order because doing so is the condition for addressing or indeed posing any others.[8]

It is not a necessary condition of a successful answer to the political question that the political framework governs according to a particular set of normative principles. It need not be just, maximise all individuals' freedom, or treat all persons equally, for example, to be an answer to the political question. Even tyrannical regimes, those that persecute particular minorities or that do not grant their members rights that liberals would take to be fundamental, such as to freedom of religious practice, free speech or association, are responses to the political question even though their political frameworks might be deeply unjust, unequal, intolerant, etc. There can be, properly speaking, tyrannical politics.[9] In this sense, and when elaborating on de Maistre's claim that 'Any government is good once it is established', Schmitt drew attention to a key feature of realist political thought when he wrote that 'a decision is inherent in the mere existence of a governmental authority, and the decision as such is in turn valuable precisely because, as far as the most essential issues are concerned, making a decision is more important than how a decision is made'.[10] The initial purpose of politics is to provide a framework that delivers order and principles of co-existence.

While it is the case that a response to the political question need not be just, or fair, or equal, and so on, it does have to be legitimate in order to count as an instance of *politics* rather than mere domination.[11] The concept of legitimacy is central to realist thought. While the *realpolitik* caricature of realism would have us believe that it reduces the practice of politics to the successful exercise of power, realists adamantly reject this.[12] Might, quite unequivocally, does not equal right. Realists insist that there is a distinction between raw power and legitimate authority, mere force, and political rule.[13] This distinction is most often established by claiming that there are standards internal to politics itself that have to be met if an instance of rule is to be properly thought of as political. Bernard Williams, for example, insists that what he calls the Basic Legitimation Demand (BLD), which arises whenever one agent claims authority over another, 'is inherent in there being such a thing as politics'.[14] Only when the BLD has been met do we have an instance of political order (of which more in chapter 5). Mark Philp links legitimacy more closely to the distinctive nature of political rule: 'it has force where those involved are engaged in the set of practices that we recognise as politics and which claim, in some way or another, *a right to rule others*. This makes their action intelligible, both to themselves and to others, and offers the prospect of internal criteria, simply in virtue of their attempt to order the relations of others and to claim *some remit or right to do so*. Those who are merely violent can make no such claim; whereas those who use politics implicitly claim, in a very general way, a degree of legitimacy'.[15] Those who claim the right to rule, not merely the ability or power to do so, are making some claim as to the legitimacy of their ruling over others. Thus if a ruling group is unwilling to provide a legitimating story then they are not claiming that they have a right to rule. Likewise, if they are unable to provide a sufficient response then they do not, strictly speaking, have a right to rule. In either case, realism insists that their rule is illegitimate and hence non-political. While the regime might provide a framework for co-existence, it is not, strictly speaking, a *political* framework but rather a structure of successful domination.

Realists stress that political disagreement extends to the very normative principles and values of politics, ensuring that persons endorse a variety of different and competing conceptions of the political ideal, and hence prefer different political frameworks, many of which could provide a sufficient answer to the political question. Liberalism is but one form of political framework, or more specifically one family of different political frameworks, that people support and which has the potential to provide a legitimate response to the political question. It is an important truism, however, that no political framework, even a liberal one, can be normatively neutral. Every framework will embody or represent the pursuit of particular substantive ends and values, and often make difficult, or even impossible, the pursuit of others (not always purposefully). The fundamental terms of our shared political association will always be one of the topics on which individuals will inevitably and permanently disagree. Realism takes disagreement to go 'all the way down (in theory as well as practice), not only over different conceptions of the good within a framework of fundamental principles of justice, procedures of deliberation or constitutional essentials, but over any such framework as well'.[16] In modern parlance, we disagree about the right as well as the good. And because the nature of the political framework is itself a matter of perpetual and persistent disagreement between persons, the universal consent or endorsement of that framework cannot be a condition of its legitimacy.

This is a point that Williams stressed most emphatically. While legitimacy does require that a justification be *offered* to each person over whom the state claims to have the authority to rule, it is not the case that that justification must be accepted by each person.[17] As Williams put it,

> when it is said that government must have 'something to say' to each person or group over whom it claims authority – and this means, of course, that it has something to say which purports to legitimate its use of power in relation to them – it cannot be implied that this is something that this person or group will necessarily accept. This cannot be so: they may be anarchists, or utterly unreasonable, or bandits, or merely enemies. *Who* has to be satisfied that the Basic Legitimation Demand has been met by a given formulation at one given time is a good question, and it depends on the circumstances.[18]

This, Williams believed, was one of the key reasons why the satisfaction of the Basic Legitimation Demand could not coincide with the 'insatiable ideal of many a political theoretician: universal consent'.[19]

Even recent attempts to offer more realistic accounts of political frameworks in conditions of radical disagreement by shifting focus to the character of the procedures that generate mutually binding decisions have failed to properly appreciate how the values that underpin proceduralism are themselves controversial, contested, and often rejected. Waldron, for instance, has advocated majoritarian democratic procedures as an appropriate response to the circumstances of politics on the grounds that majority-decisions *respect* the individuals whose votes they aggregate, both in the sense that 'it does not require anyone's sincerely held views to be played down or hushed up because of the fancied importance of consensus', and because 'it embodies a principle of respect for each person in the process by which we settle on a view to be adopted as *ours* even in the face of disagreement'.[20] Likewise, Andrew Mason has advocated democracy as a response to the circumstances of politics, but for him the legitimacy of the decisions that it generates relies upon the *inclusivity* of democratic procedures.[21] There is certainly something to the thought, which underpins both arguments, that procedural issues and substantive issues are separable, in the sense that I can think about the question of the appropriate manner in which we reach common decisions separately from my own considerations as to what those decisions should be. But this does not mean that the sort of disagreements that plague the latter will not apply to the principles and values, such as respect and inclusivity, that underpin democratic procedures also.[22] So even political frameworks that are largely procedural in character, or which are generated by procedures that deliver commonly binding decisions, will fall short of unanimous consensus. They themselves will be controversial and contested elements of a political framework.[23]

This said, for a response to the political question to be legitimate there must be some sense in which the political framework can be justified in terms of beliefs and values that both the rulers and at least a substantial proportion of the ruled share. If this is the case then those persons will recognise the right of the association to expect their obedience, because they take it to be a political entity that has authority (not just power) over them, one whose commands should be taken as having normative force in guiding their actions in virtue of the fact that they were issued by an authoritative political source and regardless of their own independent judgements about those commands. Legitimacy is therefore still a matter of a political framework's conformity with norms, beliefs and values that both the dominant and the subordinate hold in common. But though realism recognises that not everyone will accept the legitimacy of the framework, this does not undermine its legitimacy as long as at least a significant proportion of the citizenry at large endorse the norms and values through which it is justified. This is a realistic account of legitimacy insofar as it accepts that no society is characterised by complete uniformity of beliefs. Yet, as David Beetham rightly notes, 'without a shared minimum of the appropriate beliefs ... being shared between the dominant and the subordinate, and indeed among the subordinates themselves, there can be no basis on which justification for the rules of power can find a purchase'.[24] Disagreement as to what counts as an adequate or sufficient justification will continue and be perpetually open to dispute. There is no authority above the political association that can settle this question, or at least not one that all accept to be ultimately authoritative. But nevertheless, appealing to the beliefs, norms and values of a given society does give us some clear limits as to which justifications will count as plausible or credible within it.[25]

It is interesting, again contrary to the 'might is right' caricature of realism, that the classic realists such as Carr, Morgenthau, and Reinhold Niebuhr were sensitive to the fact that 'Just as within the state every government, though it needs power as a basis of its authority, also needs the moral basis of the consent of the governed, so an international order cannot be based on power alone, for the simple reason that mankind will in the long run always revolt against naked power. Any international order presupposes a substantial measure of general consent'.[26] So the legitimacy of any political association must stand in some relation to the normative nature of its political framework, the ends that it pursues and the values or principles that inform its practices, procedures and institutions and, importantly, this framework must enjoy 'a substantial measure of general consent' from those over whom it applies. Consent need not be understood here in a strongly voluntaristic or explicit sense. This would repeat Weber's mistake of equating the legitimacy of a regime with people's belief in its legitimacy.[27] What matters is rather that the framework can be justified with reference to the beliefs of a substantial proportion of those over whom it applies. So if the values, beliefs and norms that underpin the framework are shared by at least a significant proportion of the citizenry at large that is sufficient to ensure that the state will represent a legitimate political authority, and hence an answer to the political question.

Finally, it is worth emphasising that the very accomplishment of creating a political order that provides a sufficient and legitimate response to the political question is, realists emphasise, a fragile and hence a valuable one. No answer to the political question fixes or resolves the points of contention once and for all. Every answer is temporary and likely to be contested, in both theory and practice.[28] Furthermore, the political question is one that we are constantly called upon to answer and will often need to alter our response to as circumstances change or challenges arise.[29] 'Political stability and order are not once-and-for-all achievements'.[30] That we, at the beginning of the twenty-first century, may be lucky enough to have inherited a relatively stable and established political order, one which is comparatively free from sustained challenges to its political framework and authority more generally, should not lead us to take it for granted as a now permanent feature of Western life. '[H]uman interaction', Geuss says, 'is not something that can ever be taken for granted; it is always potentially disrupted, unstable, and conflict-ridden'.[31] Or in Philp's words, 'the institutionalisation of political rule and its regulations with procedures, rules, and norms to produce a stable and moderate regime is a fragile achievement – one that is, historically, the exception rather than the rule – and even where it exists there remain tensions among the dynamic, innovative, and open-ended character of political rule, the attempt to regulate such forces in a well-ordered state, and the potential for political agency and decision making to generate new constituencies of opposition and contention.[32] The hubris we must avoid is to think that simply because liberalism has successfully entrenched itself as the dominant form of political order, at least in the West, it therefore comes stamped with some sort of guarantee, be it from Truth, God, Reason, or Human Nature, which ensures its survival against current or future instability or challenges. The provision of order and stability is always, according to realism, a magnificent achievement. As such, the extraordinary stability of liberal orders is an incredible accomplishment worthy of much praise, especially when set against the history of mankind. Yet once we fully appreciate the presence and permanence of political disagreement, realists believe we should come to recognise even the order provided by liberal states as a fragile and delicate accomplishment constantly in need of reform and adjustment and by no means certain to last long into the future.

Political disagreement and political conflict

The realist emphasis on disagreement and conflict leads to the obvious question of the origin of such discord. Here realists do not speak with a single voice. Several of the classic realists have tended to see the origin of political disagreement and conflict in features of human nature. Niebuhr argued that disagreement arises out of the inevitable partiality of man's reasoning, a partiality that is most evident and powerful when he is part of some social grouping. As he put it in *Moral Man and Immoral Society*, 'the limitations of the human imagination, the easy subservience of reason to prejudice and passion, and the consequent persistence of irrational egoism, particularly in group behaviour, make social conflict an inevitability in human history, probably to its very end'.[33] Pride, in particular collective pride, is particularly formative in creating conflict.[34] Elsewhere he argued that even racial prejudice can be explained not as a form of ignorance but as the result of 'racial pride' (which he admits is still a form of irrationality, but one which cannot be overcome by 'an enlightened education').[35] It is foolish, Niebuhr believed, 'to regard racial pride as a mere vestige of barbarism when it is in fact a perpetual source of conflict in human life'.[36] There is no such thing as an unprejudiced mind or judgement which is not at least partially corrupted by pride.[37] But groups also tend to pervert our reasoning by limiting the human capacity to envisage the interests and needs of our fellows as clearly as we do our own. This is especially true when a group's economic interests are at stake.[38] Uniquely amongst the realists, Niebuhr argued that the aim of politics should be the development of social justice, and that such development depended upon the extension of rationality. Yet the fact that men would never be wholly reasonable, nor be able to put aside their partial perspectives, ensures that power, force, and coercion will be necessary tools for the achievement and maintenance of social justice.[39]

Schmitt and Morgenthau identified the cause of political disagreement and conflict in the more dangerous facets of human nature. Schmitt took man to be a 'dangerous being' driven by hunger, greed, fear, and jealousy, all of which are evident in the exceptional circumstances of civil wars which reveal the normally concealed realities of political life.[40] Hence 'all *genuine* political theories presuppose man to be evil, i.e. by no means an unproblematic but a dangerous and dynamic being'.[41] As Strauss astutely recognised in his review of *The Concept of the Political*, Schmitt saw man as inherently possessed of the need and desire to dominate and struggle with others. This aspect of human nature ensures that politics is a basic characteristic of human life insofar as the need or desire to engage in struggle between those we consider our friends and those we consider our enemies is the binary distinction that distinguishes the political from all other spheres of human life. In large part, Schmitt's affirmation of the political was an attempt to affirm the struggles and conflicts that he took to be necessary for man to be truly human.[42] Morgenthau, who was deeply influenced by Schmitt (though the relationship between the two thinkers is a complex one), likewise believed that 'The drives to live, to propagate, and to dominate are common to all men', the latter being a tendency that 'is an element of all human associations, from the family through fraternal and professional associations and local political organisations, to the state'.[43] The struggle for power, Morgenthau thought, was simply one of the universal truths that ensured that political conflict was an ineliminable feature of the human condition.

Other realists have been at pains not to blame human nature as such but to locate the cause of disagreement and conflict in the fact of pluralism, either of interests or of values. Carr is a good example of the former position. He argued that the utopianism that dominated international politics between the two world wars assumed (with disastrous consequences) that states enjoyed a natural 'harmony of interests which identifies the interest of the whole community of nations with the interests of each individual member of it'.[44] Such an assumption obscured the fact that nations' interests were plural and conflicting. The doctrine of the harmony of interests was really a moral cover to mask the fact that the interests being pursued served the dominant group which had identified itself with the community as a whole after the First World War.[45] Even the common interest of peace, Carr argued, functions as a means to maintain the status quo against those whose interests would be better served by a different order.[46] As he pointed out, prior to 1918 the notion that war profited no one would have fallen on the deaf ears of numerous nations whose recent experience indicated otherwise.[47] As long as our interests conflict, as Carr thought they inevitably will, political disagreement and conflict will be a perennial feature of human life to which we will constantly need a response.

But much contemporary realism has tended, in a way that undoubtedly draws upon the recent discussions and theories of pluralism in liberal thought, to shy away from making grand claims about human nature or to focus on material interests, and to link disagreement and conflict to theories of the nature of normative value and judgement. Many focus on the close relationship between the presence of plural and conflicting values and the persistence of political disagreement. The exemplar of this way of thinking is undoubtedly provided by Max Weber and he saw, possibly more profoundly than anyone else, just how constitutive of politics the conflict between values is. In one of his most famous passages that address this issue, Weber argued that:

> That old sober empiricist, John Stuart Mill, once said that, simply on the basis of experience, no one would ever arrive at the existence of *one* god – and, it seems to me, certainly not a god of goodness – but at polytheism. Indeed anyone living in the 'world' (in the Christian sense of the word) can only feel himself subject to the struggle between multiple sets of values, each of which, viewed separately, seems to impose an obligation on him. He has to choose which of these gods he will and should serve, or when he should serve the one and when the other. But at all times he will find himself in a fight against one or other of the gods of this world.[48]

Weber's warring gods, and sometimes demons, are the numerous ends, values, and principles to which humans commit themselves. Politics is thus an endless struggle between persons and is so largely because the substantive goals that politics can be put in the service of are several and competing (which is why Weber defined the state according to the unique means that it employs, legitimate violence, rather than the ends that it pursues). As such, the conflicts that exist between persons, groups, classes, and states are struggles to obtain power in order to achieve but one possible value, or but one set of possible values (and thereby, and necessarily, neglect and maybe even undermine the possibility of achieving others). Even more problematically, there is no rational way in which we can come to decide between these competing values: 'as long as life is left to itself and is understood in its own terms, it knows only that the conflict between these gods is never ending. Or, in nonfigurative language, life is about the incompatibility of ultimate *possible* attitudes and hence the inability ever to resolve the conflicts between them. Hence the necessity of *deciding* between them'.[49] Or as Morgenthau rephrased this in relation to the international sphere, 'We find ourselves under a sky from which the Gods have departed'.[50] Without any transcendental standards against which we can assess the competing values, the disenchanted world of modernity leaves individuals with nothing but their own choice to determine which gods and demons to follow.

Yet despite the realist's emphasis on disagreement, one might argue that, at least prima facie, there exists at both the domestic and global level a much higher degree of consensus on political, and specifically liberal, values, principles, and ends than they recognise. While liberals might disagree with conservatives, libertarians with Marxists, and so on, nevertheless they are all committed to human rights, to freedom, to equality, to justice, to democracy, and so on. In fact, therefore, politics seems to be characterised more by agreement on the ends and values of politics than disagreement. The realist response to this is to emphasise that such consensus only applies at the most abstract of levels and as soon as any interpretation of these values is required, or detailed exploration of what they consist of and what they mean politically, what we discover is that even those who are ostensibly committed to the same values nevertheless often radically disagree.[51] '[P]olitical disagreement', as Williams rightly saw, 'includes disagreements about the interpretation of political values, such as freedom, equality, or justice'.[52] And this is because every political value is open to radically different interpretations. While this means that, at the level of particular values, principles, or ends, individuals are likely to disagree or conflict, their 'essential contestability' (to use a now somewhat hackneyed term) ensures that such disagreement and conflict occurs at the level of value systems also. Different value systems are constructed out of different interpretations of the same values. Libertarians and Marxists both believe in freedom and equality – but they disagree as to how those values are to be interpreted and what they demand morally and politically. And even where value systems contain the same or similar interpretations of values, nevertheless different relative priority can be given to different values and hence crucial divisions between persons' moral and political ideals created. This is most evident between different positions within the same moral and political traditions. Libertarians and egalitarian liberals, Trotskyists and Stalinists, are liberals and Marxists respectively insofar as they hold similar enough interpretations of the same values and largely give priority to the same values such that they are part of the same tradition or 'family', but both in theory and practice their differences can still be profound.

Developing this, I want to draw a distinction between political disagreement and political conflict. This is not a distinction that maps onto the terms as employed in common-day usage, but it does draw attention to two different localities of political difference, which is interesting in itself but will also be important for understanding the realist challenge to liberalism. Political *disagreements* are contestations between those who are largely committed to the same form of political framework (e.g. liberal, fascist, theocratic, socialist, communist, etc.) yet whose interpretations of the same values and/or their relative priority differ. Such disagreements often characterise differences between people within the same political parties ('new' and 'old' Labour, the 'left' and 'right' wings of the Conservative party) or who come from similar political traditions (Marxists, liberals, etc.). Political *conflicts* occur between persons who because of their disagreements about values, ends, and principles are led to endorse different forms of political framework, or hold what we might also call different conceptions of the political good. The differences between liberals, Marxists, republicans, theocrats, fascists, libertarians, and so on, are, on this account, best thought of as political conflicts rather than disagreements.

The distinction between political disagreements and conflicts is not a hard and fast one. Crucially, at which point the differences between parties and people become disagreements within the same political framework or conflicts about what form it should take are made indeterminate by the fact that it is very difficult to know at what point a political difference is one of degree or kind. Furthermore, the point at which reform tips into revolution of a constitutional settlement is something that is very difficult to determine, especially in advance. Yet though these distinctions do not match up in any neat way to the reality of political differences, they are useful in helping draw attention to the forms that such differences can take. Most importantly, they allow us to recognise a distinction between political differences that nevertheless take place within a commonly shared political framework (disagreements) and those political differences which are about the political framework itself (conflicts). Or, maybe more simply, there are disagreements between those who broadly share the same conception of the political good and conflicts between those who hold competing conceptions of the political good. Both forms of political difference will exist simultaneously throughout any political association.

When an association is particularly stable, often there will be widespread endorsement of the political framework and so differences will mostly take the form of political disagreements. This is obviously the case in many Western liberal democratic states today. Less stable political associations will probably experience a higher degree of political conflict than political disagreement. But even when a state is relatively stable, the inevitability of political differences means that there will always be some persons within the association who reject the political framework in favour of a different set of political principles and institutions. Though they might not pose an existential threat to the political association as it is currently configured, such conflicts are likely to always be present even if only represented by a minority.

Power, coercion, and the unity of political associations

What we properly call politics includes what goes on within a political framework, such as the creating and amendment of legislation, competitions for office and patronage, etc., as well as attempts to change the rules, institutions, practices, principles, and so on of the framework itself. One of the main functions of a political framework is to determine the manner in which the struggle for power that is politics is to be conducted at both levels; it provides the principles, practices and procedures that regulate the struggle for power, determines the boundaries of what counts as legitimate pursuit of that power and often limits the ends that can be lawfully pursued. Politics is the sphere of contest between human wills competing for the power or influence to determine what decision is taken in the circumstances of politics. It is, as Weber put it, the 'striving for a share of power or for influence on the distribution of power, whether it be between states or between the groups of people contained within a single state'.[53] Whereas politics must, at the most basic level, provide a commonly binding decision on a matter on which there is disagreement, it is also the struggle for the power to determine which decision is reached, where power is essentially defined as the ability or capacity to get people to act in ways, or work towards ends, that they otherwise would not.

Whereas realism is often accused of fetishising military power and reducing politics to a crude game of *realpolitik* in which what matters in determining whose will triumphs is simply the question of who has the greatest military capabilities, realists have actually tended to appreciate the plethora of forms that power can take and which can be employed to achieve the ends that persons and states pursue. In fact they have tended to see the actual use of violence as to abscond from politics, rather than as a practice internal to it. Morgenthau, for example, explicitly distinguished the use of physical violence from political power. 'Political power', he wrote 'is a psychological relation between those who exercise it and those over whom it is exercised. It gives the former control over certain actions of the latter through the influence which the former exert over the latter's mind'.[54] Political power derives from three sources, he thought: expectation of benefit, the respect or love for men or institutions, and the fear of disadvantages. Only in the latter source of political power does physical violence play any part (so the threat of police action, imprisonment, capital punishment, and war) and even then it is only the threat of it that counts as political: as soon as 'violence becomes an actuality, it signifies the abdication of political power in favour of military or pseudo-military power'.[55] And much of Morgenthau's *Politics among Nations* is a discussion of the numerous non-military forms of power that a state might have at its disposal, such as its geographical location, natural resources, industrial capacity, population, national morale, propaganda, and the quality of its diplomacy and government. Carr was equally concerned not to equate power simply with military force, though he did, contra Morgenthau, see it as one aspect of the indivisible whole that is power, along with economic power and 'power over opinion'.[56] Niebuhr even viewed property as a form of power.[57] Working with a broad definition of power enables us to include as arenas of politics those sites other than the state, and which lack any military capacity or functions of physical coercion, that we often refer to as political. And so we speak of 'church politics', 'office politics', or 'family politics', by which we mean the attempts by individuals within these associations to have their will prevail in determining the policies or objectives that they will pursue. But nevertheless, realists have tended to focus on politics as the attempt to gain control or influence of the coercive functions that are today peculiar to the state. While this will, of course, include its 'monopoly of legitimate physical violence', the forms of power that are specific to the state, and which we most often think of as the object of political struggle, are non-violent in character also (though one might still say coercive, even if only minimally so).[58]

But while power is always the immediate aim of politics, it is only very rarely the objective of politics. Though there is something to the thought that those who go into politics do so for the feeling and prestige that power confers upon them[59], or out of mere thirst for the ability to impose their will upon others, a simple will-to-power, most of the time politicians (sincerely) define their goals in terms of a religious, philosophic, economic, or social ideal.[60] As Weber said, 'if politics is to be a genuinely human action, rather than some frivolous intellectual game, dedication to it can only be generated and sustained by passion', and in particular 'the passionate commitment to a 'cause', to the god or demon who commands that cause'.[61] Even Morgenthau, whose second principle of political realism defined interest in terms of power and hence has done much to fuel the caricature of realism as the amoral struggle for control over the will of others, accepted that 'the kind of interest determining political action in a particular period of history depends upon the political and cultural context within which foreign policy is formulated. The goals that might be pursued by nations in their foreign policy can run the whole gamut of objectives any nation has ever pursued or might possibly pursue'.[62]

It is worth stressing this point a little further. Realism, so we are often told, seeks to provide an amoral account of politics: what matters is whose will triumphs and normative or moral considerations are either irrelevant to the primary task of obtaining and using power or indicative of the sort of naïve theorising that characterises the utopianism that much realism attempts to refute. It is strange that such a view has taken hold when we find, amongst the classic texts of twentieth century realism, passages such as this one from Carr's *The Twenty Years' Crisis*:

> The exposure by realist critique of the hollowness of the utopian edifice is the first task of the political thinker. It is only when the sham has been demolished that there can be any hope of raising a more solid structure in its place. But we cannot ultimately find a resting place in pure realism; for realism, though logically overwhelming, does not provide us with the springs of action which are necessary even to the pursuit of thought. ... The impossibility of being a consistent and thorough-going realist is one of the most certain and curious lessons of political science. Consistent realism excludes four things which appear to be essential ingredients of all effective political thinking: a finite goal, an emotional appeal, a right of moral judgement and a ground for action.[63]

Carr's denunciation of 'consistent realism', the focus solely on power and coercion, is echoed across numerous pages of the realist literature. Niebuhr, for instance, in his *The Children of Light and the Children of Darkness* identified the latter as those 'who know no law beyond their will and interest' and, furthermore, as '*evil* because they know no law beyond the self'.[64] Morgenthau even went so far as to claim that fascism had failed as a practical philosophy because it mistook individuals to be simply the object of political manipulation rather than moral persons endowed with resources that cannot be controlled by political power. In other words, fascism failed because it relied almost exclusively on violence and coercion; it was possibly too realist.[65] It would be deeply unrealistic of a realist theory to imagine that politics is the amoral struggle for power devoid of any regard for the values and normative goals that persons hold, or to think of human beings as mere physical objects out of whom any edifice can be constructed if only the right amount of force is applied. It is often forgotten that the focus of much classical realist literature was not to highlight the role or importance of power for its own sake, or to glory in the possibilities that coercion and violence enable, but to provide a realistic understanding of politics which can then serve as a more suitable basis upon which to try to achieve the normative goals to which we aspire. Morgenthau and Carr tried to instruct us as to how to develop a more peaceful world order, which ironically requires a better understanding of the nature and inevitability of political conflict, and Niebuhr sought a more realistic account of politics so as to better promote social justice and democracy. Realism does not offer a vision of politics as merely the naked struggle for power. Rather it seeks to acknowledge that the struggle for power occurs as the means to achieve a plethora of different and often conflicting normative ends. In this sense, politics will always contain both realist (power) and idealist (normative) elements.

If, however, politics is the struggle between wills pursuing power in order to achieve competing ends, principles, and values, then politics is inevitably a realm of domination. Since the natural condition of human beings does not tend towards harmony and agreement, and yet our co-existence depends upon decisions being made, politics will unavoidably involve the predominance of some wills, values, and choices over others. 'Properly political questions always involve decisions which require us to make a choice between conflicting alternatives'.[66] This ensures that politics will always be exclusionary in the sense of favouring some values, ends, or principles over others, and will always involve imposing those upon some who reject them. Philp captures this well when he explains that, 'The point of trying to rule politically is to use authority, not domination, to negotiate, conciliate, and further the interests of those within the state, rather than to seek to impose one set of interests over all others. That said, not every conflict can be resolved, nor every difference settled; domination is a recurrent element in most political systems, and while some cases are evidence of political failure, it also can be evidence of the intractability of the problems faced'.[67] All order will therefore require at least some imposition of values.

This has important ramifications for the role of coercion in political life. Where, as is inevitable in relation to at least a minority of citizens, some reject that the state is legitimate, then their recognition of its authority, and hence their obligation to obey its laws, will of course be absent. As no political framework will ever enjoy the endorsement of all those subject to it, there will always be a sense in which the unity of a political association will need to be maintained through a variety of mechanisms, several of which will be coercive to greater or lesser degrees. No state can maintain its unity purely through the use of coercion but, in the face of the fact of political disagreement, no state can maintain its unity without the use of coercion either.[68] This is why, as Carr noted, 'Power is a necessary ingredient of every political order'.[69] In such cases, coercion, either as a threat or the actual employment of physical violence, plays a crucial function in providing these persons with good reason to do what they otherwise would not and obey the law. Coercion is therefore a necessary fact of political life. All political associations will involve coercion of some sort and no proper form of political understanding can eschew the truth that forms of coercion will be necessary for political order to be possible at all. Of course, more often than not the threat of coercion is sufficient to ensure individuals' obedience and allegiance. But for this threat to provide sufficient solidarity it must be backed up with effective institutions of law and its enforcement agencies such as a police force, judicial system, legal processes, etc. The threat cannot be an empty one.

Coercion can obviously be employed in more or less covert ways. One of the unique characteristics of modernity is the plethora of advanced covert methods rulers now have at their disposal, from the strong use of propaganda and public education through to the more subtle processes and norms of socialisation into any community. It is admittedly difficult to fully demarcate the different forms of coercion, physical and non-physical, covert and explicit, that maintain this order-amongst-disorder. The numerous physical coercive features of social life become most apparent in moments of crisis and especially through the political association's policies towards recalcitrant individuals. Otherwise coercion is usually more covert, but it is not, and never can be, totally absent.[70] As such it is impossible to extricate the consensual and coercive reasons why individuals respect the political framework and obey its laws:

> The coercive factors, in distinction to the more purely moral and rational factors, in political relations can never be sharply differentiated and defined. It is not possible to estimate exactly how much a party to a social conflict is influenced by rational argument or by the threat of force. It is impossible, for instance, to know what proportion of a privileged class accepts higher inheritance taxes because it believes that such taxes are good social policy and what proportion submits merely because the power of the state supports the taxation policy. Since

political conflict, at least in times when controversies have not reached the point of crisis, is carried on by the threat, rather than the actual use, of force, it is always easy for the casual or superficial observer to overestimate the moral and rational factors, and to remain oblivious to the covert types of coercion and force which are used in the conflict.[71]

What Niebuhr said of classes is equally true of individuals.

But in an important sense, an association that relies exclusively or even heavily on actual coercion as the means to maintain its unity and stability is failing. This is not because the use of such coercion has no place in politics but because it will be indicative of the fact that it is failing to provide a sufficient account of the legitimacy of its rule. Hence the question of legitimacy is raised at this point in realist theory also. Legitimacy plays a role in helping secure political rule and the allegiance of sufficient numbers such that the act of governing (rather than dominating) can take place and, importantly, the potential destabilising effects of those that reject that rule can be contained, by force if necessary.[72] Legitimacy, and the process of legitimation, is therefore embroiled in the fray of political struggle rather than normatively independent from it.[73] But while legitimacy is part of the struggle to secure power, to be sure, it does so in the name of moral and political ideals. As we have seen, legitimacy demands that the political association can be justifiable in terms of values, beliefs, principles, etc. that the rulers and the ruled share in common. It is therefore too crude to say that legitimacy is either a servant of individual wills or an independent normative standard that should regulate the will of the rulers. It is, as is so often the case in politics, a precarious balance of moral considerations and the interests of the rulers.

The essential point is that political unity, order, and stability are not natural features of the human condition but must be worked at and created through the sort of coercive political power that the state (as the primary form of political association in modernity) has at its disposal. Politics must create harmony if no natural harmony exists.[74] Political unity is therefore an achievement of politics. It is, as Stears has noted, an 'artefact' of politics, a human creation forged with the tools of coercion. '[O]nly political power', as Schmitt said, 'which should come from the people's will, can form the people's will in the first place'.[75]

The necessity of coercion draws attention to the fact that politics has a special relationship to ruling, the rule of one group over another and, importantly, the rule of one agent's will over all others. Insofar as political rule takes place in conditions of political disagreement, coercion becomes a mechanism not just for ensuring political unity but of imposing the will of the rulers on the ruled that is a condition of such unity. Where decisions must be made, as in the circumstances of politics, the impossibility of absolute consent or consensus means that political life will inevitably involve the predominance of some will, values, and choices. Carr goes too far when he states that 'coercion is regularly exercised by a governing group to enforce loyalty and obedience; and this coercion inevitably means that the governors control the governed and 'exploit' them for their own purposes'.[76] This is only true of some of the ruled – those that do not share the values, ends, and principles of their rulers. For those that endorse these, coercion will feature much less as a factor in their loyalty as they will not be forced to pursue ends that are not their own. But it is this fateful combination of the necessity of coercion, combined with the inevitability of it being put into the service of ends which not all those subject to it will endorse, that gives politics its distinct and potentially tragic ethical dimension. This is something that Weber saw most astutely but which many later realists who were influenced by his work, Morgenthau maybe most importantly, also recognised. Politics mixes partiality with power and, in doing so, turns the political into a sphere of human freedom and creativity that can easily turn into despotism, oppression, and violence.

The autonomy of the political

A paradigmatic feature of realist political theory is the notion that politics is a distinct and autonomous human activity that, as such, requires a mode of thinking that cannot be merely derivate of some other sphere but must itself reflect the particularity of the political. As Morgenthau put it, political realism 'sets politics as an autonomous sphere of action and understanding apart from other spheres, such as economics (understood in terms of interests defined as wealth), ethics, aesthetics, or religion'.[77] This is not to denigrate the existence or importance of these other modes of thought, but rather to insist that each be recognised as distinct and assigned its proper sphere and function.[78] The distinctiveness of politics derives from the fact that the particular problems that it addresses are unique and specific and are not reducible to those of other spheres. Politics arises as a necessary response to conditions that we do not encounter in other spheres of life, in circumstances where we need to reach a common decision, undertake a joint action or agree to a framework in conditions where we disagree about what the decision, action or framework should be – the circumstances of politics. As such, politics is not to be understood as epiphenomenal, a secondary activity generated by some deeper and more basic human activity such as economics or morality, but as responding to its own unique set of questions and concerns (which is not the same as saying that it cannot draw upon the resources of other spheres of human life to address these concerns). And because politics is a discrete human activity, the mode of thinking appropriate for politics cannot be merely derivative of some other sphere but must itself reflect the distinctiveness of the political.

More often than not the autonomy of the political is asserted in reference to morality.[79] For Williams, political realism is to be understood primarily as an alternative to what he called political moralism, which he believed takes two forms: the first is that of an 'enactment model' in which political theory formulates principles, concepts, values, and ideals and politics is then tasked with expressing these in action.[80] According to the second model of political moralism, the 'structural model', political theory sets prior moral conditions for the exercise of political power.[81] While these two models have important differences, what they have in common 'is that they both represent the priority of the moral over the political. Under the enactment model, politics is (very roughly) the instrument of the moral; under the structural model, morality offers constraints ... on what politics can rightfully do. In both cases, political theory is something like applied morality'.[82] As such, Williams wanted to develop a theory of politics which contrasted with political moralism, 'an approach which gives a greater autonomy to distinctively political thought'.[83] At the heart of Williams' political realism is a series of claims which he believed could be derived from within politics itself: that might does not equal right, that politics is an activity which is intended to replace conditions of disorder, chaos, and the terrorisation of one group over another with the conditions for peace, security, and co-operation, and that what distinguishes between war and politics is whether the political order is one that meets the Basic Legitimation Demand (BLD), i.e. that it offers a sufficient justification of its power to each and every person subject to it. These claims, Williams believed, were basic premises of politics, presuppositions which we are required to make in order for there to be such a thing as politics in the first place, and, importantly, claims that are not generated by moral considerations external to the political.

This concern about ensuring that political theory puts adequate distance between politics and morality can be found echoed in the work of several other realists. Geuss' realism begins in the same rejection of politics as applied ethics:

> When I object to the claim that politics is applied ethics ... I intend a ... specific view about the nature and structure of ethical judgment and its relation to politics, and in particular a theory about where one should *start* in studying

politics, what the final framework for studying politics is, what it is reasonable to focus on, and what it is possible to abstract from. 'Politics is applied ethics' in the sense I find objectionable means that we *start* thinking about the human social world by trying to get what is sometimes called an 'ideal theory' of ethics.[84]

Likewise Glen Newey has coined a nice phrase, the 'sovereignty of morality', in order to describe a particular way of doing political theory which realism should avoid, one in which 'moral considerations take precedence over others, and therefore the task of political philosophy is to attempt the project of political design guided by what theory takes to be its fundamental moral commitment or value – justice, autonomy, rights, equality, and so on.'[85]

For both Geuss and Newey, a further problem with the 'ethics-first' view or the sovereignty of morality is that it diverts the attention of political theorists from the real motives upon which people *do* act to the motives which moral philosophy ascribes to people on which it thinks they *should* or *ought* to act, what Galston called 'psychological and motivational realism.'[86] Part of what the distinctiveness of politics rests upon, at least in relation to morality, is that it responds to people's motives, dispositions, values, etc., as they are, which is at the heart of Geuss' claim that 'political philosophy must be realist. That means, roughly speaking, that it must start from and be concerned in the first instance not with how people ought ideally (or ought 'rationally') to act, what they ought to desire, or value, the kind of people they ought to be, etc., but, rather, with the way the social, economic, political, etc., institutions actually operate in some society at some given time, and what really does move human beings to act in given circumstances.'[87] Newey echoes this when he writes that 'The tendency is for theory to retreat from explaining political actors' real motives into an account of how they *would* behave if their motivations conformed to the prescriptions of ideal theory, while politics, most of the time, has to work with *given* motivations.'[88] And so, while Geuss' and Newey's realism develops in a different direction to that of Williams they nevertheless begin with a similar claim about recognising the autonomy of the political from the moral and from that explore the requirements of a mode of theorising that is appropriately sensitive to the distinctiveness of politics.

That realism seeks to assert the autonomy of the political from the moral does not mean that it sees no place at all for moral considerations or reflections upon politics.[89] As Coady says, the target of realism is not morality per se but particular distortions of morality, distortions that he calls 'moralism', 'a kind of vice involved in certain ways of practising morality or exercising moral judgement, or thinking that you are doing so.'[90] In many ways part of what realism seeks to do, especially by highlighting the centrality of struggle, conflict, and power to politics, is give a better account of the unique moral and ethical dilemmas that arise within the political sphere. Weber went to great lengths to explicate how the legitimate violence that is the specific means of the state generates the ethical problems that give politics its particular character.[91] 'Anyone who gets involved with politics', Weber said, 'which is to say with the means of power and violence, is making a pact with diabolical powers' and they must be conscious of the 'ethical paradoxes' of politics.[92] Chief amongst these are 'that it does *not* hold true of his [a politician's] actions that only good can come of good and only evil from evil, but rather that the opposite is often the case'.[93] The achievement of good ends might require the politician to employ morally suspect or morally dangerous means, especially given that the decisive means of politics is violence itself, the so-called problem of 'dirty hands'.[94] And the politician will need to continuously reckon with the possibility that the pursuit and maybe achievement of good ends might generate evil side effects.[95] There is no way in which the 'ethics of conviction' and 'ethics of responsibility' can be united and so politicians must always use their own judgement to decide which end justifies which means and bear responsibility for its consequences, a responsibility that Weber continuously stressed can weigh heavily upon us and determines who truly does have a 'vocation for politics'.[96]

Realism is not amoral in thinking that there is no place for morality in politics but it does want to try to put clear distance between morality and politics such that the latter is not simply subsumed into the former. It denies that the question 'What should we do?' can simply be answered with reference to what we think is the morally right thing to do in any given political situation. The circumstances of politics ensure that we will disagree on what we think the morally right thing to do will be. Politics takes place in conditions where we don't agree what the right course of action is. The prevalence of disagreement and conflict, alongside the fact that power and violence will be a constituent part of any answer to this question, ensures that politics cannot be simply 'applied morality', the mapping of the good or the morally desirable onto the political.

Notes

1   Waldron, *Law and Disagreement*, p. 102. Emphasis in the original
2   R. Bellamy, 'Dirty hands and clean gloves: Liberal ideals and real politics', *European Journal of Political Theory*, 9:4 (2010), 412–30, p. 415

3   Newey, *After Politics*, pp. 7–8, 53–4

4   'We have come to recognise that the political is the total, and as a result we know that any decision about whether something is *unpolitical* is always a *political* decision, irrespective of who decides and what reasons are advanced', C. Schmitt, *Political Theology* (USA: University of Chicago Press, 2005), p. 2

5   Bellamy, *Political Constitutionalism*, pp. 24–6

6   C. Schmitt, *The Concept of the Political* (London: University of Chicago Press, 1996), p. 22. Mouffe, heavily influenced by Schmitt, also writes that 'it is impossible to determine a priori what is social and what is political independently of any contextual reference' (*On the Political*, p. 17). And according to John Dunn, 'Anything about which human beings have come to care is apt to become part of politics: to enter its field and modify its dynamics and outcomes' (*The Cunning of Unreason*, p. 133)

7   P. Lassman, *Pluralism* (Cambridge: Polity, 2011), pp. 10–11

8   Here I adapt Williams' thoughts regarding his Basic Legitimation Demand. See *In the Beginning was the Deed*, p. 3

9   As we shall explore in more detail in chapter 5, Williams denied that this was the case. He was not alone in thinking that politics and tyranny were antithetical: the notion that politics was an alternative to tyranny was also central to Sir Bernard Crick's defence of politics (*In Defence of Politics* (London: Continuum, 2005), ch. 1

10   Schmitt, *Political Theology*, pp. 55–6

11   As such, politics can be thought of as a legitimate response to the political question. Politics is therefore the alternative to the disorder that pertains when the political question remains unanswered, *and* when there are illegitimate responses to the political question

12   Bell rightly points out that '*realpolitik* does not exhaust 'realism'; indeed it has little in common with sophisticated understandings of it' ('Under an empty sky: Realism and political theory', p. 2)

13   Carr even went as far as to claim that 'It is a basic fact about human nature that human beings do in the long run reject the doctrine that might makes right' (*The Twenty Years' Crisis*, p. 130)

14   Williams, *In the Beginning was the Deed*, p. 5

15   Philp, 'What is to be done? Political theory and political realism', p. 471. Emphasis added. See also Philp, *Political Conduct*, p. 56: 'authority becomes expressly political in character when it invokes a more or less explicit claim that the right to rule rests on some specific or principled ground'

16   J. Tully, 'The unfreedom of the moderns in comparison to their ideals of constitutional democracy', in his *Public Philosophy in a New Key – Volume II: Imperialism and Civic Freedom*, 91–123, p. 110

17   Williams, *In the Beginning was the Deed*, p. 6

18   *Ibid.*, pp. 135–6

19   *Ibid.*, p. 136

20   Waldron, *Law and Disagreement*, p. 109

21   A. Mason, 'Rawlsian theory and the circumstances of politics', *Political Theory*, 3:5 (2010), 658–83

22   'Even a procedural device, such as voting, will be subject to these sorts of disagreements, such as those relating to the fairness and appropriateness of different voting procedures' (Bellamy, 'Dirty hands and clean gloves: Liberal ideals and real politics', p. 415)

23   This is the central thrust of my own critical response to Mason's article (M. Sleat, 'Legitimacy in a non-ideal key', *Political Theory*, 40:5 (2012), 650-56)

24   D. Beetham, *The Legitimation of Power* (Hampshire: Palgrave, 1991), p. 17

25   *Ibid.*, p. 17

26   Carr, *The Twenty Years' Crisis*, p. 216

27   See Weber, 'The profession and vocation of politics'. For a critique of Weber's account of legitimacy see Beetham, *The Legitimation of Power*, ch. 1

28   '[F]or any number of reasons, the best of agreements remain potentially open to reasonable disagreement and dissent' (J. Tully, 'The agonistic freedom of citizens', in Tully, *Public Philosophy in a New Key – Volume I: Democracy and Civic Freedom*, 135–59, p. 147)

29   What Williams says of his 'first political question' is therefore true of the political question also: it 'is not (unhappily) first in the sense that once solved, it never has to be solved again. This is particularly important because, a solution to the first question being required *all the time*, it is affected by historical circumstances; it is not a matter of arriving at a solution to the first question at the level of state-of-nature theory and then going on to the rest of the agenda' (*In the Beginning was the Deed*, p. 3)

30   Philp, *Political Conduct*, p. 62

31   Geuss, *Philosophy and Real Politics*, p. 21

32   Philp, *Political Conduct*, pp. 5–6

33   R. Niebuhr, *Moral Man and Immoral Society* (London: Continuum, 2005), p. xvii

34   'The conflicts between men are thus never simple conflicts between competing survival impulses. They are conflicts in which each man or group seeks to guard its power and prestige against the peril of competing expressions of power and pride', Niebuhr, *The Children of Light and the Children of Darkness*, p. 20

35   *Ibid.*, pp. 138–9

36   Niebuhr, *Moral Man and Immoral Society*, p. 143

37   *Ibid.*, p. 144

38   *Ibid.*, pp. 6–7

39   *Ibid.*, p. 24

40   Schmitt, *The Concept of the Political*, pp. 58–9. Here I follow McCormick's excellent analysis of the relationship between Schmitt and Hobbes in his *Carl Schmitt's Critique of Liberalism* (Cambridge: Cambridge University Press, 1999), ch. 6

41   Schmitt, *The Concept of the Political*, p. 61. Emphasis added

42   L. Strauss, 'Notes on Carl Schmitt, *The Concept of the Political*', in *ibid.*, 81–107, p. 95

43   H. J. Morgenthau, *Politics among Nations – The Struggle for Power and Peace*, 4th ed. (New York: Alfred A. Knopf, 1967), pp. 31–2

44   Carr, *The Twenty Years' Crisis*, p. 57

45   *Ibid.*, pp. 74–8

46   *Ibid.*, pp. 50–1

47   *Ibid*, p. 50. This point is developed a little further in chapter 4

48 M. Weber, 'Between two laws', in Weber, *Political Writings*, 75–9, pp. 78–9

49 M. Weber, 'Science as a vocation', in M. Weber, *The Vocation Lectures*, eds. D. Owen and T. B. Strong (Cambridge: Hackett, 2004), 1–31, p. 27. See also Weber, 'The profession and vocation of politics' in his *Political Writings*, p. 355

50 Morgenthau, *Politics among Nations*, p. 249

51 See, for example, Tully, 'The unfreedom of the moderns' in his *Public Philosophy in a New Key – Volume II: Imperialism and Civic Freedom*, pp. 94–5

52 Williams, *In the Beginning was the Deed*, p. 77

53 Weber, 'The profession and vocation of politics' in *Political Writings*, p. 311

54 Morgenthau, *Politics among Nations*, p. 27

55 *Ibid.*, p. 26

56 Carr, *The Twenty Years' Crisis*, ch. 8

57 Niebuhr, *The Children of Light and the Children of Darkness*, ch. 3

58 Weber, 'The profession and vocation of politics', pp. 310–11

59 *Ibid.*, p. 352

60 Morgenthau, *Politics among Nations* p. 26

61 Weber, 'The profession and vocation of politics', pp. 352–3

62 Morgenthau, *Politics among Nations*, pp. 8–9

63 Carr, *The Twenty Years' Crisis*, p. 84

64 Niebuhr, *The Children of Light and the Children of Darkness*, pp. 9–10. Emphasis added. Of course, Niebuhr also thought that the children of darkness were wiser than those of light because they knew the power of self-interest whereas the latter naïvely believed that self-interest could be brought under the discipline of a higher law

65 H. J. Morgenthau, *Scientific Man vs. Power Politics* (Chicago: Chicago University Press, 1946), pp. 8–9

66 Mouffe, *On the Political*, p. 10

67 Philp, *Political Conduct*, p. 62

68 Niebuhr, *Moral Man and Immoral Society*, pp. 4–5. As Sabl notes, this is true of democratic regimes too: 'Because democratic institutions are not always universally popular, and their decisions are typically thought illegitimate by someone, they must sometimes be established and defended by force and must enforce their decisions through coercion' (Andrew Sabl, 'History and reality: Idealist pathologies and 'Harvard School' remedies', in Floyd and Stears (eds), *Political Philosophy versus History? Contextualism and Real Politics in Contemporary Political Thought*, 151–75, p. 151)

69 Carr, *The Twenty Years' Crisis*, p. 213

70 Niebuhr, *Moral Man and Immoral Society*, p. 5

71 *Ibid.*, p. xviii

72 Philp, 'What is to be done? Political theory and political realism', p. 471

73 See B. Honig and M. Stears, 'The new realism: From modus vivendi to justice', in Floyd and Stears (eds), *Political Philosophy versus History? Contextualism and Real Politics in Contemporary Political Thought*, 177–205

74 Carr, *The Twenty Years' Crisis*, p. 50

75 C. Schmitt, *The Crisis of Parliamentary Democracy* (Cambridge: MIT Press, 1985), p. 29

76 Carr, *The Twenty Years' Crisis*, p. 91

77 Morgenthau, *Politics among Nations*, p. 5

78 *Ibid.*, p. 13

79 '[P]olitics is a distinct sphere and type of activity that is not reducible to morality', Philp, *Political Conduct*, p. 1

80 I take this also to be Philp's understanding of the assumed relationship between morality and politics in contemporary political theory when he writes, 'the relationship between moral philosophy and politics is not deductive, and ... many of the abstract values found in moral philosophy and much liberal political philosophy are profoundly inflected by their interpretation, implementation, and realisation in political action ... Politics, and political conduct in this view, needs to be understood largely, although not entirely, on its own terms', *ibid.*, p. 4

81 Williams, *In the Beginning was the Deed*, p. 1

82 *Ibid.*, p. 2

83 *Ibid.*, p. 3

84 Geuss, *Philosophy and Real Politics*, p. 6. See also R. Geuss, 'Moralism and realpolitik', in his *Politics and the Imagination*, 31–42

85 Newey, *After Politics*, p. 106–7. See also Mouffe's claim that 'What is happening is that nowadays the political is played out in the *moral register*. In other words, it still consists in a we/they discrimination, but the we/they, instead of being defined with political categories, is now established in moral terms. In place of a struggle between 'right and left' we are faced with a struggle between 'right and wrong' (*On the Political*, p. 5)

86 Galston, 'Realism in political theory', p. 398

87 Geuss, *Philosophy and Real Politics*, p. 9

88 Newey, *After Politics*, p. 107

89 Bell reminds us that 'while some realists have made implausible claims about the irrelevance of morality, they are the exception not the rule. Realist theorising encompasses a range of ethical arguments' (*Ethics and World Politics*, p. 94)

90 Coady, *Messy Morality – The Challenge of Politics*, p. 15. Bell likewise insists that 'Realism is best seen as a position that challenges *moralism*, not *morality*' (*Ethics and World Politics*, p. 99)

91 Weber, 'The profession and vocation of politics', p. 364

92 *Ibid.*, pp. 362, 365

93 *Ibid.*, p. 362. Morgenthau makes a similar point when discussing the irrelevance of motives or intentions of statesmen in judging whether their policy will be either morally praiseworthy or politically successful (Morgenthau, *Politics among Nations*, pp. 5–6)

94 See, for example, Bellamy, 'Dirty hands and clean gloves: Liberal ideals and real politics'

95 Weber, 'The profession and vocation of politics' in *Political Writings*, p. 360

96 *Ibid.*, pp. 366–8

3

The realist challenge to liberal theory

The recent resurgence of interest in realist political theory has often been presented as essentially little more than the latest in a long line of critiques of liberalism.[1] This is unfortunate and obscures the extent to which realism is a distinct and compelling form of political theorising in its own right. Nevertheless, it is indeed the case that realism does present an alternative and competing theory of politics to liberalism and challenges it on some of its most fundamental theoretical and normative commitments. In this chapter I want to highlight the nature of this challenge and to counter three potential liberal claims as to why this challenge is misguided. In the final section, I shall set out, in light of the reflection upon the two theories that has already taken place, the obstacles and difficulties that a realist theory of liberal politics will inevitably face. This will then act as a guide in the chapters that follow.

Consensus and conflict

'What is distinctive about liberalism', Geuss writes, 'isn't ... so much its openness to pluralism as its view that all societies should be seen as capable of attaining consensus, despite a lack of homogeneity in the manners, beliefs, and habits of their members.'[2] 'What is characteristically liberal', he writes elsewhere, 'is the attempt always to see society *sub specie consensus*.'[3] Though this is a characteristically unsympathetic judgement of liberalism from Geuss, he is right to highlight the sense in which alongside a recognition of religious and moral disagreement runs a notion in liberal thought not only that persons can reasonably be expected to reach consensus on fundamental political principles but that politics properly understood is an arena of (at least relative) concord and harmony. Liberalism sees politics almost like a haven of agreement, even if only on the most basic yet fundamental principles of freedom, equality, justice, etc., in an otherwise chaotic world of deep and radical disagreement. As we have seen, this is underpinned by a particular normative commitment: in conditions where persons who hold different moral comprehensive doctrines seek to live together on terms that respect their status as free and equal moral beings, the only way in which this can be achieved is if they live according to political principles that can be understood as representing the will of each person, which, if this is to be truly universal, means that there must be some set of political principles that all do or can reasonably be expected to endorse. A society whose political framework does not meet this criterion is necessarily oppressive.

Realism challenges liberalism by offering a vision of the political that undercuts the plausibility or appropriateness of thinking about politics in terms of consensus, agreement, or universal endorsement. The realist vision of politics challenges liberalism by conceptualising politics as an activity that takes place in conditions of ubiquitous, perennial, and ineradicable political disagreements and conflicts, including about the very fundamental terms of the political association itself, and hence accuses liberals of being too sanguine about the possibility of achieving either normative or practical consensus.[4] Realism takes pluralism to extend beyond moral and religious diversity to conceptions of the political ideal also. As Williams put it, 'the idea of the political is to an important degree focused in the idea of political disagreement … [and] political difference is of the essence of politics'.[5] Liberalism therefore fails to take seriously the fact that politics takes place in conditions of political discord rather than consensus, including conflict over the very terms or principles of the political association. As such, if we accept that persons will persistently and perennially have disagreements that go all the way down to their most fundamental normative moral and political commitments, leading them to endorse very different political frameworks, then theory cannot be orientated towards the search for reaching final agreements on political principles.[6] Nor can politics be understood to be demarcated or limited by such principles.

This challenge has most often been expressed in terms of liberalism's attempt to 'displace',[7] 'repudiate',[8] or 'abolish'[9] politics, or to describe a world that is 'after' politics in the sense that the disagreements and conflicts that politics responds to have effectively been resolved once and for all.[10] Bonnie Honig, for example, has argued that 'the task of [liberal] political theory is to resolve institutional questions, to get politics right, over, and done with, to free modern subjects and their sets of arrangements [from] political conflict and instability'.[11] By identifying and fixing 'once and for all' a core set of political principles, liberties, rights, constitutional essentials, etc., not only is politics constrained by these but any decision making that touches upon these is effectively depoliticised.[12] Mouffe describes liberalism's central political deficiency as 'its negation of the ineradicable character of antagonism'.[13] The aims of contemporary political philosophy are anti-political, Newey argues, insofar as they aim at 'a philosophical description of a state of the world in which political engagement over fundamental issues no longer exists – a world after politics'.[14] From the realist perspective, with its emphasis on the presence and permanence of political conflict and disagreement, any theory which assumes the actual or hypothetical possibility of consensus is not a theory of *politics* at all. Rather in trying to settle fundamental political matters pre-politically via philosophical argument liberals are effectively attempting to evade or escape from politics.

At this point, the liberal may well object. After all, they might argue, much of what motivates *political* liberalism, especially as presented in Rawls' 'The idea of public reason revisited', is exactly the realisation that people can reasonably disagree about justice. The concept of public reason is introduced exactly because Rawls accepted that citizens reasonably disagree as to which conception of justice is the most reasonable, i.e. most consistent with the demands of reciprocity.[15] His theory does not require that each person comes to recognise the conception of justice that regulates the basic structure of their society as the *most* reasonable. As long as it is presentable in terms of public reason then it is at least minimally reasonable and hence a conception that we can reasonably expect others to accept.[16] It is also, therefore, politically and morally binding on them.[17] Far from overlooking political discord, contemporary liberal theory takes it very seriously indeed, and has adapted the demands of public justification accordingly.

If the realist charge is simply that liberalism fails to recognise political discord, then this can only be a half-truth. To employ terms introduced in the previous chapter, Rawls clearly accepted the presence of political *disagreement* insofar as persons can hold different yet nevertheless still reasonable, and hence liberal, conceptions of justice and his later philosophy was directed towards responding to that. The procedures and values that underpin public reason, which are accepted by all reasonable citizens, provide the political framework for reaching future legitimate and commonly binding decisions. Public reason addresses and is directed towards the resolution of political disagreements. And politics takes place within the framework of principles of justice consistent with public reason.

But political disagreements are only one fragment of the discord that politics is called upon to address. The circumstances of politics do not just include disagreements within a shared political framework, in Rawls' case a constitution designed along the lines of a political form of liberalism, but the political conflicts between persons who endorse different forms of political framework. What Rawls excludes from politics is political *conflicts*, disputes between liberals and those that hold illiberal conceptions of justice (by definition, unreasonable persons).[18] Such differences are not regulated with reference to values and procedures shared in common because unreasonable persons are not committed to the values and procedures of public reason. If we are to make sense of the realist claim that liberalism fails to take the political seriously enough, that is to say without caricaturing or misrepresenting liberalism, this must mean that liberalism excludes political conflicts as part of politics itself. This is not to say that liberals do not recognise that there exist within even well-organised liberal states people who endorse non-liberal political frameworks. They clearly do. What matters is that, from a theoretical perspective, such differences are somehow external to politics. Given the liberal understanding of politics as living in common with or acting according to principles that are shared, the relations between liberals and non-liberals is clearly not political.[19] So non-liberals fall outside of the political. And hence questions relating to them, such as how liberal political associations respond to, deal with, or treat those who reject its framework are not, strictly speaking, questions that a *political* theorist need address.

Of course, very little liberal philosophy assumes that politics takes place in reference to principles that all do accept but has often insisted that they be principles that all can reasonably be expected to accept (or justified according to reasons all can reasonably be expected to accept). The manner in which such arguments proceed is usually to imagine what political fundamentals people who held different and conflicting conceptions of the good *yet shared a particular moral disposition or commitment*, such as reasonableness, equal respect, impartiality, fairness, autonomy, or equality, would agree to. In this sense, a liberal political framework is what one would accept if one held the right sort of moral beliefs. And from this we can defend liberalism's consensus vision of the political as grounded in the recognition of a liberal political framework as what all people should endorse (even if they actually do not).

There are four problems with this hypothetical approach from a realist perspective, all of which stem from or are related to the problem of not taking pluralism seriously enough. First of all, there is indeed something compelling in the thought that what matters is not what political arrangements people would, as a matter of fact, mutually endorse but what settlement is most consistent with the moral demand one emphasises. Liberal political theory, on this view, tells us which constitutional essentials or principles of justice we should endorse if we want to treat others as free and equal, for instance. Such a way of looking at the issue does not require us to worry too much about whether persons do actually endorse such principles or not. What matters is simply identifying what justice demands. The trouble with this response is that it sits in some considerable tension with the liberal account of legitimacy, for that *does* demand that we are able to connect the political principles with the will of each and every person subject to them. Schmitt pressed this point, and the dangerous logic it entails, in relation to democracy, freedom, and the individual will:

> In democracy the citizen even agrees to the law that is against his own will, for the law is the General Will and, in turn, the will of the free citizen. Thus a citizen never really gives his consent to a specific content but rather *in abstracto* to the result that evolves out of the general will, and he votes only so that the votes out of which one can know this general will can be calculated. If the result deviates from the intention of those individuals voting, then the outvoted know that they have mistaken the content of the general will ... And because ... the general will conforms to true freedom, then the outvoted were not free. With this Jacobin logic one can, it is well known, justify the rule of a minority over the majority, even while appealing to democracy. But the essence of the democratic principle is preserved, namely, the assertion of an identity between law and the people's will. For an abstract logic it really makes no difference whether one identifies the will of the majority or the will of the minority with the will of the people if it can never be the absolutely unanimous will of all citizens (including those not eligible to vote).[20]

What Schmitt says of 'the democratic principle' is true also of the liberal principle of legitimacy. Liberal legitimacy requires that individuals are able to recognise the political framework as something that they have willed, rather than had imposed upon them. This vision of politics without oppression, in which all people can live according to principles that they endorse, is at the normative core of liberal political theory. So while there is nothing wrong with this line of reasoning as a way of thinking about how we theorise justice, it does sit awkwardly with the demands of liberal legitimacy. The freedom of non-liberals is preserved in a liberal regime, and the legitimacy of that regime to rule over them, only by equating their will with the will of liberals. But this is, in effect, to ignore their will completely. Hence the question of the legitimacy of coercing non-liberals, and how they are treated as free and equal in a liberal order that they reject, remains.[21]

Secondly, it does seem strange to begin with the position of moral pluralism, indeed the reasonableness of moral pluralism, as the problem that liberal politics is intended to address yet then prioritise one moral value as an answer to that problem. On the one hand, if all persons did give priority to that value then the fact of moral pluralism is not really much of a problem at all. Yet no norm, or general moral framework, enjoys universal endorsement; nor, given moral pluralism, should we ever expect any to do so. Whereas liberals have awarded priority to freedom, respect, or toleration, others might prioritise other values, such as glory, equality, or order, which lead in non-liberal directions. On the other hand, to start theorising from a particular commitment might tell us something about what that norm demands, which is undoubtedly of interest, but it again leaves unclear how we are then to identify the political principles that this generates with the will of those subject to them, especially when they might not share this original commitment. As such, it is unclear how this approach is consistent with the liberal principle of legitimacy. All in all, starting political theory from one particular value, commitment, or disposition, looks like a strange and self-defeating strategy to employ when moral pluralism presents the problem that liberal political theorising is intended to address. 'It seems', as Newey has put it, 'like a journey up the hill, and back down again'.[22]

Thirdly, it is worth noting that even if it were the case that people do share particular moral norms and dispositions, they nevertheless disagree about the meaning of those norms, the demands that they generate, and how they are to be enacted or embodied in political practice. One needs only look at the vast literature by liberal theorists that has been amassed, and the lack of consensus that has been reached, on the meaning of reasonableness, respect, reciprocity, and public justification, as well as the institutions, norms, and practices that they justify, to see that this is true. Even if we were all reasonable, all committed to reciprocity and public justification, we would mean different things by these. To assume not only that all people are or should be reasonable, but that they are or should be reasonable in a way that not even all liberals accept, is clearly to overlook the extent to which persons can reasonably hold different interpretations and meanings of the same concept.

Another realist consideration that is relevant here is the insistence that political theory addresses people's motivations as they are rather than as they should ideally be. To assume that our moral disposition or commitments always trump other non-moral considerations in guiding our actions, to assume that morality is sovereign, is to assume what is empirically false. But the deeper and less pessimistic point to take from this is not that people are essentially bad, more likely to act on self-interested or prudential motives rather than what is morally right, but rather, and here we meet the final objection, that even if it were the case that fully decisive moral or philosophical justifications could be provided in favour of one political framework, the fact is that people would still disagree, our responses to that disagreement will require politics, and we would still need guidance as to how we should respond to that conflict. Nothing would be solved, *politically*, if someone were to achieve tomorrow what has so far eluded those many philosophical minds that have come before us and successfully demonstrate the undeniable, philosophically incontrovertible, truth of any particular form of political association. There will still be some who do not accept the argument and promote and support some alternative and we will still need political procedures in place which respond to this conflict. A *political* philosopher, one might think, should know better: 'A good theory may make idealistic assumptions about people's motivations, but even if it does, it should hold on to a sense that in the real world, even after deliberation, people will continue to disagree in good faith about the common good, and about the issues of policy, principle, justice, and right which we expect a legislature to deliberate upon.'[23]

Waldron has rightly warned us against a dangerous temptation

> not to pretend an opposing view does not exist, but to treat it as beneath notice in respectable deliberation by assuming that it is ignorant or prejudiced or self-interested or based on insufficient contemplation of moral reality. Such an attitude embodies the idea that since truth in matters of justice, right, or policy is singular and consensus is its natural embodiment, some *special* explanation – some factor of deliberative pathology, such as the lingering taint of self-interest – is required to explain disagreement, which explanation can then be cited as a reason for putting the deviant view to one side.[24]

A tempting response at this point, especially for a philosopher, is to argue that those who reject this irrefutable form of political association are being irrational and so their views can justifiably be ignored, which must, at least in part, mean that we can legitimately coerce those who reject it to live according to its laws and constitutional essentials. Imagine if this argument were made in relation to either morality or religion. Just imagine if a liberal theorist argued that the truth of a particular conception of the good legitimated coercing persons to live according to it. They wouldn't be much of a liberal. It is now commonly accepted by liberals that religious and moral pluralism is not just an empirical fact of modern liberal democratic societies but that such disagreement is reasonable, inevitable, and ineradicable. Liberals accept that individuals will disagree about matters of the good without being irrational or guilty of any cognitive error. It is a puzzle why liberals do not accept that the same is true when it comes to politics, the most fundamental normative questions of politics in particular. Indeed it seems somewhat absurd to hold that people can reasonably disagree about the fate of one's eternal soul yet disagreements about the fundamentals of politics must necessarily be the result of irrationality, bias, prejudice, self-interest, or some other unreasonable source. And here I do not just mean the disagreements that exist between liberals, regarding principles of distributive justice, the requirements of multicultural citizenship, or the conditions for developing autonomy, but between liberals and those who endorse non-liberal normative frameworks also. So unless liberals want to make the incredible case for thinking that one can only reject liberal political associations on pain of irrationality, they must accept that political disagreement *and* political conflicts are reasonable and, being reasonable, are as inevitable and ineradicable a feature of modern liberal democratic societies as moral or religious pluralism.[25]

The nub of the realist challenge to liberalism, then, centres on the issue of political discord: though liberalism takes very seriously the political problems generated by moral and religious pluralism, and indeed has recently given much greater recognition to political disagreement also, it does not take seriously enough the diversity of different and conflicting conceptions of the political good, the fact of political pluralism. As such, the notion of a political consensus that sits at the very heart of liberal theory is both unrealistic, in the sense of overlooking the actual deep and permanent disagreements and conflicts that typify political life, and an inappropriate way to think about the nature and character of politics. Liberalism essentially misunderstands the political.

From this fundamental point of difference stem two ancillary considerations that further emphasise the importance of this challenge for liberal theory. Because liberalism fails to recognise the conflictual nature of politics, it is led to overlook both its own status as a partisan and contested political position in the struggle for power that is politics, and, hence, the necessity of coercion in the sense of forcing people to live according to principles they reject. These are not minor oversights. Rather they highlight the extent to which the fundamental normative commitment of liberalism, that liberal politics is a non-oppressive form of co-existence in which each and every person is able to recognise the terms of the shared association as representing their own will rather than the coercive imposition of another, is thrown into doubt by realism's conflictual vision of the political. Far from being set apart from alternative forms of political life by the fact that it is non-tyrannical or oppressive, liberals also use coercive power to impose their will upon those over whom they rule. So not only does realism challenge liberalism's vision of the political, it begs the question of how its very self-understanding and fundamental normative commitment is sustainable in conditions of political disagreement and conflict.

Three objections

It would not be surprising if staunch defenders of liberalism disagreed with the analysis offered in the previous section and, though little time has yet been dedicated to addressing the charges made by realists, in this section I want to examine three potential liberal counter-challenges.

The indeterminacy of realism

If, as realists claim, politics is characterised by endemic disagreement, then this does not in any way preclude the normative vision of political liberalism. Rather, and this is the point made by Paul Kelly, 'All it does is preclude that vision being elevated into an exclusive account of the political ... it [liberalism] merely needs to defend the priority of its approach as an important corrective to the contingencies of political power'.[26] Realists claim too much for their theory if they believe it gives liberals good and compelling reasons to stop being liberals. In an important sense, nothing normatively follows from accepting political disagreement and conflict. All it tells us is that people have differing views about how the political question should be answered, and liberalism is one possible and often viable answer to that question. Realism is plainly indeterminate when it comes to selecting which of the possible responses to the political question we should endorse. This is right. But rather than undermining the realist challenge, I want to claim that this way of thinking about liberalism as a form of politics and realism as a vision of the political against which liberal politics takes place is central to a theory of liberal realism.

To elaborate a little further, realism often challenges liberalism on the grounds that it is a form of political moralism. On such an account, liberal theory is little more than applied ethics in which pre-political moral considerations determine political questions, and modest space is left for thinking about politics as a distinct or autonomous sphere of human activity. If we distinguish between the political question and liberalism-as-a-response-to-the-political-question then this criticism is weakened. First of all, it is difficult to know how any realistic theory could possibly offer a solution to the political question except with reference to moral principles that are taken to have antecedent validity and authority. This does not mean that morality is prior to politics. But it does mean that realism underdetermines how we respond to the political question and must make appeals to moral values in order to do so. Once we accept this then we can appreciate how liberalism does not claim to offer an exclusive account of the political, but rather presents itself as a distinct form of political association that addresses the political question by appealing and giving priority to a particular set of moral considerations, such that, and for example, it understands the legitimacy of a political association to turn on whether it respects the freedom and equality of all its subjects by being acceptable to each and every one, or it takes there to be a series of pre-political moral rights that individuals possess which governments must not violate. It not only provides a framework that settles many of the most controversial and contested fundamental questions of politics, it also places significant constraints on the sort of political decisions that can be deemed legitimate or appropriate in the future. In this sense, from the realist perspective the moral commitments underpinning a liberal framework are a specific response to the political question, a political settlement that entrenches a particular and contestable set of values, principles and ends and a way of managing and controlling such discord in the future. It goes without saying that not all forms of political association share this commitment to a morally constrained politics (or at least not so heavily a morally constrained politics). Indeed, at the extreme we might think, following certain interpretations of Hobbes, that our considerations as to how to respond to the conditions of politics need not make any concessions to morality at all. But liberalism is a moralistic response to the political question at the heart of which lies a series of fundamental moral commitments. And these commitments put very serious constraints on what sort of political association, policies, institutions, etc., make for a morally suitable response to the conditions of politics. Therefore to criticise liberalism on the basis that it is a form of moralism is really only to restate a key, and many think very attractive, characteristic of liberal politics as a response to the political question.

But there are two crucial and related caveats to this which mean that Kelly's response to Newey cannot be the end of the story. Firstly, in keeping with realism's emphasis on political understanding, where there are aspects of liberal thinking that overlook important features of political life then there is no question that liberalism does need to become more realistic. Williams' reminder that the rights and wrongs of humanitarian intervention must take into account several important political considerations which do not feature when we think about the moral principle of rescue, is a good example of this.[27] One could argue that many liberal discussions about its core normative commitments, questions surrounding censorship, toleration, governmental truthfulness, human rights, the limits of freedom, and so on, could also benefit from taking more seriously their political dimensions. Secondly, and as I have been trying to emphasise, there is an important sense in which liberalism's understanding of politics is ill-matched to many of our contemporary political problems, especially those that stem from the sort of political disagreement and conflict that realism emphasises. If such matters fall outside of the political then there is simply no way in which liberal theory can offer us any normative political guidance as to how to respond to them.

Most importantly, however, Kelly seems to assume that liberalism need make little further concession to realism than accepting that political disagreement and conflict does exist. With this small matter accepted liberal theory can carry on business as usual. I fear that this is not the case. Not only does this concession require liberalism to jettison its consensus vision of the political, it also means that the strategy of universal agreement that has been adopted in order to realise liberalism's central normative commitment to being a non-oppressive form of political association has to be abandoned also. In this sense, realism represents a much greater challenge to liberalism than Kelly recognises. And, as such, if one really does want to accept the realist vision of the political yet retain a consistent and compelling liberal theory, then some deep re-theorisation of some of liberalism's central normative commitments and its overall structure is required.

To bring this back to the question of the indeterminacy of realist theory: the surer ground for the realist challenge to liberalism is not the accusation of political moralism, but rather that it attempts to respond to the political question by essentially insisting that politics takes place with reference to an accepted political framework, and in doing so excludes political conflict, that is to say conflict between liberals and persons endorsing non-liberal values, principles, and political frameworks, from the sphere of the political.[28] At best, therefore, liberalism is an incomplete response to the circumstances of politics; it brings order to but one segment of the circumstances of politics, political disagreement, while leaving political conflict essentially outside of the political framework and the purview of politics (theoretical and practical) itself.

Over-emphasising conflict?

There is a potential worry that realists make too much of the fact of political pluralism, that they see societies as characterised by radical and drastic political conflict and instability where, in reality, citizens of Western liberal democracies have largely converged on at least the most basic liberal beliefs and commitments. Those who reject them, on this view, are either too small in number to concern ourselves with (from either a theoretical or practical perspective) or simply weird, mad, or irrational and hence of no normative interest to us. Realists are effectively making a theoretical mountain out of a practical molehill (which would, of course, be a rather unrealistic thing to do).

There are several things that can be said in response to this challenge. The first is that, at an empirical level, disagreement with liberal values and norms is likely to be more prevalent even in liberal societies than liberals like to admit. Even without going to either extreme of the political spectrum, conservatives, socialists, libertarians, and many more, reject one or more of the central tenets of liberal theory (otherwise they would be liberals). The familiar differences that exist between liberal egalitarians, social democrats, and libertarians over justice, for example, undercut the sort of consensus on political principles that the liberal vision of the political requires. Even the most basic liberal commitment, say to public reason or to the liberal principle of legitimacy itself, is rejected by many whom we would (or should) usually be reluctant to call unreasonable or radical. So focusing solely on these more normal or familiar conflicts is still enough to get the realist challenge going. And then there are also those more radically minded individuals, anarchists, communists, fascists, religious fundamentalists, who reject liberal values also. Realism does not need to go the further step and insist that all these non-liberals are potential threats to the stability of the liberal state, through either violent or non-violent means. It is merely to point out that not everyone is a liberal and this should be sufficient, given liberalism's self-image as a non-oppressive form of political authority, to cause them concern.

Nevertheless, I do not think we should lose sight of the presence of political radicalism and the threat that it poses. It seems an obvious mistake to make to simply disregard those who reject liberalism as either mindless thugs or idiots and madmen who do not represent, properly speaking, a political problem. Political extremism and radicalism is a problem facing almost all liberal democratic societies today, one which is increasingly recognised by politicians as a threat that needs to be taken incredibly seriously. Given liberal theorists' concern about coercion, the fact that any response to these people is likely to require the use of force and possibly the suspension of civil rights means that it should be of particular interest to them. In light of this, reflection upon how such issues affect their account of the political should be expected also. Political radicalism is, of course, but one political problem that we face amongst many others. But while political theorists have written reams and reams providing normative guidance on a whole host of other issues, they have so far had very little assistance to offer in relation to radical political conflict.

Finally, there is a worrying ahistoricism to this position, a failure to adequately recognise that liberal democracies are a precious achievement that throughout the twentieth century battled, with both ideas and weapons, those who held rival ideologies. That liberal democracy prevailed in the West should not blind us to the fact that it crumbled, sometimes worryingly easily, in several Western countries and only returned, or in some cases appeared for the first time and with still worrying fragility, after horrific wars or large-scale economic collapse backed by the most powerful political association the world has ever known. That it has been challenged in the past and lost, sometimes to those who were equally dismissed as an irrelevant, farcical, and weird minority, should mean that theorists think more and think harder about how the challenges of political conflict are addressed today so that they do not become serious threats to the stability of liberal democratic societies tomorrow.

Consensus as aspiration

The third possible objection I want to consider is that the role of the consensus on political fundamentals in liberal thought is not, as realism interprets it, a necessary prerequisite of the political but rather an aspirational ideal towards which liberal politics strives. On this view, liberal thought is not so unrealistic as to assume that unanimous agreement between citizens is, as a matter of fact, possible. But it does realise that a society in which all persons can affirm its fundamental political principles would be better, and maybe more legitimate, for it. So rather than providing the foundational assumption of liberal politics, consensus represents an aspiration of liberal societies towards which it is directed and against which the legitimacy of the state can be judged at any one time.

This is a very tempting liberal line of response. But it begs two crucial questions. The first is essentially the question of how liberal theory explains the legitimacy, here and now, of coercing those persons who actually reject liberalism. How, on their own terms, can liberals explain the legitimacy of the liberal state and its use of coercion vis-à-vis these people? As argued above, I am deeply sceptical about the potential success of any appeal to hypothetical consent once you accept that persons can reason sincerely and properly yet nevertheless still reasonably disagree. In what sense can those that live in liberal regimes today yet reasonably reject liberalism be said to nevertheless live according to their own will? I am open to the possibility that this question has an answer, but the point is that it *needs* an answer unless liberals want to accept that liberalism is, until the point that full consensus is reached, oppressive (if only in relation to a minority of people). Furthermore, and as Waldron points out, the fact that liberals believe that politics ideally needs a common view 'does not make the fact of disagreement evaporate. Instead it means that our common basis for action in matters of justice has to be forged in the heat of our disagreements, not predicated on the assumption of a cool consensus that exists only as an ideal'.[29] The question of how we proceed here and now still requires an answer even if consensus is an aspiration.

The second question is somewhat related: Rawls said of comprehensive moral doctrines that such consensus would only be possible via the widespread and unacceptable use of coercive force, what he called the fact of oppression.[30] Again, the comparison with morality or religion is instructive. Political liberals would not countenance arguing that a particular moral or religious framework, Kantianism, utilitarianism, Christianity, or Islam, for instance, provides a moral worldview that politics should look to foster amongst its people in the hope of developing a normative consensus. The fact of reasonable moral and religious disagreement precludes this as inappropriate. The same would therefore be true of political consensus if you accept that political disagreement is inevitable, ineradicable, and reasonable. If this is right then the very achievement of the political consensus that liberalism requires would be deeply illiberal and illegitimate insofar as it would be a vision of political life in which persons live according to principles that they only accept because their potential to freely employ their reason has been violated. This throws significant doubt on the extent to which political consensus can even be considered an aspiration, especially an action-guiding aspiration, in conditions of political pluralism.

Problems for a more realistic liberalism

Liberalism is a vision of the political which seeks to protect the freedom and moral equality of all persons in conditions in which the modern state has the ability to severely violate that status while respecting the fact that citizens hold a plurality of different and conflicting moral and religious beliefs. The central objective of this monograph is to make the case for a more realistic liberalism, a form of liberal theory which acknowledges and attempts to ground itself in an essentially conflictual vision of politics. It should be clear from what has already been said why this is likely to be fraught with some considerable difficulty. As we saw in chapter 1, much of what is distinct and desirable about liberalism is derived from its consensus-based vision of politics. Crucially, the appeal to consensus is contemporary liberal theory's favoured strategy for respecting the freedom and equality of all persons. In abandoning consensus, liberal realism is thereby necessarily eschewing appeal to this strategy for achieving liberalism's central normative objective. But in order to be a theory of *liberalism* at all, liberal realism will therefore have to find a way of responding to those same moral concerns without recourse to political consensus. Those moral commitments will have to find some different form of political expression, one which is consistent with an understanding of politics as characterised by conflict, disagreement, and discord.

Any attempt to create a theory of liberal realism is likely to draw criticism from both liberals and realists. Some liberals will think that the realist challenge to liberalism somehow misses the mark or is not so significant that it warrants the sort of sustained theoretical response that I am giving it here. While obviously I hope the arguments of this first part of the monograph would dispel these doubts, if liberal theorists want to deny the significance or cogency of realist insights then the onus is on them to show why this is the case, which will require them to engage with realism in a much more sustained and serious manner than they have so far. But the liberal response I am more concerned about would be one which accepts the challenge of realism as I have presented it here yet thinks that in developing a theory of liberal realism I effectively secede too much liberal ground to the realist camp. Again, the aim is to try as far as possible to present a theory which is distinctively liberal, but I recognise that there is a significant question regarding how consistent or successful a liberal theory can be if it jettisons its commitment to political consensus. This cannot be determined a priori but must be borne out in attempts to do so. Crucial to judging the success of such endeavours, and what I believe should be a decisive litmus test for liberals, will be the way liberal realism understands how those whose political views do not win out through the processes of politics, both liberals and non-liberals, are nevertheless seen as and, more importantly, treated as free and equal persons despite the fact that they are living in a political association the fundamentals of which they reject. Stears nicely sums up the dilemma here when he writes that what he calls the politics of compulsion 'is deeply sceptical of the contention that the basic terms of the social and political order can be justified to everyone, and it certainly does not believe that an order that could be so justified can be attained *now*. Liberals in response have been loath to concede the first point. Indeed, they cannot do so without ceasing to be liberals at all. The notion that individuals should lead their own lives and be subject only to laws that they can be said, in some way, to have made themselves, has always been the basis of the liberal tradition and will continue to be so'.[31] Further than this, accepting that liberal politics necessarily coerces some to obey laws they reject via the use of state power would be an uncomfortable truth for many liberals to accept, especially as its conception of politics and political legitimacy were designed in order to counter this possibility.[32]

Realists' concerns will come from the other direction. Some are likely to think that the very attempt to develop a theory of liberal realism fails to appreciate just how radical and damaging a challenge to liberalism realist political theory is. There is nothing to be salvaged from the liberal wreckage once realism is taken seriously and any attempt to do so is the theoretical equivalent, to adapt Lord Salisbury's famous metaphor, of clinging to the shreds of a mast that has fallen overboard rather than cutting the hamper away altogether. Again, I think one can only really be certain if a critique is fatal or not if all attempts to provide defences or rejoinders fail, and the fact of the matter is that liberals have yet to respond to realism in any sustained fashion. The other concern will be that in order to ensure the stability of liberal realism, political consensus is not reintroduced into the theory via some philosophical subterfuge or sleight of hand. The recognition of the realist challenge to liberalism must be genuine and pursued to its proper conclusion.

What follows is an attempt to chart a theoretical route to a more realistic theory of liberalism which successfully navigates these obstacles. And, at least in part, the stability and consistency of liberal realism can be judged against how well it addresses these issues. There are two possible strategies that we could employ to develop a theory of liberal realism. Taking into account the vital role that consensus plays in the liberal vision of politics, the first strategy would be to try to modify the agreement required to sustain the political in such a way that it is sufficient for liberal purposes yet somehow not subject to the realist challenge. The second strategy would be to abandon entirely the consensual vision of the political yet find an alternative way of responding to the normative concerns that motivate liberalism. The first strategy is undoubtedly tempting and the least labour intensive insofar as it would allow us to do more tinkering with the fundamental structure of liberal thought than wholesale reform. Our alternative option is the more ambitious and the most likely to result in a political theory that is more realist and less liberal. The next chapter will explore two possible ways of executing the first strategy, though both will be found wanting. The final three chapters then pursue the strategy of abandoning the consensus vision of politics and explore how far it can do so in a way that still meets the sort of normative concerns that any liberal politics must respond to.

Notes

1   Or, when realism is elided with non-ideal theory, simply a corrective to some of liberalism's more abstract or idealistic tendencies

2   Raymond Geuss, 'Liberalism and its discontents', p. 16

3   Geuss, *History and Illusion in Politics*, p. 4

4   Galston, 'Realism in political theory', p. 396

5   Williams, *In the Beginning was the Deed*, pp. 77–8. Bonnie Honig and Marc Stears likewise insist that 'disagreement, conflict and division are constitutive elements of politics' ('The new realism: From modus vivendi to justice', in Floyd and Stears (eds), *Political Philosophy versus History?*, p. 22)

6   Tully, 'The unfreedom of the moderns' in *Public Philosophy in a New Key – Volume II: Imperialism and Civic Freedom*, p. 110

7   Honig, *Political Theory and the Displacement of Politics*

8   Morgenthau, *Scientific Man vs. Power Politics*, p. 75

9   J. Gray, 'Agonistic liberalism', in his *Enlightenment's Wake* (London: Routledge, 1995), 64–86, p. 76

10 Newey, *After Politics*

11 Honig, *Political Theory and the Displacement of Politics*, p. 7

12 See Bellamy, 'Dirty hands and clean gloves: Liberal ideals and real politics', p. 420

13 Mouffe, *On the Political*, p. 10

14 Newey, *After Politics*, p. 134. See also Gray, 'Agonistic liberalism', p. 76

15 Rawls, 'The idea of public reason revisited' in *Collected Papers*, p. 578

16 *Ibid.*, p. 581

17 *Ibid.*, p. 578

18 Unreasonable persons may, but need not, endorse illiberal conceptions of justice according to Rawls; any liberal conception of justice that is grounded in and justified with reference to a particular comprehensive moral doctrine, be it Kantian or utilitarian for instance, will be unreasonable in the sense that we cannot reasonably expect others to accept it

19 I am using non-liberals, and shall do from here on in, to mean those who endorse non-liberal political frameworks. It should be noted, however, that from the perspective of political liberalism, the same questions that I pose here in relation to non-liberals also arise vis-à-vis those who hold liberal yet unreasonable conceptions of justice (comprehensive or perfectionist, for instance)

20 Schmitt, *The Crisis of Parliamentary Democracy*, p. 26

21 I further develop this line of criticism of the liberal principle of legitimacy in my 'Coercing non-liberal persons: Considerations on a more realistic liberalism', *European Journal of Political Theory*, forthcoming

22 Newey, *Hobbes and Leviathan*, p. 4

23 Waldron, *Law and Disagreement*, p. 93

24 *Ibid.*, p. 111

25 The reasonableness of political disagreement will be discussed in greater detail in chapter 6

26 P. Kelly, *Liberalism* (Cambridge: Polity Press, 2005), pp. 106–7

27   Williams, *In the Beginning was the Deed*, ch. 12

28   See, for example, Philp, *Political Conduct* ('Rawls starts by stipulating that his society
      will be extremely homogenous and that any pluralism is "reasonable", and, I would
      suggest, by underestimating the potential lines of conflict that may affect societies',
      pp. 61–2)

29   Waldron, *Law and Disagreement*, p. 106

30   Rawls, *Political Liberalism*, p. 37

31   Stears, 'Liberalism and the politics of compulsion', p. 552

32   As Marilyn Friedman put it, 'This is a foundational concern for any theory that calls
      itself "liberal"' ('John Rawls and the political coercion of unreasonable persons', in
      V. Davion and C. Wolf (eds), *The Idea of a Political Liberalism: Essays on John Rawls*
      (Oxford: Rowman and Littlefield, 2000), 16–33, p. 17)

4

Liberal alternatives

The liberalism of fear and modus vivendi

The liberal vision of the political set out in the first chapter emphasised but one strand of liberalism's rich tradition and history, one in which Kant is the key figure. As I said then, I am conscious that this might draw accusations of selectivity though I think it is fairly undeniable that it is this Kantian strand which is and has been for some time the most influential in contemporary liberal thinking. Even those liberals, such as Charles Larmore, who reject the truth of the broader structure of Kantian metaphysics or moral philosophy, nevertheless find themselves thinking about politics and political legitimacy in ways which are clearly derived from this theoretical heritage.

One consequence of the multi-faceted nature of the liberal tradition is that it is very possible that the resources to develop a theory of liberal realism could be found in those non-Kantian strands of liberalism which have been relatively neglected by contemporary theorists. It might well be that one of these theoretical roads not taken, so to speak, might provide a form of liberalism that is not vulnerable to the realist challenge. There is a certain intuitive appeal to this strategy; after all, if the realist challenge to liberalism were directed towards its Kantian variant then a simple solution would be to endorse a different version which does not share those theoretical features which realism rejects. Of particular interest to us is whether there is a different understanding of the sort of political consensus that liberalism requires which is not vulnerable to the realist challenge. If so, this would allow us to simply alter, rather than abandon, the consensus view of politics at the heart of liberalism in order to make it more realistic.

There are two promising candidates which it is worth exploring, especially given that they have been pursued by realists of a more liberal persuasion also. The first is the liberalism of fear as initially espoused by Judith N. Shklar but which has recently enjoyed something of a revival of interest from other theorists, some of it explicitly in connection with realist political thought.[1] The second is the black sheep of the liberal family, the theory of modus vivendi. It has become commonplace when writing about modus vivendi to begin with a comment on how maligned an approach to liberal political theorising it has been. The publication of several important explorations and defences of modus vivendi in recent years means that this is no longer necessary.[2] This does not change the fact, however, that most liberals continue to follow Rawls' disparaging view of modus vivendi as an inadequate response to the problem of justifying the political order. They have interpreted its attempt to make possible a consensus on fundamental political principles in conditions of pluralism grounded in the prudential reasoning of citizens as some sort of second best achievement, falling short in several important ways from the deep moral and political consensus that liberals hanker for. It is a consensus that is political in the undignified sense of the term; it emphasises compromise and negotiation between citizens with conflicting viewpoints and interests, and hence the principles that persons come to agree upon are little better than temporary and unstable moments of accord, precariously balanced until their various interests and power relations shift.[3] This is anathema to how liberals want us to come to converge upon and understand our relationship to the fundamental principles of our shared political association.

Despite liberalism's near unanimous disapproval of modus vivendi, a few dissenting liberal voices have defended its virtues in conditions of deep moral and political disagreement. What is emerging is a theoretical approach to politics which has more to be said for it than most liberals have so far given it credit for. But importantly for our purposes of developing a realist theory of liberal politics, while modus vivendi is, like liberalism, a consensual view of politics, it has a different understanding of the nature of the agreement that is required to sustain the political. As such, a modus vivendi approach to liberal realism might provide us with the means of maintaining the consensus vision of politics though in a way that is not vulnerable to the realist challenge. The same is potentially true of the liberalism of fear also.

Both theories pursue a very similar theoretical strategy and, because of this, and for the same reasons, unfortunately neither account is fully satisfactory for our purposes either. It therefore makes sense for me to discuss them both together in a single chapter. In the first three sections I shall set out the two theories, focusing firstly on the liberalism of fear, secondly modus vivendi, and then the moral minimum that many recent theorists of modus vivendi have introduced as a condition of political legitimacy. The following section will then argue that neither theory is immune to the realist challenge insofar as the areas of consensus they require are actually the subject of deep disagreement and conflict between persons. Finally I shall focus specifically on modus vivendi's employment of a moral minimum and suggest that it too would be the focus of disagreement, and hence is unable to coherently act as a condition of legitimacy if we accept the realist vision of the political. Ultimately, the failure of these accounts to provide the sort of theoretical framework we require will justify the need to fully abandon the consensus vision of politics in developing a theory of liberal realism.

The liberalism of fear

'Liberalism', Judith N. Shklar wrote, 'has only one overriding aim: to secure the political conditions that are necessary for the exercise of personal freedom'.[4] Her unique contribution to liberal theory was the insight that a necessary political condition for the exercise of personal freedom is the absence of fear: 'Every adult should be able to make as many effective decisions without fear or favour about as many aspects of her or his life as is compatible with the like freedom of every other adult. That belief is the original and only defensible meaning of liberalism'.[5] The fear that Shklar had in mind here as an obstacle to freedom was the fear that cruelty provokes as well as the fear of fear itself. She thought that the absence of fear was a *political* condition for freedom because she took the state, and the agents of the state, to be the most threatening and likely source of fear in modern life, largely because they have unique and often overwhelming resources of physical might and persuasion at their disposal.[6] While there are undoubtedly numerous other sources of fear, such as those created by social oppression or economic insecurity, none can match the modern state's capacity to engage in the sort of irresistible and systematic acts of cruelty which she believed made freedom impossible. This is not to say that states historically developed in order to engage in such activities, or that agents of the state are necessarily motivated by this purpose, only that the system of coercion upon which all governments have to rely in order to fulfil their essential functions makes possible such activities in a way that is not true, for instance, of other institutions such as churches, families, or private businesses.[7] In that sense, and as Hobbes recognised, fear of coercion has to be implied in any system of law. But the liberalism of fear wants to prevent the fear that 'is created by arbitrary, unexpected, unnecessary, and unlicensed acts of force and by habitual and pervasive acts of cruelty and torture performed by military, paramilitary, and police agents in any regime'.[8] There is therefore a strong emphasis in the liberalism of fear on the rule of law.[9]

Identifying the state as a threat, potential or actual, to individuals and their possibility for free agency undoubtedly places the liberalism of fear very squarely in a tradition which harks back to the very earliest liberals. Shklar reminds us how the history of the world since 1914 has been one of continual hope that torture and warfare might be gradually but finally eliminated from the practices of governments, though in actuality 'We say "never again" but somewhere someone is being tortured right now, and acute fear has again become the most common form of social control'.[10] But running parallel to this historical contextual claim regarding the prevalence and possibility of state-generated fear today is a universal, cosmopolitan claim about human psychology: 'Of fear it can be said without qualification that it is universal as it is psychological. It is a mental as well as physical reaction, and it is common to animals as well as to human beings. To be alive is to be afraid, and much to our advantage in many cases, since alarm often preserves us from danger'.[11] More than that, 'putting cruelty first' 'is simply a first principle, an act of moral intuition based on ample observation, on which liberalism can be built, especially at present. Because the fear of systematic cruelty is so universal, moral claims based on its prohibition have an immediate appeal and can gain recognition without much argument'.[12] But Shklar was more than philosophically astute enough to recognise that either of these justifications is susceptible to the charge of falling foul to the naturalistic fallacy, and so she insisted that 'Liberals can begin with cruelty as the primary evil only if they go beyond their well-grounded assumption that almost all people fear it and would evade it if they could. If the prohibition of cruelty can be universalised and recognised as a necessary condition of the dignity of persons, then it can become a principle of political morality'.[13] So while Shklar utilised two justifications for putting the avoidance of fear at the heart of the liberalism of fear, one grounded in a claim about human psychology and the other on moral intuitions, both need to be supplemented by a moral claim regarding the dignity of persons if they are to generate a political morality.

While Shklar did not try to distinguish between these two justifications in any particular detail, nor indicated which of them she believed provided the strongest basis for her theory, either could provide the grounds for the liberalism of fear making what Shklar called a universal, cosmopolitan, claim (which she believed liberalism always has).[14] While the insight that fear, and in particular the fear that governments can engender over those whom it rules, does not provide a *summum bonum*, a notion of the moral or political good towards which we should strive, Shklar did believe that it gives us a *summum malum*, a series of evils 'which all of us know and would avoid if only we could'.[15]

And, further than this, not only do we know what these evils are and seek to avoid them ourselves, but we know that our fellow citizens also understand and fear these evils too. In this sense 'We fear a society of fearful people'.[16]

In terms of the sort of political institutions and practices which guard us from cruelty and the fear of cruelty, Shklar provided a familiar list of liberal commitments: to the rule of law, to a distinction between the private and the public, to toleration, to democracy, to the division of powers, and to a strong defence of equal rights and their legal protection. Importantly, and as a way of further distinguishing the liberalism of fear from other interpretations of liberal politics, citizens' rights are not to be understood as fundamental, given, self-evident or pre-political; nor are they to be thought of as the theoretical foundations of liberalism. Rather they are 'licenses and empowerments that citizens must have in order to preserve their freedom and to protect themselves against abuse'.[17] All in all, what Shklar provided is a reinterpretation of liberalism, one which she believed is more attuned to the original historical concerns that motivated the development of liberal politics yet also has contemporary resonance in a century of unprecedented human tragedy at the hands of the modern state.

There is no doubting that, as Shklar herself recognised, the liberalism of fear is a more pessimistic and negative vision of liberalism than the dominant contemporary offering. It is grounded in avoiding the worst of human experience rather than achieving the best or the ideal. It is an operation in 'damage control'.[18] It takes the basic political units of political life not to be fellow discursive reflecting persons, reasonable others, or Jeffersonian bearers of rights, but the weak and the powerful.[19] Indeed she accepts that insofar as 'it is based on common and immediate experiences, it offends those who identify politics with mankind's most noble aspirations'.[20] The liberalism of fear 'is entirely nonutopian. In that respect it may well be what Emerson called a party of memory rather than a party of hope'.[21]

Yet it is precisely this negative aspect of the liberalism of fear that makes it potentially useful in responding to the realist challenge to liberal political theory. As we have seen, at the heart of realism's challenge to liberalism is the idea that its vision of the political assumed the hypothetical possibility of a consensus on the fundamentals of our shared political association, such as the purposes to which government should rightly be put, the just principles for distributing the benefits and burdens of social co-operation, and the line between the political and the non-political. While realism argues that such political questions are and inevitably will be the subject of disagreement and conflict, thus undermining the possibility for political consensus, what the liberalism of fear offers is the possibility of shifting the content of the agreement to political commitments which can more plausibly be thought of as universally held, from the goods that politics should pursue to the evils that it should protect us against. It seeks to ground liberalism on a series of negative commitments which it hopes that citizens who hold different and conflicting positions on a vast range of political, moral, and religious issues can nevertheless still endorse. If this is indeed plausible then it would provide the sort of political agreement necessary to sustain the liberal vision of politics in such a way that circumvents the realist opposition to consensus-based theories.

Modus vivendi and the political framework

Despite the disdain with which many contemporary liberal theorists have viewed it, several recent advocates have been keen to locate a theory of modus vivendi as congruent with the liberal tradition, though it works against that tradition in a variety of ways. John Gray, for example, has argued that modus vivendi represents the 'second face' of liberalism while, likewise, Patrick Neal has interpreted modus vivendi, or what he calls 'vulgar liberalism,' as the 'third party' in the liberal conversation, along with Rawlsian political and Razian perfectionist liberalism.[22] Insofar as it seeks authoritative political principles of co-existence between individuals that enjoys, or can be represented as enjoying, the acceptance of all those subject to them, despite their broader moral and religious disagreements and conflicts, modus vivendi clearly aspires to a similar political ideal to that of liberalism.[23] Consensus on the political framework is still the overriding objective.

That said, modus vivendi's starting assumptions about the conditions in which politics, and political theorising, take place are thoroughly realist. Proponents of modus vivendi have tended to criticise liberal theory on the grounds that though it gives appropriate attention to the problems generated by religious and moral pluralism, it nevertheless fails to take seriously enough the fact of political disagreement.[24] While liberals accept as a fact of modern societies that citizens will hold conflicting and irreconcilable moral and religious views, they have tended to underestimate the profound political disagreements which separate citizens also, and the specifically political problems that these conflicts generate. These do not just take the form of disagreements between those who are essentially liberals, say on the limits of free speech or to privacy, but include conflicts with persons whose comprehensive normative commitments lead them to endorse illiberal forms of political association, such as those who hold that the state should play an extensive role in guiding individuals towards particular moral or religious ends which many might reject.[25] Gray has put this best when he writes:

> In reality, though there is unprecedented lip-service to them, most late modern societies contain little consensus on liberal values. Many people belong at once in a liberal form of life and in communities which do not honour liberal values. At the same time, many who stand chiefly in liberal ethical life do not subscribe to some of its traditional values. The liberal ideal of personal autonomy is the idea of being part-author of one's life. For some, the pursuit of autonomy comes into conflict with allegiance to an established community. For others, it is in tension with the freedom to respond to the needs of the present. For all these kinds of people, 'traditional', 'liberal', and 'postmodern', ethical life is inescapably hybrid … Most late modern societies are far from exhibiting an overlapping consensus on liberal values. Rather, the liberal discourse of rights and personal autonomy is deployed in a continuing conflict to gain and hold power by communities and ways of life having highly diverse values. Where it exists, the hegemony of liberal discourse is often skin-deep.[26]

Modus vivendi recognises 'that many citizens endorse normative frameworks that recommend as ideal illiberal models of political association. Those frameworks may imply, for instance, that persons should be prohibited from pursuing certain misguided goals, or that the state should be more active in directing citizens towards specific virtues and goals'.[27] So modus vivendi shares the realist description of the background pluralism, of radical moral, religious, and political conflict, against which politics and political theorising is understood to take place.

This affects how modus vivendi theorists understand politics and its purpose. As McCabe has put it:

> Persons inhabiting a common world frequently make conflicting claims, face joint tasks, participate in an interdependent economy – in numerous ways come into contact and conflict with each other. If these encounters are to be manageable, stable, and productive, some consistency and uniformity in rules and overall decision-making is necessary. This means that citizens have ample motivation to establish laws and institutions all can agree upon, even if they do not match the ideal arrangements specified by many of their own normative frameworks.[28]

The objective of a political framework is to provide 'common institutions in which many forms of life can coexist'.[29] It does this by ensuring the conditions of peace and security that are sufficient to enable those subject to them to live at least minimally worthwhile lives. This means that the political framework will always inevitably have a sort of 'second best' quality; it is not what any citizen would ideally choose but they accept and endorse it on the grounds that it secures peace amongst radical disagreement and conflict. So whereas liberal political theory understands the political consensus as essentially reflecting an underlying moral agreement on the ends or values that the state should pursue, embody, or protect, modus vivendi views the agreement as largely prudential in nature. That is to say, on the modus vivendi account, what makes the political framework valuable is purely that it makes possible peaceful co-existence between people with different values and ideals. The objective of politics is 'to reconcile individuals and ways of life honouring conflicting values to a life in common'.[30] Or, as McCabe states, modus vivendi 'grounds political life not via its consonance with citizens' deepest moral ideals but instead as something diverse citizens can agree to as an acceptable compromise'.[31] Modus vivendi therefore views the political framework as essentially 'a compromise among citizens who recognise the value of ordered political life but realise that the political vision recommended by their distinct normative frameworks cannot be achieved'.[32]

Often, as is the case with Gray and McCabe, this background of disagreement is explained as the inevitable consequence of value pluralism. As a theory of the origin and nature of disagreement, the central tenets of value pluralism are that there are myriad different values, ideals, and ways of life, that these can often conflict, and that when they do there is no common standard or currency against which to judge which should take precedence. This is the thesis of value incommensurability. Though Gray and McCabe obviously assert value pluralism because they believe it to be an accurate description of the nature of the moral universe and of our moral experience, a central feature of this account of disagreement and conflict over others is that it understands pluralism to be an inevitable and non-regrettable feature of human life (unless one is to regret that morality takes the form that it does). In this sense, value pluralism can account for the permanent character of conflict not as the result of human frailty or weaknesses, such as ignorance, bias, prejudice, irrationality, or error, but as the foreseeable consequence of the plural and incommensurable nature of moral and political ideals. Like realism, therefore, modus vivendi takes conflict to be an inevitable, permanent, and ineradicable feature of both moral and political life.

Modus vivendi assumes a less ambitious account of the objectives of political theory than is currently dominant; it rejects the project of discovering the right, correct, just or true principles of co-operation, principles that all persons should or would accept if they were reasonable, and so on, and focuses primarily on showing how individuals with conflicting views can nevertheless agree to live according to a common political framework on the prudential ground that it enables peaceful co-existence. In circumstances of disagreement and conflict, concentrating on creating stable conditions in which those who conflict can nevertheless co-exist peacefully is no small or insignificant feat. And it is an achievement that is realised not pre-politically, by reason or political philosophy for instance, but through the familiar processes of politics themselves (bargaining, compromise, etc.). Modus vivendi does not, therefore, displace or theorise away politics, nor does it take politics to be a version of applied moral theory, but makes the very achievement of political order an artefact of politics itself. And, as such, the fundamental principles of our shared political association are not to be viewed as permanent features of the political landscape but as provisional sanctuaries of peace and stability, always liable to be disturbed by the winds of radical conflict. Political disagreement and conflict is never fully overcome, even in contemporary liberal democratic states, and we must always be prepared to alter even the most fundamental terms of our shared associations in response to the disruptive forces of disagreement.

Theorists of modus vivendi are agreed that the terms of our shared political association must not be understood as universal principles of politics discovered by reason or constructed out of basic moral intuitions and commitments which all individuals share (or should share) such as autonomy, reciprocity, or respect for persons. They cannot be for, as we have seen, individuals disagree about exactly these matters, which moral values are most fundamental for designing political institutions, what political demands such values give rise to, and what rational procedure it is appropriate for persons to follow. And we should not expect otherwise. Despite this, and though the principles of the political order might be arrived at via compromise, negotiation, and bargaining, we still have significant reason to endorse the political order, according to theorists of modus vivendi, on the grounds that stability and peace are preconditions of many human goals and needs. Not all ways of life are guaranteed to pursue peace but the majority will undoubtedly have good reason to do so.[33] And hence though the terms of the political order might come about via a process of bargaining and negotiation between parties, which will inevitably require individuals to compromise on their ideal vision of politics, all will have good reason to endorse it on the grounds that it allows them to live together peacefully on terms they can all endorse. And the authority of that political order is derived from it successfully providing the conditions for peace and stability in conditions of conflict.

Modus vivendi, legitimacy, and the moral minimum

Theories of modus vivendi cannot be prescriptive as to the form that the political framework should take or which principles of co-operation persons should endorse. This is because modus vivendi assumes that what counts as an acceptable compromise will be contingent on the actual beliefs, values, interests, and power that individuals or groups actually possess. We cannot determine pre-politically or solely via philosophical argument which form of political order will or should be endorsed for the simple reason that the political framework is the outcome of the processes of politics itself. And while what counts as an acceptable compromise will be dependent upon persons' actual account of the political ideal, it is also important to bear in mind that while 'the spirit of compromise is the spirit of resigning oneself to the idea of the second best', nevertheless it is often the case that the second best requires us to do something very different from the ideal.[34] To use the example offered by Avishai Margalit, the Catholic Church believes that being a nun is the ideal life for a woman though it recognises that the sacrifices entailed to live such a life, giving up sexuality and motherhood, are such that most women cannot achieve this ideal. But the second best form of life is not to become a nun with a slightly more lax attitude towards sex but instead to be a good mother.[35] This is a good example of where the second best option, what one would be happy to compromise on, cannot simply be extrapolated from the ideal. The compromise that a person might be willing to reach need not be simply a watered-down version of their ideal, 'slightly-less tolerant liberalism', 'property-owning communism', or 'libertarianism with a small welfare state' for instance, but could be something radically different. This will not always be something that can be determined a priori but will be discovered through political activity.

There is an obvious but important consequence to this: any form of political order that secures the conditions of peace and stability amongst those who disagree and conflict can be deemed legitimate from the perspective of modus vivendi. Clearly there are numerous forms of political framework which can successfully achieve peace and order, liberal variants being but one family of frameworks. As has often been the case throughout human history, and continues to be the case today, many of these regimes will not be liberal.

Other, less liberal, alternatives might also provide the necessary reconciliation equally well, or possibly better depending on the circumstances.[36] So according to theories of modus vivendi, liberalism has no particular or special claim to political legitimacy.

Yet while the test of legitimacy for any regime is its success in mediating conflicts of values, modus vivendi theorists are adamant that this should not be mistaken for a theory of politics in which, in the words of John Gray, 'anything goes'.[37] The worry that it might stems from the fact that without any moral criteria for what counts as a legitimate form of political order, modus vivendi might legitimise profoundly unjust societies. There are two ways in which this might be possible. The first is if the actual political ideals endorsed by the members of the political community are themselves widely unjust (for example, if freedom of speech is not widely endorsed, or if the vast majority fail to support the political equality of women). Then it is likely to be the case that the political framework agreed will be inherently unjust also. The second possibility is if the majority of persons within a society endorse unjust relations with regard to a particular minority, wishing to deny them, for example, the right to vote, to education, or freedom of religious practice. Again it is likely that the political framework will be discriminatory in relation to that minority.

Theorists of modus vivendi have sought to avoid this conclusion by insisting that there is a minimum moral standard that any legitimate political order must satisfy. It is worth briefly outlining three different accounts of what this moral minimum consists in. On McCabe's understanding, modus vivendi is not to be distinguished by its rejection of moral ideals, as many of its critics assert, but by its commitment to a certain minimal moral universalism. This minimum is grounded in the commitment that the interests of all persons matter equally and from this McCabe derives three criteria for legitimate political order: 1) The rulers ought in some way to be accountable to the ruled; 2) Punishments should be appropriate to the crime; 3) No person should be forced to worship in a manner they reject.[38] Margalit seeks to make a moral distinction between compromises and what he calls 'rotten' compromises. A rotten compromise is an agreement to establish or maintain an inhuman regime that treats particular persons with cruelty and humiliation.[39] Rotten compromises, Margalit insists, 'are not allowed even for the sake of peace. Other compromises should be dealt with on a retail basis, one by one: they should be judged on their merit. Only rotten compromises should be ruled out on a wholesale basis'.[40] And finally, Gray argues that the limits to what counts as a legitimate modus vivendi are determined by the universal minimum of human goods and evils that it is necessary to either have or avoid for any kind of human flourishing to be possible.[41] Gray lists courage, prudence, and sympathy for the suffering and happiness of others as generically and hence universal human values which are necessary for proper human well-being.[42] Equally, there are universal human evils such as genocide and enslavement which if pursued by a state would rule out any reasonable claim to its legitimacy.[43] So only a political regime which reconciled conflicts between values within the limits of providing the space for the pursuit of universal human goods and avoiding common human evils can be legitimate, though Gray is clear that many political regimes, not only liberal ones, will meet the test of the universal minimum.

Part of what is interesting about this moral minimum of political legitimacy, the notion that politics is compromise but within moral limits, is that it seemingly makes redundant the primary criticism that liberals have levied against modus vivendi over the years: that it addresses what it is rational or prudential for individuals to endorse in light of their self-interest without any regard for normative considerations about the justness or morality of the principles on which persons agree. While liberals might still be concerned about how thin the moral minimum that theories of modus vivendi demand is (which we shall come back to in the following section), nevertheless it is clearly not the case that it endorses the 'anything goes as long as it creates peace and stability' account of politics that has often been assumed. To be fair, this misunderstanding on liberals' part can probably be put down to the fact that the resurgence of interest in modus vivendi has been very recent and, until now, the main model of compromise available was that offered by Hobbes (who obviously did not feel the need to include any moral minimum to political legitimacy at all). In this sense, though modus vivendi theories are often accredited with a deeply Hobbesian heritage, the requirement of a moral minimum for political legitimacy makes it an interesting and importantly different theory of politics. And, because of this requirement, we might also have reason to think that it will be a fruitful theory of politics from which we can develop an account of liberal realism.

Peace and fear as supreme values

Both the liberalism of fear and modus vivendi pursue a similar theoretical strategy for identifying the grounds of consensus upon which politics can then be built. In both cases, the objective is to identify a single value that all persons consider most important such that it overrides their numerous moral, religious and political disagreements. Though they might disagree about so much else, the hope is that we can identify this supreme value and in doing so provide the shared ground that a consensus vision of the political requires. This strategy remains deeply problematic from a realist perspective and, given that both theories pursue it, it makes sense to address them together in the same section.

It would be a mistake to think that modus vivendi treats peace and security as ultimate goods in the sense that they will everywhere and always take precedence over all other goods that people might pursue. But nevertheless, an assumption is made that, for the vast majority of persons at least, peace and stability are of instrumental value insofar as they are the precondition for successfully achieving almost any other good humans might pursue. In this sense, the reasons that motivate persons to seek peace and stability are many and varied and it is this that, in conditions of radical disagreement and conflict, enables co-existence and accommodation in the manner modus vivendi requires.

Importantly, the aim of politics according to modus vivendi is not to maximise peace and security.[44] It is commonly thought that a fully stable political order would demand significant losses in terms of other important values, such as freedom or rights, which most people would be unwilling to accept. The obvious response, and the one that modus vivendi pursues, is to try to indicate a level of stability that constitutes a basic minimum and then deem legitimate any political order that passes that threshold. But how are we to identify this basic minimum? Inevitably, any minimum will require us to trade off security with other goods that we value. Yet people will and do disagree as to how much security should be sacrificed in the name of, for example, the right to privacy, freedom of speech, or religious toleration. How this calculation should be made, and hence how much security and stability is to be deemed even minimally acceptable, will depend on each person's account of the political ideal. For those who think that little stability should be traded off against other values, the minimum threshold will necessarily be higher than for those who think that we can afford a greater loss. Different citizens are therefore going to assess whether a political order provides the conditions for security differently; some may judge the status quo to reach the required minimum and thus legitimate while others will judge that it falls short. The notion that persons can reach a consensus on what counts as an appropriate level of peace and stability required for legitimacy therefore runs up against the prevalence and permanence of political disagreement.

The liberalism of fear takes a slightly different route insofar as it attempts to identify a consensus on a *summum malum* rather than a *summum bonum*, the evils all humans want to avoid rather than the goods they seek to achieve. Yet it still assumes that individuals agree what the universal evils are and when they are being perpetrated. It still requires consensus. But it is highly unlikely that the realist insight regarding perennial and deep disagreement and conflict does not apply as much to the possibility of a *summum malum* as to a *summum bonum*. Yael Tamir has criticised Shklar's theory, for instance, on the grounds that it 'takes an overly narrow view' of fear:

> Fear has many faces: some have to do with the fear of suffering, of experiencing physical pain or torment; others concern more social fears, like the fear of being marginalised, silenced or ignored. Each of these fears leads in a different political direction. Individuals do not fear only bodily torture and cruelty, they fear social oppression, marginalisation and, worst of all, invisibility.[45]

Remember that for Shklar, the assuaging of individuals' fear that they will be subject to state brutality is considered the biggest threat to individuals' freedom, and, in this sense, the worst of the evils. Yet, as Tamir argues, many 'faces' of fear are non-physical in nature, such as exile, social oppression, or lack of recognition. For some, these evils might, at least in certain circumstances, be considered worse than physical cruelty. The threat of exile, social humiliation, or shame has throughout history been recognised by groups and governments as an often more effective way of ensuring obedience than the threat of death or torture ('I would rather die than have x happen to me'). Richard Rorty expanded Shklar's focus on fear and cruelty and placed great emphasis on the evils of humiliation and other psychological wrongs. In his reinterpretation of the political evil at the heart of George Orwell's *1984*, and in particular the torture scenes of the last third of the book, Rorty took the moral to be that 'the worst thing you can do to somebody is not to make her scream in agony but to use that agony in such a way that even when the agony is over, she cannot reconstitute herself. The idea is to get her to do or say things – and, if possible, believe and desire things, think thoughts – which later she will be unable to cope with having done or thought'.[46] As such, what is most despicable about O'Brien's torture of Winston is not the physical pain he causes but using that pain to get him to violate his most fundamental commitments, both about the physical ('2+2=5') and the moral world ('Do it to Julia!'), and in doing so made him incapable of having a self because he cannot weave a coherent web of beliefs and desires.[47]

More importantly, however, these sources of cruelty and fear can be understood to weaken the self-respect or the sense of membership citizens need to see their aims and goals as worth pursuing in the first place. Those who take this position are likely to support political positions in which the more familiar liberal commitments are weakened in order to accommodate the demands of recognition necessary to secure social identity and membership.[48] This is a deeper point as it challenges Shklar's claim that the absence of the fear of physical cruelty is the main precondition for individual freedom. There is no need for us to adjudicate here these competing claims regarding the preconditions of freedom; rather what matters is the very fact of disagreement on the issue: there is a plurality of different forms of cruelty and sources of fear, we disagree as to the relative wickedness of them as well as which poses the more fundamental threat to freedom, and hence even from this more negative basis we will be led to endorse different, maybe even non-liberal, forms of political association.

So one difficulty with using either the liberalism of fear or modus vivendi as the basis for a more realistic liberalism is that they rely on agreement on what the minimal universal human goods or evils of peace or fear consist of. Yet these are matters on which people disagree. Furthermore, both approaches assume that people do indeed share the commitment to peace or the absence of fear. The second reason for doubting the appropriateness of the theoretical strategy employed by these two theories is that it is questionable whether these commitments are really as universal and pervasive as they assume. Let me start again with modus vivendi. There are several points to make here. While it is undoubtedly true that all ways of life value peace very highly (I doubt if there are any that do not value it at all), there are some in which a person's fundamental interests might be understood to require or demand that they prioritise other goods above it. For example those which place high worth upon goods such as honour, glory, militaristic duty, or the salvation of their soul, may actually require conflict and, in some instances, war and violence. Such conceptions of the good are, at least today and in Western societies, rare. But they do exist. Nor should we overlook the more frequent (though that is still not to say regular) occurrence of ways of life that place high value on peace yet which see conflict and violence with particular groups, such as 'infidels', the bourgeoisie, the oppressors, or a certain religious or ethnic minority, as positively encouraged on moral or religious grounds as a means to achieving other goods (such as the favour of God, full equality, freedom, or racial or ethnic purity). In these slightly more familiar cases, the worry is not that these ways of life do not value peace at all but that they do not desire peace with particular groups, that their moral or religious doctrines rule out co-existence, and, as such, may either not desire to live according to a common framework or, at the extreme, pursue policies of repression and violence. As such, and this is the important point, advocates of these ways of life may deem the terms on which everyone else is willing to accept a modus vivendi as incompatible with the achievement of their fundamental interests.

One need only think of Georges Sorel's (chilling) justification for the use of violent means against the bourgeoisie to disrupt social order and harmony to appreciate this possibility. 'Proletarian violence', he wrote, 'carried on as pure and simple manifestations of the sentiment of class struggle, appears thus as a very fine and heroic thing; it is at the service of the immemorial interests of civilisation; it is not perhaps the most appropriate method of obtaining immediate material advantages, but it may save the world from barbarism'.[49] Sorel did not believe that violence was intrinsically valuable, but he did think that it was justified, and maybe even demanded, as a means to achieve true socialism. Likewise, Niebuhr argued that

> a social conflict which aims at greater equality has a moral justification which must be denied to efforts which aim at the perpetuation of privilege. A war for the emancipation of a nation, a race or a class is thus placed in a different moral category from the use of power for the perpetuation of imperial rule or class dominance. The oppressed, whether they be the Indians in the British Empire, or the Negroes in our own country or the industrial worker in every nation, have a higher moral right to challenge their oppressors than these have to maintain their rule by force.[50]

While Niebuhr questioned the efficacy of violent over non-violent means, especially as oppressed minorities are always likely to be disadvantaged when it comes to the use of violence, he was adamant that violence was not intrinsically immoral[51] nor that it could ever be completely ruled out as the best means to achieve justice and social equality.[52] Essentially, where the ends justify the means, violence and social conflict might be the appropriate response.

The notion that all persons have an equal and identical interest in peace formed the political aspect of the assumption that E. H. Carr called the 'harmony of interests'. This assumption, he believed, played a crucial role in inter-war years in convincing nations and statesmen that no nation could have a rational or moral claim to pursue war, and hence to 'evade the unpalatable fact of a fundamental divergence of interest between nations desirous of maintaining the *status quo* and nations desirous of changing it'.[53] The status quo is something which people will fight for and fight against. While it was easy to see how such an assumption, that war profits nobody, would be easily accepted in 'English-speaking countries', those who had benefited most from the Versailles treaty and hence had most cause to discourage disruption to the inter-war status quo, he was less convinced that other nations shared their conviction:

> The argument did not seem particularly convincing to Germans, who had profited greatly from the wars of 1866 and 1870, and attributed their more recent sufferings, not to the war of 1914, but to the fact that they had lost it; or to Italians, who blamed not the war, but the treachery of allies who defrauded them in the peace settlement; or to Poles or Czecho-Slovaks who, far from deploring the war, owed their national existence to it; or to Frenchmen, who could not unreservedly regret a war which had restored Alsace-Lorraine to France; or to people of other nationalities who remembered profitable wars waged by Great Britain and the United States in the past.[54]

Far from nations having an equal and identical interest in peace, the use of conflict and war had actually been seen by nations as a means for furthering their ends rather than hindering them. The point I want to take from this, and which emphasises the claims made above, is that while peace is something that most people value very highly, it is not something that we all value highly all the time. Sometimes peace might not be an end that we share, especially when violence and war might successfully achieve our goals and objectives. And the same goes, I think, at the domestic level also: it is a contingent matter, dependent upon the interests and values but also importantly the relative power of particular groups within society that determines the likely success of violence, whether maintaining peace rather than pursuing conflict is deemed to be the appropriate course of action.

Accepting the inevitably transient nature of any political order and the permanent possibility of disruption is, of course, one of the aspects of modus vivendi that is congruent with realist theory. As John Horton puts it: 'A modus vivendi exists only as long as the parties to it continue to accept it; when that ceases to be so, either negotiation or coercion are pretty much the only options. This is not, though, because a modus vivendi is especially unstable, as its critics allege, but because such instability, if that is what one wants to call it, is at the heart of politics'.[55] Yet modus vivendi overestimates the extent to which even a stable political order will enjoy the affirmation of all its members. Even a political order justified on the more minimal grounds of peace and stability will be home to individuals who reject the status quo. And, insofar as the legitimacy of a political order depends in a theory of modus vivendi on it being affirmed by those who are members of it, it therefore runs up against the same problems of radical disagreement that afflicted liberalism's consensus account of political legitimation.[56]

Shklar's recognition that the prohibition of cruelty must be universalised as a condition of the dignity of persons if it is to be a central principle of political morality is also problematic from a realist perspective, and on similar grounds. In referring to the dignity of persons in order to shore up this normative universalism Shklar made a conscious appeal to moral intuitions. Realism sees such appeals as largely inimical to the fact of deep pluralism. You do not have to accept the profoundly pessimistic claim that there are some people who do not share this intuition, who totally reject the notion of human dignity, for this to be troubling, only that there are some who do not think *all* others are deserving of respect. Insofar as the liberalism of fear is a party of memory, and in particular remembering the horrors of the twentieth century, it should recognise that agents of the state have all too often actively pursued policies of cruelty and fear over certain groups of their own fellow citizens, possibly even with the view that doing so was a morally worthy end in itself. The sad fact is that such people, the powerful, have regularly done so in full appreciation of the psychological and physical harm that they caused, indeed, sometimes revelling in the abhorrent and terrifying brutality they have inflicted upon those they do not consider their moral equals.

What is potentially attractive about both the liberalism of fear and modus vivendi is that they allow us to overcome the realist challenge by finding common ground on minimal normative commitments, the fear of cruelty or peaceful co-existence, which all persons can endorse. This might provide normative yet sufficiently realistic foundations on which liberal politics can then be developed. But if the arguments presented in this section are right, then there is good reason to think that both theories are still vulnerable to the realist challenge insofar as it calls into question both the universality of the values that they appeal to and the fact that not everyone is committed to them in the manner that the theories require, and draws attention to the fact that, even where there is such commitment to the values themselves, individuals will still have substantive disagreements over issues such as when peace is secure or what counts as cruelty. It is unlikely, therefore, that either theory can provide the minimal but universal normative basis necessary to address the realist challenge.

Realism and the moral minimum

The inclusion of a moral minimum into contemporary theories of modus vivendi is an intriguing development, especially for a theory that takes Hobbes to be one of its main progenitors. Gray admits that he has to 'amend' Hobbes in order to interpret him as thinking that the legitimacy of a regime depends upon how well it enables conflicts among values to be negotiated.[57] But clearly for theorists such as Gray the introduction of the moral minimum is justified on the grounds that it precludes the possibility that any regime that ensured peace and stability – even if a minority (or even majority) were oppressed or treated unjustly – could be deemed legitimate. This is not the same as saying that only liberal regimes can be legitimate; all theorists of modus vivendi accept that other (non-liberal) forms of political order might be legitimate if they meet this moral minimum. Yet clearly it does, as intended, normatively rule out several ways of political life.

Remember that both Gray and McCabe argue that modus vivendi is to be distinguished not by its avoiding relying on substantial moral claims but by its commitment instead to a minimal moral universalism that will be endorsed by any decent way of life. For McCabe this moral minimum is the presumption of moral equality, the notion that all persons matter equally, which then generates the three conditions of legitimacy we encountered above.[58] Gray's moral minimum is determined by those universal human goods (e.g. courage, prudence, sympathy for others) and evils (e.g. genocide and slavery) that any flourishing human life will either require or avoid. Hopefully by now it will be unnecessary to labour this point too long – but in the case of Gray's moral minimum there will be significant disagreement both about how to define these universal human goods and exactly what constitutes a morally acceptable minimum. These are the same problems of indeterminacy and disagreement that we encountered above in relation to peace and stability, pain and humiliation. Furthermore, persons will disagree just how these universal human goods are to be weighed and ordered. In other words, very quickly this moral minimum will become the focus of disagreement. We might think that matters will be slightly easier when it comes to the universal human evils. But unfortunately disagreements as to what constitutes genocide or slavery prevail there too (as will any attempt to determine what counts as a minimum definition of either).

McCabe's moral minimum fares little better. While it would be nice if it were true that 'any morally decent person must endorse' the commitment to moral equality, or that it cannot be plausibly denied, unfortunately many people whom I expect we would be reluctant to deny were 'morally decent' have denied this and many continue to do so (Aristotle here is a case in point – was he not a morally decent person because he denied this moral equality of persons?).[59] If we are to start from a truly realist theoretical position, we have to avoid taking this presumption for granted. And again, even if it were the case that all persons did indeed affirm such moral equality, what they would take it to demand in terms of concrete politics would inevitably differ. McCabe lists three conditions that he takes to follow from moral equality: the accountability of the rulers to the ruled; punishment must be proportionate to the crime; and religious toleration.[60] Others will think alternative or further conditions will follow. But even accepting McCabe's conditions: what counts as even a minimally accountable government? And how do we determine whether a punishment fits a crime? That depends both on how heinous the crime is interpreted to be (e.g. does it matter if a murderer killed his victim because of his race or religion?) and how severe the punishment (and indeed, how severe the punishment is interpreted to be). And, of course, we disagree as to which actions should be considered crimes (e.g. the use of drugs, blasphemy, adultery, or apostasy). And it is quite astonishing that McCabe takes the claim that 'no person should be forced to worship in a manner they reject' to be a minimal claim that no one can plausibly deny, let alone one that is and has been agreed across human communities.[61] The idea that persons should not be forced to worship in manners they reject is clearly a commendation to tolerate those with whom you disagree about religious matters and to refrain from imposing your practices and beliefs upon them. While this is far from being a commitment exclusive to liberalism, it is nevertheless not one that is, or has been, shared by all ideals of political life. And, after all, we should not overlook the possibility of certain communities in which amongst the numerous things that divide its members, religious beliefs are not amongst them. Where there is significant enough overlap of religious beliefs, religious toleration will not be a necessary component of any potential compromise.

The point of the moral minimum in theories of modus vivendi is that it is thin enough that it provides the grounds for rejecting the notion that any political order which enables the peaceful co-existence of its members can be legitimate, regardless of how immoral or unjust the regime may be. And clearly if this moral minimum is to do any serious work in helping us determine illegitimate regimes, it will need to be fairly specific about what that minimum is. Yet the inclusion of a moral minimum sits in some tension with the original justification for turning to a theory of modus vivendi in the first place, the fact of deep and radical moral and political disagreement. Alongside the difficulties identified in the previous section with the indeterminacy of peace and stability, these issues with regard to the moral minimum make modus vivendi an inadequate basis for developing a theory of liberal realism.

Notes

1   See, for example, J. Kekes, 'Cruelty and liberalism', *Ethics*, 106:4 (1996), 834–44; J. T Levy, *The Multiculturalism of Fear* (Oxford: Oxford University Press, 2000); Richard Rorty, *Contingency, Irony, and Solidarity* (Cambridge: Cambridge University Press, 1989); Yael Tamir, 'The land of the fearful and the free', *Constellations*, 3:3 (1997), 296–314. For the realist connection see K. Forrester, 'Judith Shklar, Bernard Williams and political realism', *European Journal of Political Theory*, 11:3 (2012), 247–72; F. Freyenhagen, 'Taking reasonable pluralism seriously: An internal critique of political liberalism', *Politics, Philosophy and Economics*, 10:3, 323–42; Williams, *In the Beginning was the Deed*. While Bernard Williams endorsed and developed Shklar's liberalism of fear, I will not be discussing that in this chapter given that his theory is the exclusive focus of the chapter that follows

2   See, for example, Gray, *Two Faces of Liberalism*; J. Horton, 'Realism, liberal moralism and a political theory of modus vivendi', *European Journal of Political Theory*, 9:4 (2010), 431–48; D. McCabe, *Modus Vivendi Liberalism* (Cambridge: Cambridge University Press, 2010); P. Neal, *Liberalism and its Discontents* (New York: New York University Press, 1997); E. Rossi, 'Modus vivendi, consensus, and (realist) liberal legitimacy', *Public Reason*, 2:2, 21–39

3   Larmore, 'Political liberalism', p. 346; Rawls, *Political Liberalism*, p. 147

4   J. N. Shklar, 'The liberalism of fear', in ed. S. Hoffman, *Judith N. Shklar – Political Thought and Political Thinkers* (London: University of Chicago Press, 1998), 3–20, p. 3

5   *Ibid.*, p. 3

6   *Ibid.*, p. 3

7   *Ibid.*, p. 11

8   *Ibid.*, p. 11

9   See Judith N. Shklar, 'Political theory and the rule of law', in ed. Hoffman, *Judith N. Shklar – Political Thought and Political Thinkers*, pp. 21–37. In chapter 7 I shall incorporate Shklar's account of the rule of law into liberal realism's justification of its legitimacy vis-à-vis those that reject liberalism

10 Shklar, 'The liberalism of fear' in ed. Hoffman, *Judith N. Shklar – Political Thought and Political Thinkers*, p. 9

11 *Ibid.*, p. 11

12 *Ibid.*, p. 11

13 *Ibid.*, pp. 11–12

14 *Ibid.*, pp. 10–11

15 *Ibid.*, pp. 10–11

16 *Ibid.*, p. 11

17   *Ibid.*, p. 19
18   *Ibid.*, p. 9
19   *Ibid.*, p. 9
20   *Ibid.*, p. 13
21   *Ibid.*, p. 8
22   Gray, *Two Faces of Liberalism*, p. 2; Neal, *Liberalism and its Discontents*, p. 185
23   See Horton, 'Realism, liberal moralism and a political theory of modus vivendi', pp. 348–9
24   'To conceive of the central threat to the stability of a liberal, constitutional order as disagreement about the nature of the good life is to think of liberal political life as if it were analogous to a philosophical debate amongst friends. With our attention focused upon the fact that they disagree about the concrete answers to the question of the good life, it is easy to overlook just how much social order is implicitly being assumed when we suppose that that question is the root of conflict and the threat to stability. This is not a picture of people fighting over wealth, or power, or race, or ethnicity, or selfishness, or greed, or vainglory, or – well, just about anything people actually fight over in the real world. It is in fact a picture which resembles more than anything else the, relatively speaking, genteel disagreements amongst contemporary political philosophers about the viability of liberal political theory!', Neal, *Liberalism and its Discontents*, p. 197
25   McCabe, *Modus Vivendi Liberalism*, p. 133
26   Gray, *Two Faces of Liberalism*, p. 13
27   McCabe, *Modus Vivendi Liberalism*, p. 133
28   *Ibid.*, p. 133
29   Gray, *Two Faces of Liberalism*, p. 6
30   *Ibid.*, pp. 5–6
31   McCabe, *Modus Vivendi Liberalism*, p. 126
32   *Ibid.*, p. 133
33   Gray, *Two Faces of Liberalism*, p. 20
34   A. Margalit, *On Compromise and Rotten Compromises* (Oxford: Princeton University Press, 2010), p. 117
35   *Ibid.*, p. 116
36   McCabe asks, 'what ensures that the liberal state will result from this approach [the actual deliberations of citizens seeking to reach a mutually acceptable compromise]? The answer is: nothing' (*Modus Vivendi Liberalism*, p. 160)
37   Gray, *Two Faces of Liberalism*, p. 20
38   McCabe, *Modus Vivendi Liberalism*, p. 138
39   Margalit, *On Compromise and Rotten Compromises*, p. 2
40   *Ibid.*, p. 1
41   *Ibid.*, p. 8. McCabe likewise believes that modus vivendi is committed to what he calls 'minimal moral universalism', though for him this is given by 'a core set of human rights which the MVL [modus vivendi liberal] state is committed to protect and which draw the limits of the tolerable' (*Modus Vivendi Liberalism*, p. 138)
42   Gray, *Two Faces of Liberalism*, p. 8
43   *Ibid.*, p. 111

44   In this paragraph, I am heavily indebted to and build upon the argument made by Horton, 'Realism, liberal moralism and a political theory of modus vivendi', p. 444

45   Tamir, 'The land of the fearful and the free', p. 302

46   Rorty, *Contingency, Irony, and Solidarity*, pp. 177–8

47   *Ibid.*, p. 178

48   This is McCabe's interpretation of Tamir's argument (*Modus Vivendi Liberalism*, pp. 130–1)

49   G. Sorel, *Reflections on Violence*, ed. J. Jennings (Cambridge: Cambridge University Press, 1999), p. 85

50   Niebuhr, *Moral Man and Immoral Society*, p. 154

51   *Ibid.*, pp. 112–13

52   *Ibid.*, pp. 157–67

53   Carr, *The Twenty Years' Crisis*, p. 51

54   *Ibid.*, p. 50

55   Horton, 'Realism, liberal moralism and a political theory of modus vivendi', p. 440–1

56   To be fair, Gray does accept that peace is, as he puts it, a 'contingent' good in the sense that not all persons will pursue it; but he claims that this is not a peculiar disability of modus vivendi because (as value pluralism insists) all political ideals are contingent goods, and hence this problem is really a limitation of all forms of ethical/political reasoning and not specific to theories of modus vivendi (*Two Faces of Liberalism*, p. 135). Realism would generally accept this point. But, even on Gray's own terms this does not strike me as a particularly strong defence – especially when modus vivendi's account of legitimacy depends upon consensus

57   *Ibid.*, p. 133

58   McCabe, *Modus Vivendi Liberalism*, p. 138

59   *Ibid.*, p. 138

60   McCabe does not present them as conditions of legitimacy. But insofar as they are requirements that derive from the thin moral commitment to moral equality which he thinks no one can plausibly deny, they effectively play this role within his theory. Nor does he say that these three exhaust the conditions

61   McCabe, *Modus Vivendi Liberalism*, pp. 139–40

5

Bernard Williams and the structure of liberal realism

The hankering for political consensus that lies at the heart of liberal theory is not some epiphenomenal offshoot of an underlying epistemological commitment to a form of Platonism or value monism, but is driven by the moral commitment to place theoretical and practical limitations on the ends to which political coercive power can be put. This is a noble objective. Yet as we saw in the previous chapter, even attempts to modify the nature and content of the required consensus to a set of less substantial but nevertheless sufficient moral and political principles still leaves liberalism open to the realist challenge. As such, we need to accept that any plausible theory of liberal realism will need to abandon the consensus vision in favour of realism's conflictual account of politics as taking place in conditions of inevitable and deep political disagreement. But one cannot simply tack liberal theory on to a different account of politics. This is not how political theories work. They do not float free of their normative and theoretical foundations. A change in those foundations will necessarily have wider ramifications for the structure and content of the theory itself. This is what we find in trying to develop a theory of liberal realism. If liberal theory is to incorporate a conflictual vision of the political not only must the very structure of that theory change in crucial ways but, in doing so, the strategy for realising the central moral commitment of liberalism must adapt also.

With this chapter, and the two that follow, we now turn to the issue of what a realist theory of liberal politics might look like. The specific aim of this chapter is to set out the basic structure of liberal realism in regard to one crucial aspect: the relationship between politics and domination. This is particularly important because it relates directly to the question of how liberalism can successfully respect the freedom and equality of all persons in conditions of political disagreement, in particular those that reject liberalism, and how it can reimagine itself as a non-oppressive form of politics in light of the fact that the liberal state does indeed impose its principles, values, and ends upon at least some who do not endorse them. How liberal realism answers these questions depends in large part on how it understands the role of coercion and domination in political life.

In his *In the Beginning was the Deed*, Bernard Williams offered not only what many have taken to be the most well-developed and potentially fertile theory of political realism (in spite of the fact that it was published posthumously and incomplete), but also a model for conceptualising the relationship between politics and domination in realist terms. One might naturally think, therefore, that Williams' work offers the most promising starting place for developing a theory of liberal realism. Unfortunately, I do not think this is the case. There are several facets of Williams' theory that are unrealistic in the sense of being out of kilter with other key assumptions of the realist tradition or attempts to uphold political distinctions that a realist theory cannot sustain. One could almost go as far as to say that several of Williams' key theoretical assumptions are decidedly liberal, rather than realist, in character.[1] Most important for our purposes is Williams' distinction between politics and successful domination. For Williams, and for reasons we shall explore shortly, any coercive relationship that is sustained purely through the use of power is illegitimate and hence non-political. Politics is a legitimate form of coercive relationship whereas non-political relationships occur when coercive force is employed illegitimately (and where claims to have the authority or right to wield that power are made). Successful domination is in many ways the very opposite of politics, the problem to which politics is the answer. While realism does, contrary to many of its crudest interpretations, indeed insist that there is a difference between politics and the mere imposition of order via coercive power, the manner in which Williams drew this distinction is untenable. This is because realism also accepts that successful domination has a role to play in the creation and maintenance of any (legitimate) political order. There is no political order without successful domination.[2] As such, the distinction is better understood not as 'politics as distinct from successful domination' but 'politics cannot be merely successful domination'. And this is a crucial difference because these differing realist conceptualisations of the relationship between politics and domination will inevitably lead us to think differently about exactly what problem coercion poses for the development of a theory of liberal realism and how we should respond to it. In short, I want to argue that, contra Williams, liberal realism must accept two claims (both of which are in many ways anathema to liberalism as commonly conceived): firstly, that political rule, even when that rule has been appropriately legitimated, will inevitably include instances of successful domination, forcing persons to live according to wills other than their own, and, secondly, that the mechanisms of coercion necessarily play a prevalent role in establishing and maintaining political unity and legitimacy, even in liberal regimes. The important question then becomes how liberal realism reconciles these points with a vision of liberalism as a non-oppressive form of political life.

Bernard Williams and the Basic Legitimation Demand

Consistent with much of the realist tradition, Williams' realism sought to give a greater autonomy to distinctively political thought, particularly from the sort of political moralism that he believed had dominated Anglo-American theorising in the late twentieth century.[3] To do this, Williams sought to identify normative standards of politics that were internal and specific to the political sphere itself (and hence not derived from some external non-political source like morality). The most fundamental of these internal standards is the notion that politics is not, and cannot be, merely successful domination. 'One thing can be taken as an axiom', Williams wrote, 'that might does not imply right, that power itself does not justify'.[4] It is, Williams thought, one of the few necessary truths about the nature of politics itself that there is a difference between legitimate government and unmediated power.[5] The will of the strongest is not, in and of itself, a legitimation.[6]

Williams justified this distinction with reference to the primary task of politics which is to answer what he called the 'first' political question. This question, which is first in the sense that a solution to this problem is required all the time (rather than solved once and for all) and a necessary precondition before any other political issues can be attended to, is essentially the Hobbesian one of securing the conditions of order, protection, safety, trust, and co-operation.[7] However, unlike Hobbes, Williams did not think that any solution to this first question would be sufficient; the demands of legitimacy are such that only certain sorts of resolution will be acceptable. Creating order out of chaos is a necessary but not sufficient condition of legitimacy. This is because:

> The situation of one lot of people terrorizing another lot of people is not per se a
> political situation: it is, rather, the situation which the existence of the political is
> in the first place supposed to alleviate (replace). If the power of one lot of people
> over another is to represent a solution to the first political question, and not itself

be part of the problem, *something* has to be said to explain ... what the difference is between the solution and the problem, and that cannot simply be an account of successful domination. It has to be something in the mode of justifying explanation or legitimation.[8]

The state, essentially, must not 'become part of the problem' by systematically terrorising its citizens or 'radically disadvantaging' them 'in the basic Hobbesian terms of coercion, pain, torture, humiliation, suffering, [and] death'.[9] Insofar as the point of politics is to save people from such actions, any state that itself perpetrated them, or failed to protect people from such actions, would therefore not be a solution to the first political question.

This 'something' that explains why the state is a solution to the first political question is what Williams called the 'Basic Legitimation Demand' (BLD). 'The idea', he wrote, 'is that a given historical structure can be (to an appropriate degree) an example of the human capacity to live under an intelligible order of authority. It makes sense (MS) to us *as such a structure* ... This requires ... that there is a legitimation offered which goes beyond the assertion of power and we can recognize such a thing because in the light of the historical and cultural circumstances, and so forth, it MS to us as a legitimation'.[10] Not only must the political order address the first political question, it must do so in a way that makes sense to those subject to it as an example of legitimate authority and not merely the imposition of tyrannical power.[11] The idea of making sense is, as Williams put it, a category of historical understanding which draws upon our political, moral, social, interpretative, and other concepts in this particular case to demonstrate whether we can comprehend a political regime as an example of legitimate authoritative order or not. This means that what makes sense to us cannot necessarily be used as the basis for making normative judgements about whether such reasons should guide the behaviour of others in different contexts or should have done so in the past, because what makes sense to them might be different to what makes sense to us. The category of making sense is evaluative when applied to other contexts though it is normative when applied to our own. This is because what makes sense, or makes most sense, to us as a political authority will be viewed as legitimate and guide how we react and respond to it (e.g. not resisting or opposing it). Therefore what counts as a sufficient reason for taking the political order to be legitimate will be dependent upon what makes sense as such to persons in their particular contexts.[12]

The historical and social sensitivity of Williams' realist account of legitimacy means that it cannot be the case that reasons that are deemed to be sufficient to satisfy the BLD in one context are automatically and inevitably going to be sufficient in another. Hence Williams did not think that the only form of political regime consistent with the BLD has or always will be liberalism. Rather what counts as a sufficient justification of political power, what makes sense in the appropriate manner, is going to be heavily contextualised. The supplementary and very stringent conditions which liberals require of legitimacy (i.e. disadvantage in terms of race and gender are invalid, hierarchical structures which create disadvantage are not self-legitimating), and which other regimes are not necessarily required to meet, are given by our historical and social conditions, in particular modernity's undermining of supposed legitimations which are now seen to be false or merely ideological.[13] In this sense, the slogan 'LEG [legitimacy] + Modernity = Liberalism' crudely but adequately captures the basic structure of Williams' thought. Though any legitimate state must necessarily meet the BLD (and so be LEG) it must meet the specific and unique demands of the context also (modernity), which explains why, now and around here (as Williams often put it) liberal regimes have a compelling claim to legitimacy.

Williams is clear that it is neither a necessary nor sufficient condition for the BLD to arise that someone demands a justification of power be offered. Anyone with a criticism, no matter how trivial, can raise a demand and within any political order there will always be some place for grievance. So the mere voicing of a complaint cannot be sufficient to generate a genuine BLD. Nor can it be a necessary condition because of the 'obvious truth' that people can be forced through the use of coercive power itself into accepting its exercise.[14] This is why Williams thought it necessary to introduce what he called the 'critical theory principle', which states that 'the acceptance of a justification does not count if the acceptance itself is produced by the coercive power which is supposedly being justified'.[15] It is however a sufficient condition of a (genuine) demand for legitimation arising that 'A coerces B and claims that B would be wrong to fight back, resent it, forbid it, rally others to oppose it as wrong, and so on. By doing this, A claims that his actions transcend the conditions of warfare, and this gives rise to a demand for justification of what A does. When A is the state, these claims constitute its claim of authority over B'.[16] Insofar as the modern state claims to have the authority to rule over all its subjects, the BLD itself will necessarily demand that a legitimation of the state's right to rule is offered to each and every subject.

Politics is a relationship that Williams believed is intrinsically non-tyrannical in the sense that it is designed to replace or alleviate conditions of domination and terror. Only if the relationship between the state and an individual subject to its power meets the conditions of the BLD can it properly be understood as political. It is important to note that though the BLD does require that a justification be *offered* to each person over whom the state claims to have the authority to rule[17], it is not the case that that justification must be accepted as 'making sense' by each person.[18] As William put it,

> when it is said that government must have 'something to say' to each person or group over whom it claims authority – and this means, of course, that it has something to say which purports to legitimate its use of power in relation to them – it cannot be implied that this is something that this person or group will necessarily accept. This cannot be so: they may be anarchists, or utterly unreasonable, or bandits, or merely enemies. *Who* has to be satisfied that the Basic Legitimation Demand has been met by a given formulation at one given time is a good question, and it depends on the circumstances.[19]

And Williams went on to state in a footnote that 'This is one of the reasons for which the idea of satisfying the Basic Legitimation Demand does not coincide with this insatiable ideal of many a political theoretician: universal consent'.[20] An implication of this is clearly that the state can be legitimate even if not everyone accepts that the BLD has been met, and consequently that the state can legitimately coerce those that reject the justification of its authority. Furthermore, and apart from one exception that we shall come to in a following section, the relationship between the state and its subjects is political even in conditions where consent has not been given.

Politics and successful domination

Williams' theory contains several important insights that should be incorporated into any account of liberal realism: firstly, order is a necessary but not sufficient condition of political legitimacy. This is because, secondly, it is a truth of politics that might cannot and does not equal right. The mere fact that a person or group of persons has the coercive capacity to effectively rule over others, to force them to obey their will, is not sufficient to establish their right to do so. There is something special about *political* rule, as distinct from rule as domination, which requires rulers to offer a legitimation story to those over whom they claim authority. This is a normative standard internal to politics. Thirdly, universal consent cannot be a condition of political legitimacy. It cannot be the case that every person over whom the rulers rule must accept the legitimation story if it is to be legitimate. That said, and finally, a significant proportion of those over whom the state rules must accept that legitimation story in order for it to be successful, and the values and principles that are appealed to in order to satisfy legitimation demands must demonstrate an appropriate amount of historical and contextual sensitivity.

Nevertheless, I want to argue that though Williams' conception of politics rightly defined politics in distinction to successful domination, it drew that distinction in a manner which is unsatisfactory from a realist perspective. For Williams, a coercive relationship between the rulers and those over whom they claim to have authority is either political or it is successful domination. A condition of politics is, by definition, the absence of successful domination. But though politics cannot be *only* or *merely* successful domination (because then it would be illegitimate), a truly realist theory must accept both that politics will inevitably include instances of successful domination and that the use of coercive power has an important role to play in creating and maintaining the acceptance of political authority in the first place. Hence the distinction between politics and successful domination that is crucial to realist thought cannot be cast in quite the way that Williams suggested. And I want to try to establish all of this initially via two indirect routes, by discussing Williams' critical theory test and the condition that the political order 'makes sense' as a form of political authority in modernity, and then engage with the issue more directly in the final sub-section.

The critical theory principle

Williams' critical theory principle addresses what we might think is the fairly obvious truth that the acceptance of a justification is not sufficient if the acceptance itself is produced by the coercive power which is supposedly being justified.[21] This principle is intended to rule out claims of false consciousness, and the like, but also to help put clear distance between politics, understood as legitimate coercion, and successful domination. If the critical theory principle does not hold, therefore, we would have at least one compelling reason to doubt the cogency of this distinction.

In general, a condition of legitimacy such as the critical theory principle will always run up against the difficulty of demonstrating when it has been met without resorting to counterfactuals whose truth-conditions will ineludibly be indeterminate.[22] Such counterfactuals will usually take the form of '*x* would not accept *y* if coercive power was absent' and hence would be very difficult to substantiate in practice. Interestingly, Williams seemed to accept this when he said 'the difficulty with it [the critical theory principle] … lies in deciding what counts as having been 'produced by' coercive power in the relevant sense'.[23]

Without being able to demonstrate a direct and sufficient causal link between the coercion and the acceptance of the justification, a test such as the critical theory principle will always be highly indeterminate. Yet Williams clearly did not think this was a fatal problem for the critical theory principle and believed that there were certain justifications that have at all times failed the BLD. 'Those [justifications] associated with racism, and the like', he wrote, 'are all false or by everyone's standards irrelevant. It is also important that acceptance of them by the dominating party is readily explained, while their being accepted by the dominated is an *easy case* for the critical theory principle'.[24] As intuitive to us as the thought might be that there has never been a justification of slavery on racial grounds that was or would be accepted by slaves in the absence of coercion, even an 'easy case' as this still runs up against the problems of the indeterminacy of the truth of such counterfactuals. Can we really say that no slave has ever accepted, or indeed ever would accept, the racial or other justification for his subjugation independently of the use of any coercive power? This is not just the problem of the happy slave, of a slave who happens to enjoy his life despite his subjugation, but of a slave who freely accepts that he *should* be subjugated, that it is justified in the relevant manner such that he recognises the *right* of his master to rule over him. I am not as confident as Williams seemed to be that such a case is not plausible or possible.

Yet the problem of demonstrating what counts as being 'produced by' coercive power goes deeper than the indeterminacy of the truth-conditions of counterfactuals. As realists emphasise, the motivations, beliefs, and values that generate persons' actions are multi-faceted, numerous, often incoherent, highly changeable, and sometimes incomplete. It is notoriously difficult for persons to give full accounts of why they believe what they do or act in the manner they act, or, indeed, for us to determine such matters on their behalf. These are not epistemic failings on the part of individuals, but are pervasive and inherent features of human life.[25] As such, why people accept a particular justification of a political order, even if they are radically disadvantaged relative to others within that order, is going to be an incredibly complex story. This makes it very difficult to determine the extent to which coercive mechanisms, when they have been employed, have actually influenced each person's compliance or endorsement of the political authority.[26] Unless we want to modify the critical theory principle such that it is a condition of legitimacy that coercion played absolutely no role in an individual's acceptance of the legitimation story, which would be a highly unrealistic condition that no political regime would ever meet, then the mere presence of coercion is surely not enough to demonstrate that the acceptance of the legitimation story was produced by it.

Not only are there difficulties for the critical theory principle 'in deciding what counts as having been "produced by" coercive power', as Williams put it, but there are significant questions as to what activities relevantly count as 'coercive' in the first place. What justifications people will find acceptable will be affected by a whole range of factors, such as education and wider acculturation, which would seem to involve at least a minimum degree of coercion.[27] Are these processes to be thought of as coercive in a sense relevant to the question of legitimacy? If not, why not? And if so, how far does this vitiate acceptance as a test of legitimacy?[28] Further than this, and to return to a realist theme we encountered in chapter 2, realism takes any widespread acceptance of the social order to necessarily be an 'artefact' of politics and the employment of its numerous coercive functions. In this sense, we should not expect there to be widespread acceptance *without* the presence of a whole host of coercive forces.

None of these questions have easy answers. And certainly I do not have any to offer here. But what is important for our purposes is not so much the nature of these difficulties themselves but their implications for Williams' distinction between politics and successful domination. The critical theory principle is introduced by Williams in order to help sustain this distinction by deeming impermissible the acceptance of a justification of the right to rule if it is brought about via the very power that is in need of legitimation. The acceptance must be freely given if it is to satisfy the BLD and not be itself the result of successful domination. Yet the difficulties I have drawn attention to here are indicative of the fact that it is hard to demarcate politics as a sphere of non-domination given the complications of extricating coercion from the acceptance of the social system in the way that Williams' theory requires.

Making sense of the BLD

In the slogan 'LEG + Modernity = Liberalism', Williams accepted that the last term served to delineate a range of political options all of which would make sense to us in the modern world.[29] Though we might endorse different forms of liberalism, we would nevertheless agree that liberalism makes best sense to us in conditions of modernity as a sufficient response to the BLD. But in order for this account to be plausible it has to be the case that people cannot and do not disagree about what the central characteristics of modernity are (political, moral, philosophical, social, economic, etc.) or what demands they generate or constraints they engender in relation to the conditions of legitimacy here and now. Though Williams explored in several places and in sophisticated detail the nature and limits of philosophy and morality in modernity, he did not say much about the political aspects of modern life. It is clear that a central feature of modernity he had in mind was how theological and natural law justifications for hereditary or elite rule no longer make sense in a disenchanted or secularised world in which we treat the metaphysical assumptions that these accounts rely upon as highly dubious.[30] Interpreted in this manner, claims regarding natural or divinely ordained inequalities which are used to justify policies of oppression or asymmetry between the rights possessed by members of different groups will be incompatible with the conditions of modernity and hence deemed illegitimate.

For Williams' equation to hold true, it has to be the case that modernity is a constant not a variable. But this is not the case. Modernity, as a historical epoch, is a highly contestable concept and there are several other aspects, characteristics or interpretations of modernity which might not necessarily lead us so straightforwardly to liberalism. To quickly cite but a few: a familiar Marxist argument is that the conditions of modernity, in particular the economic oppression and alienation caused by capitalism, has led to a liberal politics dominated by and geared towards fulfilling the interests of one class at the expense of all others. According to this argument, the demands of legitimacy are only going to be fulfilled in the modern world by a socialist or, at the extreme, communist political order which places property and the means of production in common hands. Much anarchist thought relies upon an interpretation of modernity in which two of the central and defining features of the modern world, the state with its monopoly of power and the value of individual autonomy, sit in irresolvable tension with one another. The modern state, anarchists often contend, cannot be justified because it is necessarily inconsistent with the autonomy of persons that any legitimate state would have to respect.[31] As such, the state, including modern liberal states, is not legitimate and only a very minimal (non-state) political order will be consistent with the demands of legitimacy in conditions of modernity. And finally, Nietzscheans and existentialists believe that the preeminent feature of modernity is the 'death of God', the absence of any objective telos of humanity or objective metaphysical framework which leaves us free to engage in radical acts of self-creation. The political implications of this position are far from clear and while some, like Rorty, have linked self-creation with liberalism this is far from a necessary connection. Nietzsche's own disavowal of liberal politics, with its un-egalitarian implications, is well known.

The list of various interpretations of modernity and their political implications, including those who comprehensively reject that it has few, if any, redeeming valuable features (such as Alasdair MacIntyre or Ortega y Gasset), is extensive.[32] The point is that there is a plurality of different and conflicting ways of interpreting and understanding modernity, not all of which when combined with the demands of legitimacy will necessarily lead to liberalism. Further than this, I can understand how many of these (though not necessarily all) *make sense* as an interpretation of modernity and hence how the politics being commended would, from that perspective, seem legitimate or more legitimate than liberalism. I can, for example, understand Nietzsche's philosophy as a response to a particular interpretation of modernity. One may think it over-exaggerates particular aspects, such as disenchantment and nihilism, at the expense of those which might lead in a more liberal direction, but it certainly makes sense as an interpretation. This does not require us to defend it, nor the anti-liberal politics which it is often used to justify, but it is not clear on what basis one could deny that it makes sense. It is important to distinguish, then, between those who reject completely that liberalism makes any sense, and hence is completely lacking legitimacy as a mode of organising political life, and the more familiar case of those who believe that liberalism does make 'some' sense as a form of political authority in conditions of modernity but that other non-liberal forms of political order make what we might call 'most sense' or 'best sense' and hence endorse those more strongly. In either case, however, the differing interpretations of modernity will lead some persons to endorse non-liberal forms of political life.

The implications of this for a realist theory of liberalism are twofold: firstly, while it is true that we must avoid the universalistic conclusion that all non-liberal states in the past (or indeed the future) were illegitimate, liberalism does not have a uniquely superior claim to legitimacy here and now either. There are indeed certain forms of political life that are inconsistent with features of modernity and which hence cannot possibly make sense. But there are a series of other ways of organising our political lives that are consistent with modernity and which, to varying degrees, make sense as a form of political order – not all of them liberal. Contrary, therefore, to Williams' belief that 'non-liberal states do not now in general meet the BLD', realism needs to comprehensively accept that there can be, today, non-liberal yet legitimate states.[33] In this sense, the criterion that the state makes sense as a form of political authority, rather than being merely an instance of successful domination, underdetermines which political orders are legitimate in conditions of modernity.

The second, and in many ways more important, implication for our purposes is that it lends further weight to the worry that the way Williams distinguished between politics and successful domination is unsustainable. If it is indeed the case that persons' differing accounts of modernity will lead them to endorse non-liberal forms of political association, or to deny that liberalism is legitimate, then politics, even liberal politics, will inevitably include instances of successful domination. For these people, liberalism will be the imposition of a form of collective life that they reject. This is not meant as a criticism of the BLD itself; after all, it is not a condition of a successful answer to the BLD that everyone accepts that the political order is legitimate. The point is rather that such differing interpretation of modernity and what makes sense as a form of legitimate authority in the modern world gives us reason to doubt whether politics can be properly thought of as, at least in part, the absence of successful domination, a point I now want to develop more directly.

Politics and successful domination

As we have seen, Williams believed that politics cannot simply be successful domination because it would not then represent an answer to the first political question. It might be an instance of order and stability but this is not sufficient for the purposes of politics: it must be a legitimate response also, which is to say that it must be a response that makes sense to those subject to it as a form of political authority. This distinction between politics and successful domination is fundamental to Williams' theory. Building upon what has been said in the previous two sub-sections, what I want to suggest here is that it is a distinction which is unsustainable both on its own terms and because it is inconsistent with other necessary features of any realist theory.

Let us start with Williams' claim that universal consent is not a condition of legitimacy. This is thoroughly consistent with realism's conflictual vision of the political. Because Williams employed a relational view of politics, in the sense that politics is a relationship between two or more persons or groups of persons in which A (usually the state) has the legitimate authority to coerce B (C, D, E, and so on), then the concept of legitimacy effectively serves to distinguish political and non-political, but specifically tyrannical, relationships. Where the BLD has been met, the relationship is political. Where the BLD has not been met (and a genuine demand for one has been made) then the relationship is one of successful domination. There can be no such thing as a legitimate political relationship of successful domination. The question I want to pose is in relation to those persons who deny that the BLD has been met (let me call them 'dissenters'). Is the relationship between such persons and the state political or tyrannical?

Williams thought that the fact that dissenters rejected a state's claim to legitimacy had no implications for its right to rule and coerce them. He did not think that the legitimacy of a state to coerce those within its territory depended upon individuals' consent. While Williams believed that politics is essentially a relationship, unlike liberals he did not believe it had to be a consensual relationship.[34] So insofar as the state is legitimate vis-à-vis dissenters, the relationship between them is political and necessarily non-tyrannical.

But let us examine this question from the perspective of the dissenters themselves. We first of all need to be clear that the state claims to have the authority to rule over dissenters and this in itself is enough to establish that the BLD must be met. Dissenters are not the same as what Williams called 'enemies'. There can exist within a state what Williams called 'internal enemies', the Helots of Ancient Sparta being the example he often referred to, who are 'radically disadvantaged' relative to others within the state insofar as, at the limit, they 'have virtually no protection from the operations of the state or other subjects'.[35] They can reasonably fear, therefore, the sort of coercion, pain, torture, humiliation, suffering, and death that other subjects need not and which politics is intended to alleviate.[36] Williams was clear that the relationship between enemies and the state is not political but simply one of 'internal warfare', i.e. successful domination.[37] His reason for this turned on the fact that states do not claim to have the authority to rule over enemies, and making such a claim is a sufficient condition of a genuine demand that the conditions of legitimacy be met.[38] In other words, the state does not claim to rule over enemies with authority and therefore the relationship between them is not one of politics but of war. And so while enemies might reside within the borders of the state, they are nevertheless strictly speaking stateless people, persons who are not members of any state, over whom the state does not have the legitimate authority to employ its coercive power (despite the fact that it might be doing so). So there is an important distinction between dissenters and enemies: the state claims to have the right to rule over dissenters, and Williams believed the BLD has been met despite their denial that this is the case, while it does not claim to have the right to rule over enemies and so the demand for a legitimation does not arise.

What is interesting about this distinction between dissenters (which is my term but identifies a category of persons who Williams explicitly acknowledged exists within his own theory) and enemies is that the BLD has not been satisfied from the perspective of either. From the viewpoint of enemies this is because the state does not claim to have authority to rule over them and so, strictly speaking, the BLD does not arise. There is no attempt to mask their relationship as political. It is war. From the viewpoint of dissenters, the state claims the right to rule over them and has offered a justification of this right that they reject. Yet, in Williams' theory, the relationship between them is nevertheless political and hence the state is a political authority that can expect dissenters' obedience and has the right to legitimately coerce them to obey if necessary. From the perspective of either dissenters or enemies, the state is insufficiently justified as a form of political authority. On Williams' terms, we should expect that both dissenters and enemies do not regard their relationship with the state as political. What makes the difference between enemies and dissenters in relation to legitimacy is not their relative treatment at the hands of the state, but the *state's* claim to have the authority to rule over the latter but not the former. This begs the question why it is more appropriate, for the purposes of legitimacy, that a response to the BLD is offered but rejected rather than not offered at all. Why can one be considered a political relationship and the other not?

The only possible response that I can think of is because the dissenters might simply be wrong in their thinking that the state does not make sense as a legitimate form of political authority. The BLD is therefore sufficiently met regardless of the fact that dissenters think otherwise. Not only does it represent a response to the first political question, in the sense of securing the conditions of order and stability, but it is also an association that adequately meets the supplementary conditions of legitimacy provided by our historical context of modernity. Let us assume that dissenters do not reject that the BLD has been met on the grounds that it does not secure order and stability. There is nothing stopping dissenters from being radically disadvantaged also, such that they lack the basic protections (like enemies) yet the state still claims authority to rule over them. But let us assume that the state does secure some form of order and stability and dissenters are thus not radically disadvantaged (though this is not to say that they will necessarily be treated equally to all others). They reject, rather, that the regime is a response to the first political question which makes sense as a form of legitimate political authority. So can they be wrong about this?

To answer yes would undermine Williams' distinction between politics and successful domination. Who, after all, would determine whether the BLD has been satisfied or not? If it is the state then it would undercut the significance of legitimacy as an internal standard of politics according to which we can assess different political orders. All states could effectively claim that the BLD has been met in relation to its subjects and legitimacy would no longer be a viable concept of assessment. More importantly, it is unclear how we can sustain Williams' distinction between politics and successful distinction if it is the case that the state, the agent whose power stands in need of legitimation, determines whether the BLD has been met. After all, no state is likely to deny that it has fulfilled the conditions of the BLD. Otherwise we might say that it is some sort of majoritarian perspective that matters, such that if the majority of subjects accept that the political order meets the BLD then this is sufficient to establish the legitimacy of the state vis-à-vis dissenters. This might give legitimacy some sort of critical distance insofar as the state can now be found to be inconsistent with the demands of the BLD according to the majority of its subjects. But nevertheless it is far from clear how this would establish that the BLD has been met in regard to the dissenting minority.

If what I have argued here is right, then it places Williams' theory in a double bind. It seems that we must accept that the judgement of the dissenters has some relevance to the question of whether the BLD has been met or not, otherwise Williams' distinction between politics and successful domination is hard to sustain. It surely matters that dissenters themselves take the political order to represent a form of successful domination not legitimate authority. It is hard to know what sort of argument one could provide in order to effectively overrule the dissenters' judgement on this matter while maintaining the definition of 'politics as distinct from domination'. And this problem would be further exacerbated if it is reasonable to expect disagreement regarding whether the BLD has been met. If people can reasonably disagree as to whether the political order makes sense in the relevant way, then it cannot be an appropriate condition for determining legitimacy. Yet if we do take into account the judgement of the dissenters, then it would seem that we also have to accept that politics does include instances of successful domination. So it is not clear, therefore, that Williams' account of politics as non-domination is consistent with the conditions of legitimacy that are intended to determine when a relationship of coercion is political or not. It would seem that there can be, even within his theory, legitimate coercive relationships that are not on Williams' own terms political. There can be legitimate but non-political relationships of successful domination. In other words, Williams' conditions of legitimacy do not distinguish relationships along the lines of politics/ domination as he had wanted. As such, the distinction between politics and domination, central to any realist theory of the political, cannot be cut in the manner Williams proposed.

Lessons for liberal realism

Taking seriously political, not just moral or religious, pluralism entails accepting that the political framework will not be universally affirmed by those subject to it. This means that politics will often take the form of a struggle between those who would defend the status quo and those who would seek to change the political framework, sometimes radically, so that it reflects different values and principles or is redirected towards realising different ends. The political framework responds to the political question but is also one of the objects of our disagreement. Consequently any answer to the political question will be seen as an imposition, and possibly an oppressive one, by those who would favour a different answer. Such persons will experience the political association as a form of successful domination. Realism does not seek to mask the imposition as anything other than what it is. Rather it takes it to be a truth of all political regimes that they combine, to various degrees, different forms of relationship with their subjects ranging from outright and wholesale rejection through to wholehearted and complete endorsement. It does not celebrate the fact that such imposition and domination is necessary, but it does take it to be an inevitable feature of any successful answer to the political question. Politics cannot be merely successful domination, but neither can we address the need to which politics is the answer without it.

It is therefore a truth of politics, one that the realist tradition has often emphasised, that political rule involves what Williams called successful domination. In conditions of radical disagreement about politics, morality, religion, etc., we should expect that any political association will contain amongst those that live within its borders individuals who reject that it is legitimate. Such people will hold that any legitimate political authority must be grounded in and appeal to a different set of values from that of the legitimation story they are offered. The relationship between the political order and these individuals is a political one notwithstanding the fact that it is essentially, from the perspective of dissenters, one of illegitimate coercion, the forceful imposition of a will other than their own. Politics cannot be simply successful domination; a legitimate political order cannot be one which nobody over whom it rules recognises its legitimacy. But it will inevitably require forcing some to live according to terms, rules, values, and principles that they reject. The political association is taken to have full and equal authority over each and every person over whom it rules, regardless of whether they accept the legitimacy of its rule or not. The fact that some reject the political framework, in whole or in part, does not mean that the state is illegitimate either *tout court* or vis-à-vis these people. The fact of the matter is that, assuming the legitimation story offered is accepted by a substantial proportion of the citizenry, the framework remains a legitimate answer to the political question.

This further supports the thought that coercion has a crucial role to play within politics insofar as it cannot be assumed that all persons will obey the law because they see it as issued by a legitimate authority. As such, the expectations of benefit or, more likely, the fear of disadvantages, in particular the threat of coercive force being used against them, will need to compensate in order to ensure the order and stability that legitimate politics must afford. But, and contrary to Williams, coercion has a double role to play with regard to the very legitimation of the power that stands in need of justification. On the one hand, because no association can literally rule by force alone, legitimating political rule shores up the allegiance of sufficient numbers such that those that reject the regime pose no threat to its stability and can be forced to obey if required. On the other hand, because even widespread agreement on moral and political issues is not something that occurs naturally among individuals, coercive techniques play an important part in creating the convergence on values necessary to ensure that a significant proportion of those subject to the political rule accept it. Contra Williams, therefore, it cannot be a condition of legitimacy that acceptance of the political order is achieved free from the presence and influence of any coercive mechanisms.

For some forms of political life, the question of how we live with dissidents or recalcitrant individuals is essentially an issue of managing them, ensuring that they do not pose a threat to the stability of the regime that they reject. This cannot, and should not, be liberalism's response. And hence it cannot be the response of a realist theory of liberalism either. This is because, as I have been stressing, liberalism is a self-consciously non-oppressive form of politics. As such, there has to be a way in which we can explain how even those that reject liberalism are respected and treated as free and equals in liberal political orders. The two substantial points on which I have raised disagreements with Williams, that politics can include instances of successful domination (and still be legitimate), and that absence of the influence of coercion cannot be a condition of successfully meeting the demand for a legitimating story that any claim to *political* authority necessarily generates, mean that a realist theory of liberalism must somehow incorporate these into its own account of politics and political legitimacy. But it seems that this would mean effectively accepting that politics, even liberal politics, *is* oppressive in exactly the manner that it seeks to avoid. These are features of politics that should deeply concern those of a liberal disposition.

So a realist theory of liberalism needs to accept that any successful liberal political order will inevitably contain instances of successful domination and that coercion has a crucial and unavoidable role to play in creating and maintaining the congruence between the values of the rulers and the ruled that legitimation demands. In developing a theory of liberal realism, therefore, it will not be sufficient to simply say that liberalism accepts the conflictual vision of politics yet everything else remains the same. It requires a more thoroughgoing amendment of its theoretical structure, including, as we have seen, assumptions about the nature of political rule and political legitimacy, and the role of coercion and domination within those.

Notes

1   As I argued in my 'Bernard Williams and the possibility of a realist political theory', *European Journal of Political Theory*, 9:4, 485–503

2   I would like to thank Enzo Rossi for helping me think through my disagreement with Williams on this point

3   Williams, *In the Beginning was the Deed*, p. 3

4   *Ibid.*, p. 5

5   *Ibid.*, p. 135

6   *Ibid.*, p. 23

7   *Ibid.*, p. 3

8   *Ibid.*, p. 5. Emphasis in original. See also p. 135

9   *Ibid.*, p. 4

10   *Ibid.*, p. 11

11   For further discussion regarding the notion of 'making sense', see B. Williams, *Truth and Truthfulness* (Oxford: Princeton University Press, 2002), ch. 10

12   There are further connections between Williams' insistence that the sufficient conditions of legitimacy be generated from more local sources and his numerous arguments regarding the need to engage in theorising and critical reflection drawing upon 'thick' ethical concepts and shared understandings which command general loyalty. See, for example, B. Williams, *Ethics and the Limits of Philosophy* (London: Fontana, 1985), pp. 116–17

13   Williams, *In the Beginning was the Deed*, pp. 7–8

14   *Ibid.*, p. 6

15   *Ibid.*, p. 6

16   *Ibid.*, p. 6

17   *Ibid.*, p. 6

18   There is some ambiguity in Williams' thought on this point however. Elsewhere he wrote 'The claim is that we can get from the BLD a constraint of roughly equal

acceptability (acceptability to each subject)' (*ibid.*, p. 7). Of course, everything hangs on what the conditions of 'roughly equal acceptability' are taken to be. The requirement of acceptability need not include the condition of actual acceptance. And so it is possible to interpret this as implying that the justification offered in response to a (genuine) BLD be one that makes sense roughly equally to each subject *regardless of whether they actually accept it or not*. Yet if this is right, then it would make the BLD even more vulnerable to the difficulty of determining what qualifies as 'making sense' that I shall outline in the following section

19 *Ibid.*, pp. 135–6
20 *Ibid.*, p. 136
21 *Ibid.*, p. 6
22 This is a criticism of Williams' critical theory principle also levied by Newey ('Two dogmas of liberalism', *European Journal of Political Theory*, 9:4 (2010), 449–65, p. 462)
23 Williams, *In the Beginning was the Deed*, p. 6
24 *Ibid.*, p. 7. Emphasis added
25 See Geuss, *Philosophy and Real Politics*, pp. 2–3
26 Niebuhr, *Moral Man and Immoral Society*, p. xviii
27 This is a point also made by Stears and Honig ('The new realism: From modus vivendi to justice', in Floyd and Stears (eds), *Political Philosophy versus History?*, p. 191)
28 Newey, 'Two dogmas of liberalism', p. 462
29 Williams, *In the Beginning was the Deed*, p. 9. The argument of this section reiterates an aspect of a similar critique of Williams' theory that I made in my 'Bernard Williams and the possibility of a realist political theory' (pp. 498–500)
30 Williams, *In the Beginning was the Deed*, pp. 40–51
31 See, for instance, R. P. Wolff, *In Defence of Anarchism* (London: University of California Press, 1998)
32 A. MacIntyre, *After Virtue* (London: Duckworth Press, 2004); J. Ortega y Gasset, *The Revolt of the Masses* (London: Unwin Books, 1969). See also Michael C. Williams, 'Morgenthau now: Neoconservatism, national greatness, and realism', in Williams (ed.), *Realism Reconsidered: The Legacy of Hans J. Morgenthau*, 216–40
33 Williams, *In the Beginning was the Deed*, p. 7. Though, of course, the 'in general' might be interpreted in a generous manner so as to provide Williams with some judgemental leeway on the question of the legitimacy of non-liberal states. However, the basis on which they are legitimate would still need to be spelt out
34 It should be said that the fact that Williams explicitly denied that universal consent is a necessary condition of legitimacy does throw into question the germaneness of the critical theory principle. Insofar as some people can reject the justification offered in response to the BLD without that undermining the legitimacy of the state, it is not totally clear why it need be the case that those that do accept it do so free from coercive influence. What is the difference that bears on the issue of legitimacy between not accepting the justification for a state's authority and acceptance produced via coercive force? Why is one acceptable and the other not? I'm not sure if there is an answer to this question and so I have treated these two aspects of Williams' thought,

the critical theory principle and the non-condition of universal consent, as integral and consistent features

35 Williams, *In the Beginning was the Deed*, p. 5
36 *Ibid.*, p. 4
37 *Ibid.*, p. 6
38 *Ibid.*, p. 6

6

The partisan foundations of liberal realism

The aim of this chapter is to explore the ramifications for liberal theory of taking seriously the fact of political pluralism that incorporating the realist vision of politics demands. Any political theory that requires addressing or managing pluralism, be it moral, religious or political, will need to have an account of the origin and nature of that disagreement, for this will be crucial in determining the appropriate response. Realism has offered several different such accounts ranging from the clash of interests to human beings' inherent need to engage in struggle and competition with others. None of these are appropriate for a theory of liberal realism. Instead what I shall suggest is that we adapt the account of reasonable disagreement that is employed by political liberals to explain the origin and nature of moral and religious pluralism. Importantly, I want to argue that the notion of reasonable disagreement offers a plausible explanation of both political disagreement and conflict, in which case those who reject liberalism, conservatives, socialists, Marxists, libertarians, and so on, are not irrational, misguided, or simply driven by partial interests, bias or prejudice, but rather people whose political disagreements and conflicts we can understand as reasonable. In the following section, and building upon the reasonableness of political disagreement, I want to discuss how liberal theory needs to explicitly accept that liberalism is a controversial and contested account of politics over which persons can *reasonably* disagree and, in doing so, recognise the deeply partisan nature of its own normative foundations, with all the consequences that this gives rise to. The third section will then – given the accusation made of liberalism by realists that they seek to avoid, abandon, or overcome politics – explore the manner in which a theory of liberal realism that accepts its own partisanship can be said to 'affirm the political'. Finally, I shall bring the discussion of the previous three sections together and examine the way in which liberals should conceptualise their relationship with those who endorse non-liberal political frameworks, adapting the Schmittian/agonism inspired categories of friends, adversaries, and enemies.

The reasonableness of political disagreement

Any explanation of the origins of political disagreement that is to be consistent with the realist vision of the political will need to include several features, in particular the inevitability and permanence of disagreement. Realism does not celebrate pluralism; it takes it to be a fact that politics must address. A liberal account of pluralism also need not celebrate diversity and disagreement for its own sake. But it cannot regret it either. It cannot be viewed as an unfortunate aspect of social life that needs to be overcome. After all, liberalism is committed to the notion that people are able to adopt their own diverse life plans and should be as free as possible to pursue those (consistent with others having the same degree of freedom). It is for this reason that many of the realist accounts of the origins of political disagreement and conflict, such as our inherent partiality or bias, cannot provide the sort of explanation we need here. If this were the case, then as a manifestation of an undesirable and morally lamentable human trait, pluralism would be something that we should regret and which we potentially should seek to overcome in practice. Hence a theory of liberal realism cannot adopt a realist account of this ilk. So in this section I want to suggest that not only are the burdens of judgement that lie at the heart of Rawls' own account of reasonable pluralism consistent with realism, but that it can with little effort be extended to provide a compelling and plausible account of disagreement and conflict in politics.

The burdens of judgement tell us that it is reasonable to expect persons to disagree about the most important and fundamental matters, including morality, religion, and justice, because of the inherent difficulties and limitations of human reasoning about such complex matters. This means that pluralism is inevitable in the sense that it is what we should reasonably expect to occur when human beings employ their reason in conditions of freedom. This qualification is important because it points to the fact that pluralism is permanent unless the state employs significant coercive force in order to create and enforce a universal consensus of belief, what Rawls called the fact of oppression. This proviso aside, Rawls makes it very clear that reasonable pluralism is a *fact*, a feature of modern life that we must reconcile ourselves to rather than something that we must foster or celebrate.[1] The burdens of judgement simply tell us something important about the inevitable and permanent limits of human reasoning; no normative judgements about the value of pluralism necessarily follow. The features that are required for a consistently realist account of the origins of political pluralism are therefore present in the burdens of judgement.

Once we accept, as many contemporary liberals have, that the burdens apply to a central political concept such as justice, only a small step is then required to see our disagreements regarding the interpretation and understanding of other political concepts and values as being reasonable also. Disagreements, for instance, as to where we place the limits of toleration, the scope of liberty, the meaning of equality, or the content of human rights, seem eminently plausible candidates for being subject to the burdens of judgement. This already takes us some way to providing an explanation of the origin and nature of political disagreements. Yet while Rawls seemed to limit (at least implicitly) the scope of reasonable disagreement about justice to disagreement between those who hold reasonable conceptions, i.e. those consistent with reciprocity, there is no good reason why the burdens cannot offer an equally plausible explanation as to the origin and nature of conflict between liberals and non-liberals also. Such a possibility is slightly obscured within Rawls' theory by the fact that his use of the notion of reasonable pluralism often elides the reasonableness of disagreement and a plurality of reasonable comprehensive doctrines. As such, he largely discusses reasonable pluralism in terms of the reasonable disagreement that exists between those who hold reasonable comprehensive moral doctrines. Yet if we distinguish the reasonableness of the disagreement from the reasonableness of the positions reached (the comprehensive doctrines) then we can see more clearly the possibility that one's disagreements can be reasonable, in the sense that it comes about via the burdens of judgement, even if one holds non-liberal comprehensive doctrines. If we accept this possibility then we can plausibly employ the burdens of judgement to explain the origin of radical political conflict. As Tully put it, purposefully employing Rawlsian vocabulary, 'Reasonable disagreement and thus dissent are inevitable and go all the way down in theory and practice'.[2]

To develop this, we should expect that each comprehensive doctrine offers at least some guidance to those who hold them as to how they should answer most of politics' most fundamental and urgent questions (the demands of justice, the conditions of legitimacy, the limits of freedom, the relative priority of values, etc.). We should expect that each rival comprehensive doctrine will generate an answer to these questions and that these answers will, given the burdens of judgement, differ. Many of the answers that these comprehensive doctrines provide will conflict with those of others. So, and to expand upon and adapt an argument made by Waldron, among a range of rival comprehensive doctrines we should expect there to be a range of corresponding rival interpretations of political values, so C1 → F1, C2 → F2 and so on (where F1, F2 … Fn are rival interpretations of freedom).[3] Crucially, not every F will necessarily be consistent or compatible with a liberal interpretation of freedom. The same pattern will apply to equality (C1 → E1, C2 → E2 …), toleration (C1 → T1, C2 → T2 …), rights (C1 → R1, C2 → R2 …) and any other political concept. This pattern of the relationship between comprehensive doctrines and their corresponding different interpretations of political values can explain the reasonableness of political disagreements. This is true both at the very specific level where a disagreement is about the meaning of a single value, the practical demands that it generates, how it is to be instantiated in practice, etc. and, insofar as all political frameworks will be constructed out of a set of normative values, at the highest level of ideological conflict also. Amongst the totality of different interpretations of political values we will be able to identify a subset that is recognisably liberal in character. Nevertheless, though they are *liberal* interpretations, they are still likely to be engaged in the struggle for power as rival and competing political frameworks. In other words, we have here a way of understanding the origin of disagreement both between different competing liberalisms and between liberal and non-liberal forms of politics.

A question may arise here as to why a realist theory of politics would exclude from its analysis those disagreements that are unreasonable, in particular the result of prejudice, bias, the passions, self- or group-interest, or simply erroneous reasoning, especially as several realists, maybe Niebuhr most notably, have stressed that many of the problems that politics must address are generated by those disagreements whose origins are thoroughly unreasonable. The answer is that it does not. Rather realism is very conscious of the presence of such disagreement. Unlike much contemporary liberalism, it does not overlook the question of how we relate to such persons as the preserve of non-ideal theory. Its account of politics incorporates the presence of reasonable *and* unreasonable disagreements (and conflicts). Indeed the truth is that all disagreements have their roots in myriad different causes, combining rational and less rational elements, which reflects the muddled and messy way in which we come to hold many of the beliefs and values that we do. From a realist perspective, we could even question the cogency of the distinction between reasonable and unreasonable disagreements. But a crucial part of what it means to treat others as free and equal is to work with the presumption that their disagreements with us are reasonable, that they are not simply being selfish or stupid when they hold positions different from our own, and that they have reached their position through the sincere and proper use of their rationality. Just as we might think that those with whom we have profound moral or religious disagreements are nevertheless rational and genuine in their commitments, so we should presume the same when it comes to those with whom we have political disagreements and conflicts. This presumption can, of course, be proved to be false or unjustified in particular cases (via probing persons' justifications for their beliefs, for instance). And, as I say, it is unlikely that any of our beliefs are really fully reasonable. Yet it is not that liberal realism overlooks the presence of unreasonable disagreements, it is rather that it maintains the liberal notion that we respect others as free and equal at least in part by presuming that their beliefs and values have been reasonably arrived at despite our own rejection of them, and hence respect their disagreements with us as reasonable also.

Finally, it is worth being clear that the use of reasonable disagreement does not demarcate the boundaries of the political as it does in political liberalism. In political liberalism, the limits of politics are determined by what principles we can reasonably expect persons to accept. Hence if a principle is one over which persons can reasonably disagree, i.e. subject to the burdens of judgement, then it lies outside of the political and cannot form the legitimate basis for political order. This is not true of liberal realism. The fact that persons can reasonably disagree with liberal principles does not *automatically* mean that it would be illegitimate to force individuals to live according to them. This is not a condition of legitimacy in liberal realism. Accepting the fact of reasonable political disagreement does, however, confirm that even those that reject liberalism have done so through the free employment of their rational powers, and hence must be respected as free, equal, and rational beings. It tells us something basic but important therefore about how we are to conceptualise those with whom we disagree in a theory of liberal realism that will determine much of what follows.

The partisan foundations of liberalism

If politics is the activity of struggle to determine whose will dominates, either at the level of determining the political framework or decisions within that framework, and political disagreement is reasonable then this has obvious but critical ramifications for the way we must view the normative foundations of liberalism. Liberal politics is grounded in the fundamental concern to respect all persons' moral equality by protecting their liberty to pursue their conception of the good life free from state interference. Not all persons are committed to freedom and equality, many who are might interpret their moral content and political demands differently from liberals, and others might value freedom and equality but give priority to other values. In other words, liberalism is but one player, or indeed family of players, in the struggle for power that is politics. While the values and principles on which it is based, and the ends that it pursues, are taken by many to be of fundamental importance and amongst the most worthy of objectives that humans can aspire to, nevertheless many people have thought and continue to think the same of less liberal or even anti-liberal values, and, in doing so, endorse non-liberal political frameworks. Liberalism is a partisan political position grounded in contestable and contested normative values.

Accepting the partisanship of liberalism does not mean that liberals must refrain from making universal claims, such as 'the world would be a safer or more just place if all states were essentially liberal', 'liberalism is the best way of arranging and regulating political societies', or even of asserting the truth of liberalism. We can accept that liberalism is indeed a partisan political position with which others vehemently yet sincerely and genuinely disagree while also thinking that it *should* be the guiding theoretical framework for our political association or that commonly binding decisions should be made consistent with liberal values. Liberals can and should take their own side in an argument. They must admit, however, that liberalism has many genuine and sincere enemies many of whose rejection of liberal politics, and endorsement of anti-liberal alternatives, will be reasonable (in the sense discussed previously).[4] Such persons will hold their beliefs with the same passion, commitment and possibly certainty of their truth as liberals hold their own. And they do so because, as the burdens of judgement emphasise, moral and political questions are amongst the most difficult that humans have to grapple with and, in doing so, we are inevitably led to let our (different) life experiences inform our judgements, to assess evidence differently, to give priority to alternative values in a social space in which all cannot be equally realised, and so on. In other words, liberalism's enemies are not obviously or automatically to be thought of as irrational or guilty of prejudice, error, or bias in their coming to endorse non-liberal political frameworks. Politics is therefore the clash between persons who struggle for power to realise rival reasonably held conceptions of the political ideal. And in such a scenario, liberalism is one contestant amongst a plurality of reasonable others.

Liberalism, even if we include internal disputes between liberals, does not exhaust the space of politics. Amongst this field of competing conceptions, liberalism, with its variety of unique concerns and characteristics, does not have any necessary or automatic pre-eminence or authority. There is nothing about liberalism per se that means it is or should be the default appropriate response to the political question. Again, this is not to deny the possible truth of liberalism, nor the essential worthiness of the values at its heart; but others will make the same claims with regard to the normative foundations of their own favoured conception. In such a condition of competing assertions of truth, the authority of any one response to the circumstances of politics cannot come from claims to privileged philosophical justification. In an obviously circular fashion, if the authority of liberalism were tied to the truth or intrinsic worth of liberal values, then such authority would only be accepted by those who are already liberals.

The question of what follows from accepting the fact of deep and intractable pluralism has been central to contemporary liberal thought. Many recent liberal theories have advocated a sort of epistemological distance from one's beliefs, in the sense of irony, scepticism, or relativism, as necessarily following from recognition of pluralism and the fact of persistent disagreement. This distance is then itself often used as an epistemological justification, or an epistemological component of a larger justification, of liberal practices and commitments such as toleration or impartiality.[5] After all, and so the argument goes, if you cannot be sure of the truth of your beliefs then what justification can you have for imposing them upon others? Liberal realism does not take a position on such epistemological questions. The appropriate epistemological stance to take in relation to one's beliefs is itself a deeply contested issue both within and between different comprehensive moral doctrines. In part this is because questions of epistemology are often not extraneous from the content of our fundamental moral and political commitments, but deeply connected to them.[6] Many of the deepest contestations between different comprehensive doctrines are, explicitly or not, epistemological. So nothing is solved, politically speaking, by trying to ground liberal politics in philosophical arguments in favour of particular epistemological positions.[7] Hence liberal realism makes no epistemological claims regarding the manner in which citizens should hold their beliefs but, instead, takes disagreement about epistemology (and indeed meta-ethical questions connected to it) to be another facet of the discord that politics addresses.[8]

Those liberal theories that have relied upon scepticism or relativism as justificatory premises, or theories like Rorty's that advocate ironic detachment from the truth of one's beliefs as a virtue of a good liberal, have often been criticised as demanding a weakening or loosening of our commitment to liberal values. In a crucial sense, we cannot be as committed to the liberal cause if we are sceptical about the truth of its foundational values or accept their inherent contingency. Why would we want to fight for the liberal cause, especially in cases where we put at risk our own personal safety or well-being, if we cannot vouch with certainty for its truth or worth? 'As Trotsky justly reminded the democrat Kautsky, the awareness of relative truths never gives one the courage to use force and spill blood'.[9] Whatever the cogency of such arguments, accepting the partisan foundations of liberalism should not result in the loosening of persons' commitment to it in this manner (or indeed to whichever ends the person holds). Liberal realism presupposes that people can be wholeheartedly committed to their beliefs, and are willing to fight for them, even in the knowledge that others deny their truth and worth. This is because its very account of politics assumes the existence of such contests, that persons struggle for their ends as engaged partisans with a sense of passion in Weber's sense 'of *concern for the thing itself*, the passionate commitment to a 'cause', to the god or demon who commands that cause'.[10] Without this, if individuals really did hold their beliefs with the degree of insouciance which many have worried (rightly or wrongly) that liberal theory encourages, then the circumstances of politics would not pertain in such an urgent matter, and hence politics itself would lose much of its initial raison d'etre. Of course, not all persons are passionately committed to their cause in this way; many are not (and this does not just include liberals).[11] But the realist vision of the political assumes that persons are at least sufficiently committed to their causes such that they are willing to engage in the struggle for power, and in the face of deep disagreement with the ends and values they pursue.

The liberal realist will therefore be someone who sees liberalism as a fighting creed in the sense that it is engaged in a perpetual contest with rival visions of the political good but also in that it is a model of co-existence worth fighting for. This means that one important role of political theorists (though I do not think it is unique to them) is the constant articulation of the fundamental values of liberalism, to emphasise their importance, and to reinterpret them as social, economic and political conditions change. They need to remind us why liberalism is worth fighting for and what is at stake if we let it corrode in those societies where its hold on power is weakest. And they need to sketch out the various social practices that such values can justify, and the numerous institutions that can help realise, protect, or promote them. This willingness to acknowledge the partisanship of liberal values while arguing passionately and ardently for them is far from unknown in the contemporary literature. Stephen Macedo's work on the value of public justification is a good example.

'Liberals should', he writes, 'be candid about their partisanship, open in their arguments, and explicit on the need for principled moderation'.[12] Liberals must defend their partisanship rather than evade it.[13] This is particularly true, I think, for liberal politics specifically because of its emphasis on individual freedom, rationality, and transparency. If it is the case, as Macedo (amongst others) argues, that liberal political regimes engage and seek to shape our deepest and most personal values, which would be consonant with realism, then failing to spell out these controversial implications 'could lead to a conspiracy of silence and the embracement of a false liberal consciousness ... [P]ublic justification could become liberal hoodwinking, and 'political' liberalism could come to rest on a noble fib'.[14] Such deception is surely incompatible with some of the most fundamental moral values of liberalism. And so liberal realists must lay their cards on the table, be explicit in their guiding normative values, express their practical political ramifications, and defend them against those that oppose them.

But the sense in which a liberal realist will see liberalism as a fighting creed will go beyond the requirement of theoretical honesty: because liberal realists will be sensitive to the historical uniqueness of liberalism, to the fact that politics is a constant struggle for power even for those that currently possess it, to the inherent fragility of any political order, and to the partisan and contentious nature of their normative values, they will be more aware of the importance of the role that power plays in political life. This places liberal realism in the double bind that I have been stressing throughout: historically and normatively, liberalism has been guided by the desire to restrict and control political power, yet any theory of realism needs to recognise the role and importance of power in any form of political regime. This is exactly why the concept of legitimacy must remain central even to a realist conception of liberal politics.

The liberal affirmation of the political

One of the central themes of realists' critique of liberal theory is that it fails to fully comprehend the political as a space of contestation between different and competing conceptions of the political good, and hence its status as but one of these competing conceptions. A consequence of this is that liberalism takes up the logical space, so to speak, of politics, such that the political does not include contestations between itself and rival forms of political order. The political is displaced or abolished. A realistic account of liberalism must therefore affirm the political. But what does this actually mean? And what form must this affirmation take?

The best way to address these questions is probably through engaging with one of the most powerful forms of this critique, that offered by Carl Schmitt. Famously, Schmitt believed that 'the phenomenon of the political can be understood only in the context of the ever present possibility of the friend-enemy distinction'.[15] This grouping is created when particular associations, be they religious, moral, economic, etc., of human beings reach a certain intensity. Rather than defining politics according to its own particular content, 'The political', he stated, 'is the most intense and extreme antagonism, and every concrete antagonism becomes that much more political the closer it approaches the most extreme point, the friend-enemy distinction'.[16] The intensity of the antagonism between friends and enemies must include, Schmitt insisted, 'the real possibility of physical killing'.[17] Though only the possibility of such conflict is required in order to establish the friend-enemy distinction, and hence politics, he did write (in a manner clearly reminiscent of Hobbes) that 'Each participant is in a position to judge whether the adversary intends to negate his opponent's way of life and therefore must be repulsed or fought in order to preserve one's own form of existence'.[18] The possibility of conflict, including real physical conflict aimed towards the extermination of one's enemies, is not only a legitimate end of politics but a necessary precondition of politics itself.[19]

Against the backdrop of this understanding of the political, it is not surprising that Schmitt found liberalism wanting. Liberalism is guilty, Schmitt believed, of attempting to conceal its politics, which he believed was the politics of eradicating politics. 'There exists', he wrote, 'no liberal politics, only a liberal critique of politics'.[20] He rightly recognised that the theory of liberalism is directed at 'hindering and controlling' the power of the state in order to protect individual freedom.[21] The strategy that it employed to do this was essentially one of depoliticisation: 'In a very systematic fashion liberal thought evades or ignores state and politics and moves instead in a typical always recurring polarity of two heterogeneous spheres, namely ethics and economics, intellect and trade, education and property … From this polarity they attempt to annihilate the political'.[22] In doing so, liberalism presents itself as politically neutral or void of specific content, allowing any conflicts to work themselves out through the processes of intellectual debate (a liberal is a person who, 'if asked "Christ or Barabbas?" [responds] with a proposal to adjourn or appoint a committee of investigation')[23] or economic exchange.[24] It transforms enemies into debating adversaries or economic competitors.[25] But, pre-empting many more recent criticisms of liberalism, Schmitt saw that far from being neutral between different conceptions of the good, liberalism encouraged its own kind of homogeneity, a society consisting of market-orientated egotists unwilling to take their own side in an argument, the liberal individual.[26] Liberalism therefore masks or conceals its own specificity and, in doing so, the friend-enemy antagonism that lies at its political heart.

Relatedly, in following the strategy of depoliticisation, liberalism disavows itself of the resources needed to invigorate and motivate the sacrifice of life which the political entity must be able to demand. This is particularly true because of the individualism that Schmitt identifies as one of the key principles of the liberal system of thought (introduced as one of the methods for controlling political power): 'Such a demand is in no way justifiable by the individualism of liberal thought. No consistent individualism can entrust to someone other than to the individual himself the right to dispose of the physical life of the individual ... For the individual as such there is no enemy with whom he must enter into a life-and-death struggle if he personally does not want to do so. To compel him to fight against his will is, from the viewpoint of the private individual, lack of freedom and repression.'[27] Essentially liberalism, for Schmitt, fails to take politics seriously enough insofar as it is unable to properly mobilise the highest intensities and antagonisms of the friend-enemy distinction, the need to kill to preserve one's own existence. In large part this is also because Schmitt saw liberalism as a negative theory dedicated to restraining the state and hence unable to positively invigorate individuals' commitment to the public sphere. Liberal theory fails to see that politics is struggle and therefore cannot present liberalism as a fighting ideology.

If we begin with Schmitt's second criticism, liberalism apparently fails to appreciate the seriousness of politics, that it is a human activity which presupposes the potential for physical conflict and self-sacrifice. There is a frivolousness or playfulness to liberal politics which is indicative of its commitment to individualism, lack of normative core and unwillingness to properly recognise the existence of its own enemies. Here I think Schmitt simply misses one of the central historical motivations of liberal thought. Insofar as liberalism does attempt to tame the political it does so with the conscious intention of ensuring that politics does not return to the seriousness of seventeenth century European politics, with its bloody and horrific religious persecution, or of the numerous violations of individual freedom that took place in the nineteenth and twentieth centuries on behalf of some higher good like 'the people' or 'the nation'. The attempt to create a less serious politics is born out of historical memory, the knowledge of what taking politics too seriously can result in. The general sense in which liberals are committed to tolerating those with whom they disagree, and prefer compromise rather than conflict, doesn't belie the conflictual nature of the political; quite the reverse. It is because liberals understand the possibility and consequences of conflict that they prefer compromise and toleration. This does not mean that at the extreme, liberal democratic states will not go to war in self-defence, for the promotion of their values or to undermine their ideological enemies. This is quite obviously false. Liberals are very often willing to defend their position through the use of force. But nevertheless the point is that liberalism in general, and here liberal realism does not deviate, does recognise the seriousness of politics and indeed its very structure, theoretical and institutional, is geared towards controlling that seriousness for the sake of individual freedom.

The full force of Schmitt's second charge, that liberalism fails to be a fighting ideology, is better realised if we align it not to the notion that it needs to take politics more seriously but to the idea that it conceals its own political nature. Here I think Schmitt is on more secure ground. By stipulating the values that will determine the fundamental framework of the political association, and then insisting that politics is an activity that takes place with reference to that framework, liberal theorists undoubtedly conceal, or at least obscure, the fact that liberalism is a contested and very specific form of political life. It might be compatible with a wider range of conceptions of the good than many alternatives but this does not make it a neutral conception of politics. And, as many liberals have indeed conceded, life in liberal states is easier for those pursuing certain conceptions of the good rather than others and will, though this is often a source of complaint from those who want to resist such convergence, lead to a homogenisation of conceptions in the long run (even if it is a fairly wide band of homogeneity). In this sense, accepting the partisan foundations of liberal realism is to affirm both the political and the political nature of liberalism itself.

Does this then mean that liberal realism must accept Schmitt's friend/enemy distinction as at the heart of the political? And, if so, who are liberal realism's enemies? In an important sense it must. There are those who hold radically anti-liberal views that liberalism must be prepared to struggle against, potentially through the use of force, if it is deemed necessary to do so (though with the sort of self-imposed limitation I will discuss in the following chapter). These are its enemies. In this it is no different from the way any other form of political order must view those who oppose it. As I have been stressing throughout, however, any realist yet distinctively liberal account of politics will, given its emphasis on reflecting the freedom and equality of all persons, be highly concerned about the fate and status of enemies within a liberal regime. They will not be satisfied with the simultaneously vague yet extreme ramifications of Schmitt's account. As such, liberal realism needs to re-describe or tame the friend/enemy relationship in such a way that retains the essential truth of politics as conflict that this distinction illuminates (and its own partisan status within this conflict), while making it compatible with the normative demands of liberal legitimacy. Or, put differently, liberal realists must seek to affirm the political without violating the moral equality and individual freedom of those that reject liberalism. How it does this is the focus of the following chapter. Before we go on to that, however, it is worth lingering just a little longer on the question of the ramifications of the partisan foundations of liberalism for its own self-understanding and the relationship between those who hold different and competing conceptions of the liberal political ideal.

Friends, adversaries, and enemies

We might be tempted to think that all those who are committed to liberalism, regardless of their substantive differences, might fall into the Schmittian category of friends. But like all political 'isms', liberalism is not one thing. The liberal tradition is made up of several different and competing interpretations of its basic normative commitments to freedom and equality and hence a plurality of recommendations in regard to the appropriate institutions, practices, and norms that should make up the political framework. Insofar as politics is the conflict between different political ideals, at the extreme to provide the terms of co-existence that answer the political question, politics includes the struggle between competing liberalisms. Liberal realism is not to be identified as synonymous with any one of these. Rather part of what a theory of liberal realism aims to provide is a way of thinking about liberal politics specifically in a context where any one of these competing conceptions provides the political framework but in which alternative liberal ideals compete for power. This means that it is essential for liberal realism to consider further the relationship between those who hold different and competing conceptions of liberalism. So the difficulty with categorising all liberals as friends is that it obscures the fact that politics is as much about the contest between those with political disagreements as those with political conflicts. Indeed, much of normal day-to-day politics (including most party politics in democratic regimes) is about the disagreements between those who are nevertheless committed to the liberal political framework, and the focus on the 'extraordinary' struggle between friends and enemies can obscure this. So a realistic theory needs to be a little more refined than this. What I want to suggest is that liberal realism adopts a category employed by Chantal Mouffe in her Schmitt-inspired account of political agonism, that of the adversary. A brief outline of her theory will help us understand the nature of this new category.

In large part, that agonism has been subsumed into the wider category of realism is due to the fact that it takes as the starting point for political theorising the notion that persons hold fundamentally different and competing positions on the most important moral, religious, *and* political questions. It therefore rules out the possibility that the political order can be grounded in any pre-political normative consensus. Instead it takes the struggle and contest between these competing positions to be the condition that politics must somehow bring order to. Mouffe goes as far as to make a distinction between 'the political' and 'politics' in order to emphasise the manner in which politics of any form necessarily takes place within a space characterised by power, conflict, and antagonism: 'by "the political" I mean the dimension of antagonism which I take to be constitutive of human societies, while by "politics" I mean the set of practices and institutions through which an order is created, organising human co-existence in the context of conflictuality provided by the political'.[28] Other agonists do not follow Mouffe in making such ontological (or 'ontic'[29]) distinctions. But they nevertheless accept the basic point that politics takes place in conditions of deep and radical pluralism and that the first task of politics is to provide the means for persons to live peacefully together despite their disagreements. As William Connolly puts it, 'The most basic problem of political ethics ... is not how to get participants to obey a universal moral source that they already profess in common ... [W]e do not live in a time when most politically organised territories are populated by people who share one fundamental religious faith *or* one source of public morality. Even states said to be Hindu, Buddhist, Jewish, Christian, Islamic, or secular contain significant minorities who do not confess those faiths ... Thus a basic challenge of ethico-political life in late modern territorial states is how to negotiate honourable public settlements in settings where interdependent partisans confess different existential faiths and final sources of morality'.[30]

The classic agonist response to this problem is to try to tame the potentiality for violence that such partisanship can give rise to. Connolly's suggestion is that we forge 'a positive ethos of engagement between multiple constituencies coexisting on the same strip of territory'.[31] This 'bicameral orientation to political life' requires one to adopt the position of an engaged partisan in the world but to temper this with an acknowledgement that one's position is contestable and hence recognise the need to sacrifice the demand to have this view hegemonically imposed upon all others. In other words, we should all just be a little more tolerant of those that disagree with us. Mouffe's response places more emphasis on the institutions and practices, rather than personal dispositions that persons should foster. She claims that 'one of the main tasks for democratic politics consists in defusing the potential antagonism that exists in social relations'.[32] It does this by converting the friend/enemy antagonistic relationship that is constitutive of the political into an agonistic and hence adversarial one. The difference between the two is that 'antagonism is a we/they relationship in which the two sides are enemies who do not share any common ground, [whereas] agonism is a we/they relation where the conflicting parties, although acknowledging that there is no rational solution to their conflict, nevertheless recognise the legitimacy of their opponents'.[33] This legitimacy stems from the fact that both parties, while in conflict, nevertheless see themselves as belonging to the same association and share a 'common symbolic space'. Thus a democratic society requires a consensus 'on the institutions constitutive of democracy and on the "ethico-political" values that inform this commitment to democracy – liberty and equality for all'.[34] Essentially, the institutions and principles of democracy are what constitute the necessary common symbolic space and, in doing so, transform antagonism into agonism and enemies into adversaries.[35]

Mouffe describes the agreement on the ethico-political values of democracy as a 'conflictual-consensus' in which persons agree on the values of freedom and equality yet disagree as to their meaning. The various hegemonic projects that compete within this 'conflictual-consensus' will therefore include different interpretations of these values. And while any one project might succeed in securing hegemony, this will always be contingent in the sense that the democratic space must remain open to allow challenges from counter-hegemonic projects, those which strive to impose their own hegemonic practices.[36] Crucially, Mouffe does not believe that it is even conceptually, let alone empirically, possible for the shared common ground needed to create agonistic relations to include all persons within the political association. There will always be enemies. This is because, for Mouffe at least, any attempt to create a consensus will necessarily, by the very nature of the process of identity creation, be exclusionary. Any 'we' presupposes a 'they'.[37] So not all demands and practices will be legitimate, and those that challenge democratic institutions or reject the freedom and equality of all persons will be discriminated against.

Agonism does not, and despite several criticisms along these lines, assume that all persons will be included in the 'conflictual-consensus'.[38] As Mouffe states, 'The category of the "enemy" does not disappear but is displaced; it remains pertinent with respect to those who do not accept the democratic "rules of the game" and who thereby exclude themselves from the political community'.[39] But no political association can continue for long, especially not a democratic one, if the conflicts of the friend/enemy distinction remain dominant.[40] And so the point of democratic politics is not to eradicate conflict, but to channel and direct as much of it as is possible in such a way that it becomes compatible with a pluralist democracy. The struggle between different (what Mouffe calls) 'hegemonic projects' remains but they are played out under conditions regulated by democratic procedures that adversaries accept.[41] We can recognise that they are legitimate opponents, even though we disagree with the ends that they pursue. In treating them as legitimate adversaries, therefore, we recognise them as specifically *political* opponents. 'In the domain of the political', Schmitt wrote, 'people do not face each other as abstractions, but as politically interested and politically determined persons, as citizens, governors or governed, politically allied or opponents – in any case, therefore, in political categories'.[42] And in viewing others as political opponents we recognise them as equals in the political domain, despite how deeply we might disagree with them on moral or religious grounds.

Agonism is a radical theory of democracy. As such it represents a competing response to the first political question to liberal realism (or, in Mouffe's terms, a competing 'hegemonic project'). They share the general strategy of trying to tame or defuse the potential violence and conflict that radical pluralism affords. And in accepting that this can be done by identifying and developing as large a consensus as possible on particular values and institutions, while accepting that it is contingent and will never be endorsed by all, they certainly have a very similar approach to thinking about how politics functions in conditions of disagreement. But liberal realism is not a radical theory of democracy. And so while the category of the adversary is a useful one insofar as it allows us to introduce a third category between friend and enemy, it is important to recognise that the adversaries and enemies of agonism will necessarily be different from those of liberal realism. Insofar as agonism is a radical theory of democracy, its enemies only include those that reject democratic values and institutions. The category of adversaries could therefore potentially include representatives from across the entire political spectrum, liberals, fascists, communists, libertarians, ecologists, theocrats, etc., as long as they are committed to the principles of agonism. Within the framework of liberal realism we can say that a friend is someone who advocates the same version of a liberal political framework, an adversary is someone who advocates a political framework that is a variation of liberalism, while an enemy is someone who endorses a non-liberal form of political order. Not only will the enemies of liberal realism be different to those of agonism, it will also have more of them, and hence fewer friends and adversaries also.

Mouffe has been criticised on several occasions for being unable, or maybe unwilling, to properly establish the content of the 'conflictual-consensus' that one needs to accept in order to be properly counted as an adversary.[43] The same criticism could undoubtedly be applied to liberal realism's adoption of these categories: it is fundamentally vague and unclear what one needs to accept in order to be a friend, an adversary, or an enemy. There is indeed a high degree of elusiveness here, but necessarily so. While a realist account of liberalism is grounded in a basic notion of freedom and equality, there are a whole host of interpretations of these values that are consistent with liberal politics. Disagreements between liberals (or democrats, or Marxists, etc.) in regard to interpreting their fundamental normative commitments, and hence what political practices they should commend, is part of the day-to-day stuff of politics. This does beg a further question about how we can determine when an interpretation of these values is or is not consistent with liberalism. Are, for instance, libertarianism and social democracy interpretations of freedom and equality that are variations of a liberal political framework? Or are they challenges and alternatives to it? I personally think that Rawls' political liberalism, Dworkin's comprehensive liberalism, Raz's perfectionist liberalism, Kymlicka's multicultural liberalism, Wolfe's natural law liberalism, McCabe's modus vivendi liberalism and Kukathas' libertarianism, for instance, all represent variations on a liberal theme.[44] Advocates of such positions would therefore be adversaries rather than enemies. Yet, as liberal theorists well know, there has been extensive debate as to whether X's theory can really be thought of as liberal: is perfectionism too paternalistic? Does libertarianism's lack of concern about the basic structure of society render it fundamentally illiberal? Can a liberal theory appeal to comprehensive conceptions of the good? Can a liberal theory entertain the notion of group rights? And so on. These are, of course, highly contestable questions over which theorists disagree. But that is the point. There is disagreement about who is, and who is not, a liberal. The same lack of determinacy will be true in political practice also. There is often disagreement as to whether different political parties represent variations on the same theme – what strikes many as minuscule and irrelevant doctrinal differences between left-wing parties, for instance, are often seen by their members to be the crucial ideological dividing line between 'real' or 'true' Marxism and everyone else. And we are all too familiar with stories from communist or fascist countries in which holding a different sort of interpretation of Marxist or fascist principles was tantamount to being an enemy of the state, with all its horrendous consequences. Hence we cannot identify enemies independent of a particular political context. The rather fluid, transient and sometimes rapid manner in which political friends can become enemies and enemies become allies is not some contingent feature of political life that stems from the disloyal and disingenuous nature of politicians, but speaks to the fact that such categories are, apart from in the extreme cases, themselves at the behest of political circumstances and hence unable to be pinned down pre-politically. They are political questions. And this is why it is not possible to determine in advance, and with any high degree of specificity, who the friends, adversaries, and enemies of liberal realism will be.

Notes

1   Rawls 'Remarks on political philosophy', in his *Lectures on the History of Political Philosophy*, p. 10
2   Tully, 'The unfreedom of the moderns', in *Public Philosophy in a New Key – Volume II: Imperialism and Civic Freedom*, p. 96
3   Waldron, *Law and Disagreement*, p. 162
4   Of course not all persons that reject liberalism will do so on grounds that are reasonable. Many reject fundamental liberal principles, such as the moral equality of races or genders, undoubtedly on the grounds of pure prejudice or bias. But it would be crude in the extreme to think that this is true of all non-liberals, past and present. For the purposes of my argument, I will focus specifically on reasonable non-liberals. And anyway, can we really say that all liberals hold their beliefs reasonably? What about those who have never reflected on their beliefs and who endorse liberal values simply because they have been inculcated to do so, or because their parents did so, or through peer pressure, etc.?
5   See, for example, Barry, *Justice as Impartiality*; G. Long, *Relativism and the Foundations of Liberalism* (Exeter: Imprint Academic, 2004). Nagel poses the question thus: 'There is something of a paradox here: How can I believe something if I think others presented with the same grounds could reasonably refuse to believe it? Doesn't this mean I believe it but think also that it would be reasonable for *me* not to believe it – and is that possible?' ('Moral conflict and political legitimacy', p. 235)
6   Matravers and Mendus argue that there is an interconnection between conceptions of the good and the epistemological status of conceptions of the good and that even moderate scepticism (of the sort Barry endorses, for instance) will undermine some conceptions. They write that 'a conception of the good that is held with a degree of uncertainty is, in important respects, a different conception of the good from one that is held with assurance. It is not merely *what* we believe that contributes to and constitutes our ability to flourish; it is also *the way in which* we are entitled to believe

it ... The religious believer who can hold a belief in God unquestioningly is in a significantly different condition from the religious believer who can hold that belief only provisionally: the declaration "I know that my Redeemer liveth!" has a different status from the declaration "I believe that my Redeemer liveth, but since I am unable to persuade others I must entertain doubt" ... Scepticism is not itself a comprehensive conception of the good; but it is a view that has consequences for comprehensive conceptions of the good' (M. Matravers and S. Mendus, 'The reasonableness of pluralism', in C. McKinnon and D. Castiglione (eds) *The Culture of Toleration in Diverse Societies* (Manchester: Manchester University Press, 2003), 38–53, pp. 42–3)

7 For a defence of liberal neutrality that appeals directly to sceptical epistemological premises (rather than indirectly via the fact of reasonable disagreement) see G. Dworkin, 'Non-neutral principles', *Journal of Philosophy*, 71:14 (1974), 491–506

8 Though whether it is the objective of politics to take a decision specifically on epistemological matters will of course depend on which form of politics rules. For example, a theocratic politics may see it as crucial to settle such matters as a way of helping solidify support for a particular religious doctrine

9 Schmitt, *The Crisis of Parliamentary Democracy*, p. 64

10 Weber, 'The profession and vocation of politics', in *Political Writings*, pp. 352–3

11 And, indeed, we should not be misled into thinking that there is any direct link between the passion or certainty with which one holds one's commitments and the desire to impose those beliefs upon others. See M. Sleat, 'Liberalism, fundamentalism and truth', *Journal of Applied Philosophy*, 23:4 (2006), 405–17

12 Macedo, 'The politics of justification', p. 284

13 *Ibid.*, p. 298

14 *Ibid.*, p. 281

15 Schmitt, *The Concept of the Political*, p. 35

16 *Ibid.*, p. 29

17 *Ibid.*, p. 33

18 *Ibid.*, p. 27

19 'What always matters is the possibility of conflict', *ibid.*, p. 39

20 *Ibid.*, p. 70. Morgenthau made a similar claim when he said of liberalism, 'Paradoxically enough, the Western world has developed a political philosophy without a positive concept of politics' (*Scientific Man vs. Power Politics*, p. 87)

21 Schmitt, *The Concept of the Political*, p. 70

22 *Ibid.*, pp. 70–1

23 Schmitt, *The Crisis of Parliamentary Democracy*, p. 62

24 Schmitt, *The Concept of the Political*, p. 71

25 *Ibid.*, p. 28

26 Here I follow David Dyzenhaus' wonderful essay 'Why Carl Schmitt?' (in D. Dyzenhaus (ed.), *Law as Politics – Carl Schmitt's Critique of Liberalism* (London: Duke University Press, 1998), 1–20, p. 14)

27 Schmitt, *The Concept of the Political*, pp. 70–1

28 Mouffe, *On the Political*, p. 9

29 *Ibid.*, p. 8

30 W. E. Connolly, *Pluralism* (USA: Duke University Press, 2005), pp. 33–4

31   *Ibid.*, p. 34

32   Mouffe, *On the Political*, p. 19

33   *Ibid.*, p. 20

34   *Ibid.*, p. 31

35   *Ibid.*, p. 20

36   *Ibid.*, p. 18

37   *Ibid.*, pp. 14–19

38   See A. Knops, 'Agonism as deliberation – On Mouffe's theory of democracy', *The Journal of Political Philosophy*, 15:1 (2007), 115–26; F. Gürsözlü, 'Agonism and deliberation – Recognising the difference', *The Journal of Political Philosophy*, 17:3 (2009), 356–68

39   C. Mouffe, *The Return of the Political* (London: Verso, 2005), p. 4

40   Mouffe, *On the Political*, p. 51

41   *Ibid.*, p. 21

42   Schmitt, *The Crisis of Parliamentary Democracy*, p. 11

43   See, for instance, E. Erman, 'What is wrong with agonistic pluralism?: Reflections on conflict in democratic theory', *Philosophy and Social Criticism*, 35:9 (2009), 1039–62

44   Rawls, *Political Liberalism*; Dworkin, *Sovereign Virtue*; J. Raz, *The Morality of Freedom* (Oxford: Oxford University Press, 1986); W. Kymlicka, *Multicultural Citizenship: A Liberal Theory of Minority Rights* (Oxford: Oxford University Press, 1996); C. Wolfe, *Natural Law Liberalism* (Cambridge: Cambridge University Press, 2006); McCabe, *Modus Vivendi Liberalism*; C. Kukathas, *The Liberal Archipelago: A Theory of Diversity and Freedom* (Oxford: Oxford University Press, 2007)

7

The moderate hegemony of liberal realism

Legitimacy is a central concept in realist thought. Though the popular caricature of realism, especially in international relations theory, encourages the view that might is synonymous with right, that the ability to rule is the same as the right to do so, realists have often stressed that this is not the case. Rather, there is an important difference between rule as mere domination and rule as authoritative that the concept of legitimacy allows us to determine. This begs the obvious question of how liberal realism justifies its claim to be a legitimate form of political authority. What distinguishes liberal realism as a form of political rule rather than mere domination? This question is particularly pertinent and problematic, specifically from the liberal perspective of the theory, when we accept both that liberal regimes will necessarily need to rule over those that reject their right to do so and that any successful answer will in itself depend on the use of coercive power, in the sense of making people act in ways they otherwise would not. This stands in need of justification. In what sense, if any, can these truths about the political world be squared with liberalism's normative commitment to a morally constrained politics?

Building upon Stephen Macedo's notion of liberalism as a 'moderate hegemony', what I want to suggest is that the answer to this question lies in the manner in which liberalism rules, especially in relation to its non-liberal internal enemies. While in a liberal state liberals will necessarily be masters, they will be what I want to call 'restrained masters'. And it is through this restraint that they not only respect the freedom of non-liberals but do so in such a way that distinguishes liberalism as a form of political rule, even though it does necessarily dominate or have mastery over those persons. There are numerous elements to this or ways in which this self-restraint is realised in theory and practice, and this chapter will set out what I take to be the most important of these. But any regime, including a liberal one, will need two related but distinct legitimation stories, one directed towards those who reject the political framework, its enemies, and another towards the friends and adversaries who will broadly accept that framework though still might have substantial disagreements about it. The second story is no doubt an easier one to tell and in the next section I shall discuss the form that this takes in liberal realism and address one concern that liberals might have with it. In the following section, I want to set out the notion of a 'moderate hegemony' that is central to liberal realism's legitimation story as directed towards its enemies, and show how it can simultaneously accept yet interpret in a more liberal fashion the necessity of domination and coercion that the move to a realist account of the political requires. The third section then fleshes this out a little more by introducing the notion of liberal rulers as 'restrained masters' and the normative and institutional self-constraints that they place on their own use of power so as to ensure that even our enemies are respected and treated as free and equal. And then, finally, I want to incorporate the recently developed realist idea of political constitutionalism into liberal realism as another key way in which this respect is demonstrated.

Legitimacy amongst friends and adversaries

Though legitimacy is a multi-faceted concept that features differently in a myriad of aspects of our social world, the notion of legitimacy I have been employing is the right of one person or group of persons to rule over others, usually determined by their being located within a certain geographical territory, including the right to use coercive force in order to ensure compliance with their demands and laws when obedience is not, or is likely not to be, forthcoming. While the demand for legitimation arises whenever one group claims that it has the right to rule over any other, it only stands in need of a sufficient response when such rule is actually taking place. The focus on legitimacy as the right to rule means that it cannot be the case that those subject to the power of a *legitimate* state conform to its rules and demands *solely* on the grounds of its overwhelming force. For a state to be legitimate there must be some sense in which people obey its rules and demands, and recognise the right of the state to expect such obedience, because they take it to be a political entity that has authority (not just power) over them, one whose commands should be taken as having normative force in guiding their actions in virtue of the fact that they were issued by an authoritative political source and regardless of their own independent judgements about those commands.

Realists tend to be more ecumenical than liberals, especially those following Kant, in terms of what reasons are appropriate in relation to the question of legitimating the state vis-à-vis the individual. Coercive force, and the fear of coercive force, does have *a* role to play in the matrix of reasons that bind the individual to the state. But it cannot be the whole story, for then politics would be indistinguishable from mere domination. This is why it is important that at least a significant proportion of the citizenry at large endorse the political framework, ideally by sharing its fundamental normative commitments, values, ends, and principles. For those that do, the state will necessarily represent a political authority through which the values and ends they hold are realised, and indeed maybe without which their realisation would be impossible. This need not be understood in a strongly individualist sense in which the subordinates have (in some appropriate sense) freely consented to the state. Political legitimation does require, however, a certain level of 'binding in' through which the legitimacy of the rulers is established and reinforced. That their rule can be justified with reference to values, ends, and goals that are shared, at least amongst the most significant members and groups within society, is therefore essential to demonstrating and maintaining legitimacy.

This condition of legitimacy has great explanatory value insofar as it can help illuminate the sources of illegitimacy when the state cannot be justified in terms of shared beliefs, because no basis of commonly held beliefs exists, because changes in widely held beliefs have deprived the rulers of their justificatory common ground, or because changing circumstances have rendered implausible the original justificatory reasons employed (despite those shared beliefs remaining constant).[1] That said, exactly who needs to share the common ends is a political question that will depend on the political circumstances. How many constitutes a 'substantial number' will depend on the circumstances, as will which groups of persons this must include (e.g. powerful religious, ethnic, or tribal groups, the young, influential critics, etc.).[2] It certainly will not include, and cannot realistically be expected to include, all citizens within the state. And while widespread rejection of those ends could have important consequences in relation to the degree of co-operation and quality of performance that the rulers can secure from the ruled, especially when the latter are asked to make significant personal sacrifices in order to achieve that state's ends, this need not in and of itself determine the state's illegitimacy. At most one can say that it sets states on a vicious spiral of having to employ more and more coercive power so as to motivate citizens to engage in co-operative activity that is likely only to further demonstrate the lack of a common normative basis between the rulers and the ruled. But ineffectiveness is not, in and of itself, illegitimacy.

The liberal state is a political association whose fundamental political framework is both grounded in and directed towards realising or protecting liberal ends, ones which, like the normative foundations of any political order, not all its citizens endorse. These ends are in no sense assumed to be endorsed or affirmed by all but represent substantial and controversial moral and political commitments that will inevitably be partisan in their appeal. If we connect this account of the normative foundations of liberal politics with this realist condition of legitimacy then clearly it is a necessary condition of legitimacy that the liberal state promotes liberal ends, in particular respecting the freedom and moral equality of all individuals, where liberal ends are shared by a significant proportion of the citizenry of that state. Importantly, it is not the case that citizens must accept that these represent the best, right, or true interpretation of liberal values. The liberal state will, if successful, largely consist of adversaries, those who broadly endorse the liberal framework though disagree on how the fundamental liberal normative commitments are to be interpreted or demanded in practice. But, as long as the liberal political framework is widely recognised as a plausible interpretation of liberal values, then this will suffice for the purposes of morally justifying it to adversaries, even though they may still work to alter that framework so as to be more in line with their own liberal ideal.

There is something obviously tautological about this condition of realist legitimacy: the liberal state is legitimate because it pursues liberal ends, values, and moral commitments. The same condition provides a partial basis for justifying the legitimacy of other forms of political order also (socialist orders are legitimate because they are directed towards achieving socialist ends, fascist orders because of fascist ends, and so on). This is inevitable, according to the realist view I am expounding here, insofar as competing claims to legitimacy, and different accounts of the goods or values in which a legitimate state would be grounded, are necessarily part of the struggle and conflict between different visions of the political ideal that characterises politics. Different people believe that different goods are required to legitimate the political association. It would be a mistake to think that legitimacy somehow stands above political contestation, that it is a neutral arbiter in the struggle between different political positions that can determine which are permissible and which are not.[3] Insofar as there are different goods, values, and ends according to which claims of legitimacy can be justified, the question of what is and is not legitimate will be as contestable and contested an issue as questions over what justice demands, the limits of freedom, the content of rights, or the appropriate subject of human equality. Indeed legitimacy, and its many contested meanings and demands, is often at the very forefront of the struggle between competing visions of the political ideal. Claims to the legitimacy of any political regime, including liberal regimes, cannot therefore appeal to the consensus that surrounds any value or set of values but must appeal directly to those substantive values themselves. These values will inevitably be contested by some, even if, as will often be the case in the most stable of political orders, only by a minority. But in this the grounds of liberal legitimacy are no different from, and certainly no more or less self-referentially partisan than, those of other forms of political life.

Many liberals worry that a position such as this leads to a disquieting relativism in which the legitimacy of any political regime is simply relative vis-à-vis the values held by those who wield power and/or the majority of the citizenry. Realists are more comfortable with this notion. On the one hand they take it to reflect, as Geuss puts it, the fact that 'The legitimatory mechanisms available in a given society change from one historical period to another, as do the total set of beliefs held by agents ... and the widely distributed, socially rooted, moral conceptions'.[4] Williams' Basic Legitimation Demand contained the same sort of historical sensitivity. But the differences that they both highlight apply across space as well as time. Just as we, to use Geuss' example, no longer accept the idea that the Pope can dispense political legitimation as he did with Charlemagne in the year 800, so many of the beliefs that we take to be central to any successful legitimatory story, the primacy of individuals and their rights, religious toleration, equal freedom for all, etc., are not shared by all peoples today.[5] A realistic theory of legitimacy needs to be aware that the beliefs that lie at the base of forms of legitimation are part of, rather than independent from, the wider social world in which they exist. As such, there is an important sense in which the historical and cultural sensitivity of the grounds of legitimacy make some form of relativism unavoidable.

On the other hand, this relativism is an inevitable consequence of the conflictual nature of political life. A realist account of liberal legitimacy needs to come to terms with the partisan appeal of its foundational normative values and accept that liberal regimes are not uniquely or superiorly legitimate on the grounds that their normative frameworks are affirmed by all their citizens. An upshot of this is that liberal political orders will inevitably be experienced as an imposition by those that reject liberalism or several of its key tenets. But this will inescapably be true of all forms of political order in relation to those that reject its fundamental normative framework. As we have seen, the requirement that the fundamental principles of the political order are, or could be, affirmed by all those subject to it responds to liberalism's normative concern with respecting the freedom and equality of all individuals. In part, this is what distinguishes liberalism from many other forms of political order.

Liberals are people who insist that the state must respect the equal moral status of its citizens, including those who reject the liberal values on which its claims to legitimacy are based. They worry about the fate, in terms of freedom and equality, of political minorities. It would be a liberal regime of dubious legitimacy that did not show equal respect to its political minorities. In effect, therefore, it is not simply the epistemological consequences of relativism that are of concern but also the fact that the vision of politics as the conflict and struggle between competing conceptions of the political good renders implausible the standard theoretical mechanism for safeguarding the freedom and equality of all persons, in particular those that reject liberalism. As such, a realist account of liberal legitimacy must still have something to say to and about the legitimacy of the liberal state in relation to those that reject liberalism beyond a mere and brute affirmation of the values and ends that it pursues.

Liberal realism as 'moderate hegemony'

How do liberal regimes treat those members that reject liberalism as free and equal when they are clearly being forced to obey laws and principles, pursue ends and normative goals, that they do not share? Answering this question is, as we have seen, going to be a necessary condition of any realistic yet recognisably liberal theory of politics. What I want to suggest is that Macedo's notion of the 'moderate hegemony of liberalism' gives us a plausible and promising way of understanding liberalism that retains the commitment to treating others, including enemies, as free and equal while recognising the fact of political pluralism and the role that coercion plays in enabling and maintaining politics in those conditions.

Liberalism is hegemonic, Macedo states, in the sense that it is honest about the 'pervasive effects and influences of liberal political practices. "Moderate", because transformative constitutionalism confines itself to political virtues, seeks to respect freedom, and takes advantage, where possible, of indirect and nonoppressive means'.[6] On one prominent view of the role of constitutionalism in liberal theory, the role of a constitution is to provide the framework of rules and regulations that allows individuals an equal sphere of freedom to pursue whatever ends they choose. Such a view insists that it is not the role of the constitution to interfere with the private choices that persons make (as long as they do not impinge on the ability of others to determine their own ends), nor does it seek to dictate which ends they should pursue. Yet this, as Macedo puts it, 'misses the radically transformative dimension of liberal constitutionalism and is liable to obscure the extent to which a liberal constitutional order is a pervasively educative one.'[7] Crucially, the pervasive liberal view assumes that citizens' endorsement of liberalism is in some sense natural, with interests that pre-exist the constitutive effects of social and political institutions. It overlooks the extent to which a liberal regime needs to engage in the formation of liberal citizens:

> Liberal constitutional institutions have a more deeply constitutive role, which is to work at shaping all forms of diversity over the course of time, so the people are *satisfied* leading lives of bounded individual freedom. Successful constitutional institutions must do more than help order the freedom of individuals prefabricated for life in a liberal political order: they must shape the way that people use their freedom and shape *people* to help ensure that freedom is what they want. If a constitutional regime is to succeed and thrive, it must constitute the private realm in its image, and it must form citizens willing to observe its limits and able to pursue its aspirations.[8]

There are of course many ways in which a constitution can exert political influence over the formation of its citizens. As a case study Macedo focuses specifically on how public or common schools in the US throughout the mid-nineteenth century, which sought to educate all children within a certain geographical area, was a direct attempt to exercise political leverage over the intellectual development and moral character of future citizens. Schooling is a particularly important aspect in the formation of citizens insofar as it reinforces the basic beliefs and commitments that it is believed should be held by all citizens, and to reshape and supplant more cultural and religious identities that denied such beliefs (of which there were many at the time). What was happening, Macedo plausibly claims, was that political power was purposefully being exerted in order to foster and create the willingness of individuals from particular religious groups to live in peace with those they believed to be damned. But there can be more indirect methods of liberal citizen formation also, and here Macedo explores the manner in which the separation of the religious from the political sphere, effectively being prepared to regard religious views as politically irrelevant, was a price of assimilation into the American way of life that religious believers had to accept. Furthermore, the rituals that are demanded in order to be a judge or be a candidate for president also demanded that religious believers, and Catholics in particular, proclaimed the practical meaninglessness of their religious convictions as a condition of being allowed to serve.[9]

Not all liberal regimes will pursue the same means to create liberal citizens. But the point is that the use of the many mechanisms, practices, and expectations of transformative constitutionalism that have the effect of shaping and affecting our commitments and habits is not something that 'calls for regret, apologies, or adjustment'.[10] Rather it is a proper political aim to try to generate such convergence since liberalism, as any form of political order, needs the support of private beliefs and practices that are at least congruent with liberal politics. The mistake that liberal theory often makes, Macedo believes, is to think that liberal citizens – committed to self-restraint, moderation, and reasonableness – 'spring full-blown from the soil of private freedom', as if simply securing a rigid public/private divide through law is sufficient to ensure their commitment to the liberal constitution. This overlooks the fact that such allegiance is a political achievement.[11]

Macedo accepts that this view of the transformative dimension of liberal constitutionalism is one that will attract the charge of being illiberal in the sense that it explicitly aims at reducing diversity, especially of groups that reject liberalism. Macedo is characteristically unapologetic about this, insisting that what matters is not diversity per se, but 'healthy forms of diversity', i.e. a diversity of different groups that all support the basic values of liberalism.[12] 'The point of liberal constitutionalism at the deepest level is not to avoid this deep partisanship – for we could only do that by abandoning the liberal public morality itself – our aim should rather be to take care to promote the right sort of liberal partisanship in all spheres of life'.[13] And he accepts that 'high costs are born by all those whose religious or philosophical convictions are in tension with liberal democratic public values, including those whose religious or moral beliefs tend towards the totalistic'.[14] But he takes solace in the fact that the methods of transformation that liberal states employ are '*gentle* rather than oppressive, influencing the deeply held beliefs of vast numbers of people without coercion or force'.[15] Nevertheless, he accepts that some will see the transformative role of liberal constitutions as 'oppressive' but insists that this does not detract from the fact that it is necessary political work. 'Diversity', as he puts it, 'does not harmonise automatically'.[16]

There are many points of overlap between Macedo's liberalism-as-moderate-hegemony and liberal realism. In particular it accepts that politics takes place in conditions of ongoing political disagreement and partisanship in which not everyone will hold liberal visions of the political ideal, and that therefore the transformation of people's beliefs so as to be supportive of the political regime is taken to be an appropriate use of political power. Liberal realism places the first point in the wider context of the fact of reasonable political disagreement and the partisan nature of liberalism's normative foundations that was discussed in the previous chapter. Likewise, the notion of transformative constitutionalism needs to be linked to liberal realism's account of legitimacy. It is not only that we need to transform people's beliefs so that the liberal state can 'succeed or thrive', or so that people can lead 'satisfied' lives in it (though this might be a consideration), but because the legitimacy of the political regime depends on such a convergence of beliefs. But other than these small amendments, the notion of the moderate hegemony of liberalism provides us with the basis of our response to how liberalism can be conceived as a legitimate response to the political question, a form of political authority rather than mere domination. The answer is because it is a form of openly partisan hegemonic order that nevertheless seeks to ensure unity and stability through the gentler rather than more violent means available to it. It is through being honest about its partisan nature yet restrained in the manner in which it seeks to secure its ends that liberalism respects the freedom and equality of its enemies. If liberals are masters, they are, to coin a phrase, restrained masters.

Liberals as restrained masters

'Masters', Jean Hampton wrote, 'are dangerous to oneself and to others. They need respect no limits – neither the limits of good sense nor the limits of morality'.[17] In an important sense, the liberal state is the master to its internal enemies: it sets the rules and principles by which the enemies must live and punishes them if they deviate from those. These principles will necessarily be rejected by liberalism's enemies and will represent a restriction on their ability to live as they would wish. Masters can, of course, treat their subjects in a variety of different ways, many of them, as Hampton notes, both dangerous and disregarding of any moral limits. The costs of living in an association the fundamental terms of which you reject can vary and, at the extreme, though this is not to say infrequently, can include death, exile, persecution, the denial of equal rights, and so on. It is this that leads many, liberals and realists alike, to think that mastery cannot be a solution to the political question insofar as it may lead to consequences that are worse than the problems that politics is intended to overcome. While I accept that this might be true, that a world in which one is mastered can be worse than a world in which the political question remains unanswered, the conclusion that I have not wanted to share is that mastery cannot therefore represent a form of political relationship. Indeed, part of what I have argued throughout is that radical political disagreement is permanent and that hence domination, or mastery, is a necessary and inevitable feature of all forms of politics. This only goes to further emphasise the explanatory truth that all political regimes are mixtures, to various degrees, of mastery and non-mastery forms of relationships.[18]

According to the liberal principle of legitimacy, mastery or domination is a morally unjustified and illegitimate coercive relationship. It violates the freedom and equality of those being coerced by forcing them to live according to principles that they reject. The question for us is therefore how a realist account of liberal legitimacy can substantiate this commitment to respecting the freedom and equality of all persons, even in relation to those that reject liberalism. What I want to suggest in this section is that the answer to why liberals can still be thought of as respecting the freedom and equality of their internal enemies is because of the sort of masters they are. Crucially, while they recognise that there are costs involved in living under a political authority one rejects, the liberal state respects the freedom and equality of enemies by ensuring that these costs are kept as low as is reasonably possible, within certain constraints. *It is through this attempt to minimise these costs as far as is consistent with the demands of the liberal state's own normative framework and the requirements of providing an ongoing answer to the political question that liberals respect the freedom of their internal enemies.* Essentially the liberal master places on him or herself a series of normative and institutional constraints that ensure (as far as is possible) that coercive power is not used in a manner that violates the freedom or moral equality of any person, including any internal enemies. Liberals are masters, but they are self-restrained masters and it is this self-restraint that respects the freedom and equality of enemies.

I want to separate out the two ways in which liberals attempt to minimise the costs for non-liberals:

a)   The liberal state only applies additional costs to enemies when they actively seek to undermine the political framework (a subset of enemies that I shall call 'active enemies').

b)   In the case of 'active enemies', the liberal state refrains from using the more extreme costs that would violate their status as free and morally equal citizens.

The first condition tries to balance several aspects of what we have discussed so far. That the political framework be stable, in the sense that at least a significant proportion of persons endorse it and obey its laws, is a necessary condition of it being a sufficient response to the political question and hence legitimate. Protecting the stability of its political framework is therefore a legitimate aim of any (legitimate) political association and can be pursued via a number of different means, part of which can often include imposing additional costs, psychological and physical, on its enemies. While a liberal state will also need to maintain its own stability in order to continue to provide an answer to the political question, it will restrict its use of additional costs only to a particular subset of its internal enemies, those who are actively seeking to undermine it, rather than simply any person who rejects liberalism. Up until the point when enemies become threats, they will be treated no differently, no less as a free and equal citizen, from the liberal state's friends. Yet, even in the case of 'active' enemies, whom the liberal state must certainly treat differently in order to protect the stability of its political framework, liberals place on themselves a series of normative and institutional restrictions that ensure that the enemies are given the rights and protections that they are due as equal citizens to ensure that they are treated fairly and justly. Both of these conditions require emphasising and strengthening the universal and legalistic notion of liberal citizenship, in which being a citizen means being protected against the state by the law, and a distancing of liberal realism from the notion of citizenship as requiring participation in the legislative activity of the state.

'Active enemies'

It has long been a recognised normative objective of liberal theory and politics that people should be given the largest sphere of freedom to pursue their conception of the good life consistent with others having the same degree of liberty. Such a commitment is at the heart of J. S. Mill's harm principle and Kant's universal principle of right, two of the most famous statements of this key liberal tenet.[19] It is only if and when citizens act so as to infringe the liberty of others to pursue their ideas of the good that the state can legitimately interfere with their actions. This is further entrenched by the thought that politics should be concerned with the outward actions of people insofar as they affect other people, and not with internal matters such the fate of others' souls or the content of their beliefs. In Kant's words, politics should deal 'only with the external and indeed practical relation of one person to another, insofar as their actions, as deeds, can have (direct or indirect) influence on each other'.[20] Persons' thoughts are essentially their own; the state has no right to coerce or compel someone solely on the grounds of their beliefs. The importance of this position for our purposes is that for liberals the rejection of the normative framework of the liberal order can only be a necessary but not a sufficient condition for imposing costs upon individuals. Persons need to be actively attempting to undermine the normative and institutional framework of the liberal order for this to be permissible, hence they need to be 'active enemies'. Or, put differently, liberals show respect towards their enemies by not seeking to impose additional costs on them merely for their holding beliefs contrary to liberalism. In this sense all citizens are treated as free and equal citizens regardless of their moral and political views.

There are two ways in which one could attempt to destabilise a liberal state from within: by trying to obtain political power, or influence over how political power is distributed, by force or via engaging in the familiar processes and procedures of democratic politics. How the liberal state should respond to those who are pursuing the democratic route is going to be a heavily contextual matter which will equally rely upon a huge degree of political judgement. That far right groups are banned in Germany and Austria, for example, is obviously and explicitly due to their historical legacy while no such similar reasons exist that could reasonably justify banning the British National Party (BNP) in the UK, for instance. This is an example where the costs of politics differ in different political associations. Yet no British government, liberal or otherwise, could ever rule out banning the BNP, or any other radical party, in the future as a possible way of preventing them taking power. All things being equal, however, it is unlikely that a liberal state will seek to ban a particular political party that doesn't stand any meaningful chance of actually obtaining or even challenging for power. So it is an open political question whether those who seek to undermine or destabilise the liberal state via democratic means should be subject to additional costs or not.

But nevertheless the basic point for our purposes is that liberals do not seek to impose additional costs of politics on their enemies simply because they reject liberalism, by denying them equal rights, representation, toleration, liberty, etc. but only in those cases where they are actively seeking to destabilise or undermine the liberal framework. A political order could do differently; many political regimes have persecuted – and continue to persecute – persons on the grounds of their simply holding certain beliefs (religious, moral, or political). Liberals do not impose additional costs on anyone unless their actions (rather than beliefs) threaten the stability of the political order and, in this sense, respect enemies as free and equal as far as is consistent with liberalism continuing to provide a stable answer to the political question. Liberals wait as long as is possible within the contingent constraints of providing such an answer before they treat their enemies differently from their friends.

If we look at this through the notion of citizenship, the liberal state will include all its members, including its enemies, as full citizens entitled to equal civil, political, and social rights. They are all free to act according to the law and have the right to claim the law's protection from other citizens but also from the state itself. The fact that they hold rival non-liberal conceptions of the political good does not affect either their membership of the political association or their status as a full and equal citizen. As is the case with liberal citizenship, this means that the state must practise a high degree of toleration and forbearance towards its enemies, refraining from interfering in an individual's actions unless they infringe upon the freedom of others, regardless of how morally repugnant or erroneous those in political power might find their beliefs to be, or, importantly, how contradictory they might be to liberal norms and values. The practice of liberal citizenship therefore grants individuals a large degree of freedom when it comes to conscience, speech, religious practice, and association (along with a whole host of further areas as well) all of which will be defended and protected by law if the individual believes that they have either been denied these freedoms or had their right to them violated. In effect, what liberals are saying is that they will agree to disagree with their political opponents, and let them carry on their lives as normal with all the rights and freedoms enjoyed by others, up until the point they threaten the liberal political order.

Liberal constitutionalism and the rule of law

As was remarked earlier, a fairly familiar liberal vision of constitutionalism is to see a legal system as providing the impartial framework through which persons and groups can pursue their freely chosen and different ends. On this account, the law is itself 'purposeless' insofar as it seeks to impose neither ends nor purposes on those subject to it. The role of constitutional law is not to act as a coercive mechanism for imposing one particular conception of the good but to restrict the use of political power towards those ends on which persons agree (or can reasonably be expected to agree) while protecting the freedom of individuals to pursue whatever way of life they choose. Law is neutral towards substantive ends.[21] As such, the liberal state is often conceived as being ruled by law rather than persons insofar as the power employed by the state is restrained and limited by a framework of laws and regulations that protect individual freedom, though they do not promote or protect any particular way of life, and which no ruler is able to legitimately transgress (and often these constitutional laws can be enforced by judicial review).

The realist view of constitutionalism is quite different. To quote Carr, the law 'is an expression of the will of the state, and is used by those who control the state as an instrument of coercion against those who oppose their power. The law is therefore the weapon of the stronger ... Law is regarded as binding because it is enforced by the strong arm of authority: it can be, and often is, oppressive'.[22] In this sense, constitutional law is not neutral toward substantive ends but is likely to be consciously directed towards enforcing and realising the purposes of the rulers over the ruled. That law is a normative system that serves particular ends and represses others is not, in and of itself, that revelatory a claim. But it is a different claim from saying that the law is not neutral to saying that it is not fair, just, impartial, etc., which is often what it is really being accused of when critics decry the neutrality of any legal system. Indeed, one might think that the law could only achieve any of these ideals if it is not neutral in either its aims or its effects. It is not the neutrality of law that realists emphasise but its effectively politicised nature, the idea that law is political in the sense that it is used as a tool in the struggle for power between those who reasonably hold different notions of the political good and, effectively, as a means for the rulers to maintain and preserve their rule over those that reject it. Law is both the weapon of the stronger and 'cannot be understood independently of the political foundation on which it rests and of the political interests which it serves'.[23] On the realist view, a constitution, even a liberal constitution, represents the 'rule of men' not the rule of law.

Of course, it is precisely because law can be used in the sort of oppressive manner that realism envisages that liberal constitutional theory takes the shape it does, using law to restrict political power to the defence of publicly justified ends and leaving individuals free to pursue their own ways of life. This, as we have seen throughout, is a way of respecting the freedom and moral equality of all persons despite their substantive disagreements about the good. But I want to suggest that the realist view of constitutionalism is key to understanding how a more realistic account of liberalism can respect its enemies despite their rejection of the liberal constitution. This begs the obvious question of how we can square the notion of law as necessarily oppressive with the liberal ideal that all persons be treated as free and equal.

This is not that difficult. A liberal realist account of constitutionalism must accept that the law does not represent the will of all persons, rather only the will of the rulers and (if all is going well) a significant majority of its citizens. But part of the will of the liberal governors includes placing restrictions on how political power is employed, including allowing all citizens, adversaries and enemies, the freedom to pursue their way of life as far as is consistent with other citizens having an equal degree of freedom. The role of the law in the creation and maintenance of the self-restraints that liberal states place on their own use of power is of particular importance in understanding how liberal realists respect the freedom and equality of enemies, active and not. In other words, we can completely accept the realist vision of constitutionalism while making a further claim that, even in liberal political orders where the law is intended to defend a status quo that not all accept, the law can nevertheless be designed to function in a way that protects and respects the freedom and equality of *all* individuals. The liberal rule of law is, as realism contends, a political decision that represents the oppressive will of one group over all others, and hence really the rule of men. But it is a rule of men that is purposefully restricted in order to respect the freedom and moral equality of all persons.

It therefore makes sense to continue to speak of the rule of law in liberal realist theory. Indeed the rule of law is central to the way the freedom and equality of enemies are respected despite their rejecting the liberal constitution. Judith Shklar presented us with two different versions of the rule of law, the first Aristotelian and the second, the one she supported and I want to make a limited appeal to, being linked primarily to the work of Montesquieu. In this version, the rule of law is 'those institutional restraints that prevent governmental agents from oppressing the rest of society'.[24] It is specifically intended to be of benefit to and apply to each and every member of society and, in doing so, provide the spirit of a criminal law that precludes the possibility of a 'dual state':

> Such a state may have a perfectly fair and principled law system, and also a harsh, erratic criminal control system, but it is a 'dual state' because some of its population is simply declared to be subhuman, and a public danger, and as such excluded from the legal order entirely. They are part of a second state, run usually by different agents of the government, but with the full approval of those who staff the 'first' of the two states.[25]

Examples of such a 'dual state' include the obvious candidates such as Nazi Germany, though also many states that purport to be liberal, such as the United States until the success of the civil rights movement. The rule of law, on this account, is intended to stand in contrast not merely with despotism but with this possibility of a dual state.[26]

The overriding objective of the rule of law (one that Shklar believed has been largely forgotten) is to protect the ruled from the rulers, in particular and, in a manner that clearly links to her work on the liberalism of fear, to provide the ruled with the freedom from fear. Shklar believed that there were certain types of human activity that simply could not be made liable to public control and regulation without physical cruelty, arbitrariness, or the creation of fear, such as religious belief and practice, consensual sex, or expressions of public opinion.[27] As such, the rule of law includes taking these areas of human life out of the legitimate remit of political control. This is a substantive account of the rule of law. Though she argued that the rule of law was not primarily about rights, nevertheless today such a view is often expressed in terms like the law must afford adequate protection of all people's fundamental human rights, such as to life, the prohibition of torture, slavery and forced labour, the right to liberty and security, to a fair trial, to marry, to education, and so on. But there is a proceduralist element to the rule of law also insofar as it demands that the relations of rule be calibrated in such a manner that power is checked by power. Once the proper remit of the political is determined, 'the only task of the judiciary was to condemn the guilty of legally known crimes defined as acts threatening the security of others, and to protect the innocent accused of such acts. Procedure in criminal cases is what the Rule of Law is about'.[28] In this sense, the rule of law ensures that there is no 'dual state' where some are denied equality before the law.

Liberal realism cannot easily endorse the substantive element of the rule of law. Not only does it accept the basic realist point that any issue can find itself part of the circumstances of politics and hence be in need of a public decision, it also needs to recognise that liberalism has, and should have, a transformative effect on persons' private beliefs. Such matters as religious belief cannot so easily be taken off the table. Moreover, and to reiterate the line of argument made in chapter 4, the fact of reasonable political disagreement makes it hard to see just how we would decide what these non-political issues, judged on their prospect of causing fear, should be. Yet somehow, being a theory of liberalism, it does need to have some sense in which substantive individual rights are protected, especially as this is central to understanding how liberalism's enemies are respected as free and equal. This is a problem for liberal realism that I want to address in the following section.

But the proceduralist aspect of the rule of law, that which says 'all persons and authorities within the state, whether public or private, should be bound by and entitled to the benefit of law publicly made, taking effect (generally) in the future and publicly administered in the courts', is far from insubstantial in its own right.[29] Rather it is also a key way in which liberalism respects its enemies, even when it recognises that it is imposing an alien will upon them. So, for instance, the rule of law guarantees that the laws of the land should apply equally to all, regardless of whether one is a political ally or political opponent. Everyone is treated equally with regard to the law irrespective of their political views. The rule of law implies at least that the law must be prospective (not retrospective), accessible, and as far as is possible intelligible, clear, and predictable. This ensures that enemies know when their actions violate the law and when, therefore, they should expect the coercive agencies of the state to take effect against them. The rule of law requires that questions of legal right and liability should ordinarily be resolved by application of the law and not the exercise of discretion on the part of individual judges or leaders.[30] Adjudicative procedures provided by the state must be fair even in cases pertaining to enemies, maybe especially in such cases. All in all, the rule of law helps make impermissible many of the most excessive potential costs of disagreeing with the political regime, including the midnight knock at the door, the sudden disappearance, the show trial, the confession extracted by torture, the gulag and the concentration camp, the gas chamber, the practice of genocide or ethnic cleansing, and the waging of aggressive internal wars.[31] This aspect of the rule of law helps ensure that no additional costs are imposed upon enemies until the point at which their actions make them 'active'. So the rule of law has a crucial role to play in demonstrating how the liberal state respects the freedom and equality of its enemies. It ensures that all persons are respected as free and equal, treated as full citizens due the same rights and liberties before the law, regardless of whether one endorses the liberal regime or not. Enemies are not to be treated any differently at any stage of the legal process, before they have been charged with a crime, once they have been charged, and once they have been found guilty, from liberalism's friends or adversaries.

While it may be true that masters are dangerous to oneself and to others insofar as they need not respect any moral limits to their power, liberal masters are those who put great store on the freedom and equality of those over whom they rule, indeed judge the legitimacy of the use of their power according to how far they respect such freedom and equality. Non-liberals do not need to agree that they are being treated as free and equal through these means, and I expect that they will continue to insist that they are being oppressed by the liberal state. But this account does offer an explanation *to liberals* as to how non-liberals are being treated as such and thus can provide the second necessary part of a realistic account of liberal legitimacy. This does not, of course, mean that all liberal states will be ideally restrained masters all the time. Masters can only be subject to *self*-restraints and hence even the most elaborate institutional designs for ensuring that such limitations to the use of power are respected can be overcome if they so desire. What is required is above all an ongoing willingness on the part of the masters to respect and abide by those self-restraints. This is undoubtedly a big ask. After all, the allures of power are such that rulers will always feel the temptation to do away with those restraints that they might see as obstacles to achieving their goals. This is why we must care about the moral character of our rulers. It also means that the citizenry at large has an important role to play in ensuring that the rulers maintain their commitment to these self-restraints by holding them to account if they transgress them. But the uncomfortable truth is that respecting the freedom and equality of liberalism's internal enemies depends more than anything else on the will of the masters themselves. It depends on them being willing to recognise, despite their hegemony, the distinction between active and inactive enemies and to respect the rule of law even when other considerations might make it easier or possibly more desirable for them to do otherwise.

Liberal realism and political constitutionalism

The final piece of liberal realism's moderate hegemony that I want to discuss is its commitment to a form of political and democratic constitutionalism. Liberal political theory, at least as exemplified in recent years by the work of those such as John Rawls, Ronald Dworkin and Bruce Ackerman, has tended towards what Richard Bellamy has called 'legal constitutionalism'. 'This approach', he writes, 'defines a constitution as a written document, superior to ordinary legislation and entrenched against legislative change, justiciable and constitutive of the legal and political system'.[32] John Gray has likewise noted that the model employed by Rawls and his followers 'draws heavily on an idealised version of US jurisprudence, [in which] basic questions about liberty and the restraint of liberty are decided by legal and not by political reasonings; by judicial review, not by legislation'.[33] One of the central assumptions behind legal constitutionalism is that we can come to a consensus as to the specific ends, principles, and goods that the constitution should embody, protect, or pursue. In the case of a liberal regime, this would include determining specific interpretations of the ideals of freedom and moral equality and what they demand in practice, often expressed in terms of rights that should form the fundamental constitutional law of that society.

The difficulty with legal constitutionalism from a realist perspective is that it overlooks that even liberals reasonably disagree as to how the ideals of freedom and equality are to be substantiated and hence as to the content and limits of our most fundamental rights. No such consensus, even amongst liberals, exists that could inform what the fundamental constitutional principles should be. In this sense, while a liberal political framework is an answer to the political question, and hopefully also the legitimacy question, it is never one that escapes being part of the circumstances of politics. For liberals reasonably continue to disagree about both the good and the right; the framework never stops being the subject of contestation though the question of what that framework should be is one on which a collective answer is needed. The political framework, though it determines the means through which future collective decisions are made, will always itself remain the subject of political debate. But furthermore, as I have been stressing, even liberal societies are made up not just of adversaries, those who advocate different forms of liberal politics, but of those who endorse non-liberal political ideals also, enemies. Though these might only represent a minority in a successful liberal state, their presence further undermines the sort of substantive consensus that legislative constitutionalism demands.

John Gray has gone so far as to claim that the constitutional entrenchment of fundamental rights leads to what he calls 'a sort of low-intensity civil war, in which the capture of legal institutions is only an episode'.[34] This is because 'In conflicts about basic constitutional rights, there can be no compromise solutions, only judgements which yield unconditional victory for one side and complete defeat for the other. It is plain that this is not a recipe for civil peace but rather for the loss of civility'.[35] In a sense, insofar as this is true, we might think that it is more problematic in relation to adversaries rather than enemies. We want adversaries to feel committed to the political framework even if it does not represent their own liberal ideal, that they are full members of the political community, not engaged in a civil war of any intensity. But liberals should feel less concerned about declaring unconditional victory against anti-liberal political ideals. After all, politics is a struggle for power, and the maintenance of that power, in the name of a particular set of values, ends, and goods. Liberals must lament neither their victory, where it has occurred, nor their continued preservation of power at the expense of non-liberal alternatives.

But this leaves the status of the political framework in liberal realism caught uncomfortably between two alternatives: on the one hand, the fact that liberals themselves disagree about how to interpret their core normative commitments means that there is no consensus on what principles should be constitutionally entrenched. In other words, liberal realism cannot have recourse to legal constitutionalism. Yet on the other hand, liberal realism does not want to fall into the sort of agonism advocated by Mouffe in which liberalism is but one of the competing families of political order without any privileged constitutional status at all.

The standard realist response to this problem, best exemplified by Bellamy and Waldron, has been to advocate a form of political constitutionalism that essentially understands the constitution as the democratic process through which collective and authoritative decisions are made. As Bellamy puts it,

A system of 'one person, one vote' provides citizens with roughly equal political resources; deciding by majority rule treats their views fairly and impartially; and party competition in elections and parliament institutionalises the balance of power that encourages the various sides to hear and harken to each other, promoting mutual recognition through the construction of compromises. According to this political conception, the democratic process *is* the constitution. It is both constitutional, offering a due process, and constitutive, able to reform itself.[36]

On such a view, the constitution is the democratic framework through which we can resolve our disagreements – though one that is itself the subject of ongoing disagreement. It does not entrench any particular interpretation of key liberal commitments in terms of fundamental rights but sees such fundamental political questions (e.g. the limits of freedom, the nature of citizens' rights, etc.) as temporarily settled via legislation. Such settlements are always open to being revisited and renegotiated in the future but they do provide a provisional yet still authoritative decision that all persons must accept, even if they disagree with it.

A commitment to political constitutionalism is the only way in which a theory of liberal realism can square the circle of providing a specifically liberal response to the political question while at the same time accepting that persons will disagree as to how liberal values or normative commitments are to be interpreted and substantiated in policy terms. Fundamental questions regarding what rights persons have, their relative priority if and when they clash, their content and limits, will be determined through the legislative process. Political constitutionalism, therefore, takes rights to be best conceived of as political rather than moral. While we seek to give all persons rights, and to protect them all equally, because of a pre-political moral commitment to all persons as free and equal moral beings, the rights themselves are thoroughly political constructs. Hence the nature, content and limits of these rights can and will change through the legislative process also. No one understanding, liberal or otherwise, of rights will become permanent. Liberal adversaries will continue to compete on such matters. But while the political framework of liberal realism must therefore be fundamentally democratic in nature, this is tempered with the moderate hegemony of liberalism which indirectly ensures people's commitments to liberal values and hence to policy positions that support liberal interpretations of, for instance, the question of rights. This will go as far as is possible, and consistent with liberal values themselves, to ensuring that the fundamental political questions, such as the sphere of individual freedom, the limits of toleration, and so on, are answered in a manner that represents a plausible interpretation of liberal commitments.

Political constitutionalism is also crucial for further understanding the manner in which liberal realism respects the freedom and equality of internal enemies in three ways. Firstly, and to echo what was said in the previous section, enemies have exactly the same democratic rights as every other citizen. This means that not only are they treated as a free and equal citizen, and confront each other as such when they engage in debates about public issues, but that their views are treated equally too. The democratic procedures allow for all views, interests, and perspectives to be expressed and to be shown equal concern. Secondly, the principle of majoritarianism does not deny the continuing existence of enemies' beliefs:

> Majority-decision does not require anyone's view to be played down or hushed up because of the fancied importance of consensus. In commanding our support and respect as a decision-procedure, majority-decision requires each of us not to pretend that there is a consensus where there is none, merely because we think that there ought to be – whether because any consensus is better than none, or because the view that strikes *some* of us as right seems so self-evidently so that we cannot imagine how anyone would hold to the contrary.[37]

In other words, political constitutionalism respects the reasonableness of enemies' disagreements with liberalism. Finally, the fact that the constitution is constitutive in the sense that it can reform itself does mean that enemies will always have an avenue to pursue their political ideals, if they so wish. Initially this means that enemies (as with adversaries) will always have the right to challenge those decisions that they reject, including decisions regarding the procedures for reaching collective decisions. But it also allows them the chance to secure the assent and collaboration of a majority of their fellow citizens so as to change that decision in the future. Of course, it will be very difficult indeed for liberalism's enemies to make the sort of wholesale changes that would be required to bring the political association in line with their anti-liberal ideals. Thoroughgoing fundamental political reform of this sort is a very difficult thing to complete without revolution, by bypassing the existing decision-making procedures. But liberal realism need not regret this fact (at least in relation to those political associations in which liberalism is well entrenched; it may in those circumstances where liberalism is struggling to get a permanent foothold). Nor need it celebrate it. But it does mean that, unlike many other forms of political order, liberalism's enemies have the opportunity to pursue their political ideals with at least some chance of realising them. So again, while the liberal state does stand in a relationship of mastery or domination to its internal enemies, this is not a relationship that needs to be seen as permanent.

Of course, such avenues of change and challenge that are open to liberalism's enemies exist against the backdrop of the moderate hegemony that I spoke of earlier. While they are trying to construct a majority in favour of their views they will be competing against the political association's ongoing attempt to transform or reinforce citizens' beliefs so as to be at least congruent with liberal values. They are effectively struggling against the state, a struggle that is clearly in no way equal. This inequality can undoubtedly lead to despair, resentment, anger, bitterness, and even hatred. A task of the liberal state will always be to manage those persons who feel this way. But because providing a stable framework is a necessary condition of an answer to the political question, no association, not even a liberal one, can afford not to engage in the sort of transformative activities described above. This will, if successful, ensure that the vast majority of legislative decisions are consistent with at least one interpretation of liberal values. Again, the point is that liberal realism protects and demonstrates its treatment of enemies as free and equal by granting them equal right to partake in the democratic process and to at least attempt to challenge and overturn liberal legislative decisions. As Hampton put it, 'In this kind of state, disgruntled residents are confronted not with tools of mastery but with procedures laid down by the governing convention for changing their rulers or the offices they hold or these procedures themselves'.[38] The hope is that the fact that enemies appreciate that all decisions are reversible will encourage them to remain broadly supportive of the political association, at least in the sense that they do not seek to change those decisions via means other than the established procedures.

It is more than likely that all of these attempts to accommodate and respect the freedom and equality of enemies are unlikely to be either appreciated or experienced as such by those that reject liberalism. Indeed, the willingness to allow religious fundamentalists to believe what they will or engage in the practices they regard as essential to their religion might be seen not as an attempt to minimise the extent of liberalism's mastery or domination over them, but as weakness or even as the imposition of the values of tolerance and freedom that they so abhor. Taking seriously the fact of political disagreement, and the reasonableness of political disagreement also, means that such different perspectives on the moral qualities of the political framework and fundamental political decisions will always and inevitably occur. There is no way beyond this. As such, it cannot be a condition of a realist account of liberal legitimacy that enemies themselves accept that they are being treated as free and equal.

In an important sense, what it is to be treated as free and equal, alongside the issue of whether such demands are being met in practice, are some of the most fundamental questions of politics over which we will therefore disagree. But the moral and practical constraints on the use of their power that I have outlined here, in an attempt to keep liberalism's hegemony moderate and minimise the extent to which domination and mastery is exercised, are important in explaining *to liberals* why it is that they have the moral and political right to claim legitimacy over their internal enemies. This is something that, as I have stressed throughout, should deeply worry liberals given their commitment to respecting each and every person's freedom and moral equality. And it is for this reason that they place extensive constraints on the use of their own power and endorse democratic procedures that accommodate enemies' views and give them the possibility of pursuing and enacting change (albeit one that is countered by their own use of state power). It is through these constraints that they respect enemies' freedom and equality.

But, and finally, we might think this account of legitimacy addresses the wrong audience: surely we want any account of legitimacy to *justify coercion to those being coerced*, not to justify it to those doing the coercing. In an important sense what I have argued for here is a series of justifications to enemies regarding their treatment as free and equal despite being forced to live according to principles they reject. They might not, indeed likely will not, be accepted as successful justifications by the internal enemies; but they are still justifications nonetheless. In conditions of radical yet reasonable political disagreement, universal consent is no longer a realistic or plausible avenue to pursue. Furthermore, because I have adopted a realist account of 'politics cannot be merely successful domination' rather than 'politics as distinct from successful domination', that such persons reject the justifications does not detract from the fact that the regime is an authoritative political order (even though the nature of the rule over them is properly speaking a form of domination). Political rule, even liberal rule, requires ruling over a group of people some of whom will disagree with you, your decisions, or even your right to rule in the first place.

Notes

1   See Beetham, *The Legitimation of Power*, pp. 17–18
2   Here I adapt Williams' thoughts about the similar question of who has to be satisfied that the Basic Legitimation Demand has been met (*In the Beginning was the Deed*, pp. 135–6)

3   See Sleat, 'Legitimacy in a non-ideal key'
4   Geuss, *Philosophy and Real Politics*, p. 35
5   *Ibid.*, pp. 35–6
6   S. Macedo, 'Transformative constitutionalism and the case of religion: Defending the moderate hegemony of liberalism', *Political Theory*, 26:1 (1998), 56–80, p. 76
7   *Ibid.*, pp. 56–7
8   *Ibid.*, p. 58
9   *Ibid.*, pp. 60–9
10 *Ibid.*, p. 69
11 *Ibid.*, p. 59
12 *Ibid.*, p. 69
13 *Ibid.*, p. 65
14 *Ibid.*, p. 70
15 *Ibid.*, p. 70
16 *Ibid.*, p. 72
17 Hampton, *Political Philosophy*, p. 91
18 *Ibid.*, p. 93
19 J. S. Mill, 'On Liberty', in ed. S. Collini, *On Liberty and Other Writings* (Cambridge: Cambridge University Press, 1989): 1–115; Kant, *The Metaphysics of Morals*
20 Kant, *The Metaphysics of Morals*, pp. 23–4
21 See, for example, L. Fuller, *The Morality of Law* (Virginia: Yale University Press, 1969)
22 Carr, *The Twenty Years' Crisis*, pp. 163–4
23 *Ibid.*, p. 166
24 Shklar, 'Political theory and the rule of law' in ed. Hoffman, *Judith N. Shklar – Political Thought and Political Thinkers*, p. 22
25 *Ibid.*, p. 22
26 *Ibid.*, p. 22
27 *Ibid.*, p. 22
28 *Ibid.*, p. 25
29 T. Bingham, *The Rule of Law* (London: Penguin Books, 2011), p. 8
30 It is this aspect of the rule of law as protection against discretionary and arbitrary rule that is most prominent in Hayek's discussion of this issue (F. A. Hayek, *The Road to Serfdom* (Oxon: Routledge, 2001), ch. 6)
31 Bingham, *The Rule of Law*, p. 9
32 Bellamy, *Political Constitutionalism*, p. 1
33 Gray, *Enlightenment's Wake*, p. 74
34 *Ibid.*, p. 77
35 *Ibid.*, p. 77
36 Bellamy, *Political Constitutionalism*, pp. 4–5
37 Waldron, *Law and Disagreement*, p. 111
38 Hampton, *Political Philosophy*, p. 108

Bibliography

Ackerman, B., 'Why dialogue?', *The Journal of Philosophy*, 86:1 (1989), 5–22

Barry, B., *Justice as Impartiality* (Oxford: Oxford University Press, 1995)

Barry, B., 'John Rawls and the search for stability', *Ethics*, 105:4 (1995), 874–915

Beetham, D., *The Legitimation of Power* (Hampshire: Palgrave, 1991)

Bell, D. (ed.), *Ethics and World Politics* (Oxford: Oxford University Press, 2010)

Bell, D. (ed.), *Political Thought and International Relations – Variations on a Realist Theme* (Oxford: Oxford University Press, 2009)

Bellamy, R., 'Dirty hands and clean gloves: Liberal ideals and real politics', *European Journal of Political Theory*, 9:4 (2010), 412–30

Bellamy, R., *Political Constitutionalism – A Republican Defence of the Constitutionality of Democracy* (Cambridge: Cambridge University Press, 2007)

Benson, P., 'External freedom according to Kant', *Columbia Law Review*, 87:3 (1987), 559–79

Bingham, T., *The Rule of Law* (London: Penguin Books, 2011)

Carr, E. H., *The Twenty Years' Crisis* (Basingstoke: Palgrave, 2001)

Coady, C. A. J., *Messy Morality – The Challenge of Politics* (Oxford: Oxford University Press, 2008)

Cohen, G. A., 'Facts and principles', *Philosophy and Public Affairs*, 31:3 (2003), 211–45

Connolly, W. E., *Pluralism* (USA: Duke University Press, 2005)

Crick, B., *In Defence of Politics* (London: Continuum, 2005)

Davion, V. and Wolf, C. (eds), *The Idea of a Political Liberalism: Essays on John Rawls* (Oxford: Rowman and Littlefield, 2000)

Dunn, J., *The Cunning of Unreason* (London: HarperCollins, 2000)

Dunn, J., 'Review of *Political Theory and the Displacement of Politics* by Bonnie Honig', *International Affairs*, 70:2 (1994), 321

Dworkin, G., 'Non-neutral principles', *Journal of Philosophy*, 71:14 (1974), 491–506

Dworkin, R., *Sovereign Virtue – The Theory and Practice of Equality* (London: Harvard University Press, 2002)

Dyzenhaus, D. (ed.), *Law as Politics – Carl Schmitt's Critique of Liberalism* (London: Duke University Press, 1998)

Erman, E., 'What is wrong with agonistic pluralism?: Reflections on conflict in democratic theory', *Philosophy and Social Criticism*, 35:9 (2009), 1039–62

Estlund, D., 'The insularity of the reasonable: Why political liberalism must admit the truth', *Ethics*, 108:2 (1998), 252–75

Farrelly, C., 'Justice in ideal theory: A refutation', *Political Studies*, 55 (2007), 844–64

Floyd J. and Stears, M. (eds), *Political Philosophy versus History? Contextualism and Real Politics in Contemporary Political Thought* (Cambridge: Cambridge University Press, 2011)

Forrester, K., 'Judith Shklar, Bernard Williams and political realism', *European Journal of Political Theory*, 11:3 (2012), 247–72

Freeden, M., *Ideologies and Political Theory: A Conceptual Approach* (Oxford: Oxford University Press, 1996)

Freyenhagen, F., 'Taking reasonable pluralism seriously: An internal critique of political liberalism', *Politics, Philosophy and Economics*, 10:3 (2011), 323–42

Fuller, L., *The Morality of Law* (Virginia: Yale University Press, 1969)

Galston, W., 'Realism in political theory', *European Journal of Political Theory*, 9:4 (2010), 385–411

Gaus, G. F., *Contemporary Theories of Liberalism* (London: Sage, 2003)

Gaus, G. F., 'Reasonable pluralism and the domain of the political: How the weaknesses of John Rawls's political liberalism can be overcome by a justificatory liberalism', *Inquiry*, 42:2 (1999), 259–84

Gaus, G. F., *Justificatory Liberalism: An Essay on Epistemology and Political Theory* (Oxford: Oxford University Press, 1996)

Geuss, R., *Politics and the Imagination* (Oxford: Princeton University Press, 2010)

Geuss, R., 'Realismus, Wunschdenken, Utopie', *Deutsche Zeitschrift für Philosophie*, 58:3 (2010), 419–29

Geuss, R., *Philosophy and Real Politics* (Oxford: Princeton University Press, 2008)

Geuss, R., *Outside Ethics* (Oxford: Princeton University Press, 2005)

Geuss, R., *History and Illusion in Politics* (Cambridge: Cambridge University Press, 2001)

Gray, J., *Two Faces of Liberalism* (New York: New Press, 2000)

Gray, J., *Enlightenment's Wake* (London: Routledge, 1995)

Gürsözlü, F., 'Agonism and deliberation – Recognising the difference', *The Journal of Political Philosophy*, 17:3 (2009), 356–68

Hampton, J., *Political Philosophy* (USA: Westview Press, 1998)

Hayek, F. A., *The Road to Serfdom* (Oxon: Routledge, 2001)

Holmes, S., *The Anatomy of Anti-Liberalism* (London: Harvard University Press, 1996)

Honig, B., *Political Theory and the Displacement of Politics* (New York: Cornell University Press, 1993)

Horton, J., 'Realism, liberal moralism and a political theory of modus vivendi', *European Journal of Political Theory*, 9:4 (2010), 431–48

Jackson, B. and Stears, M. (eds), *Liberalism as Ideology: Essays in Honour of Michael Freeden* (Oxford: Oxford University Press, 2012)

Kant, I., *Groundwork of the Metaphysics of Morals*, ed. Mary Gregor (Cambridge: Cambridge University Press, 1997)

Kant, I., *Political Writings*, ed. Hans Reiss (Cambridge: Cambridge University Press, 1997)

Kant, I., *The Metaphysics of Morals*, ed. Mary Gregor (Cambridge: Cambridge University Press, 1996)

Kant, I., *Logic* (New York: Dover Publications, 1974)

Kekes, J., 'Cruelty and liberalism', *Ethics*, 106:4 (1996), 834–44

Kelly, P., *Liberalism* (Cambridge: Polity Press, 2005)

Kirkland, P. E., 'Nietzsche's tragic realism', *The Review of Politics*, 72:1 (2010), 55–78

Knops, A., 'Agonism as deliberation – On Mouffe's theory of democracy', *The Journal of Political Philosophy*, 15:1 (2007), 115–26

Kukathas, C., *The Liberal Archipelago: A Theory of Diversity and Freedom* (Oxford: Oxford University Press, 2007)

Kymlicka, W., *Multicultural Citizenship: A Liberal Theory of Minority Rights* (Oxford: Oxford University Press, 1996)

Larmore, C., 'The moral basis of political liberalism', *The Journal of Philosophy*, 96:12 (1999), 599–625

Larmore, C., 'Pluralism and reasonable disagreement', *Social Philosophy and Policy*, 11:1 (1994), 61–79

Larmore, C., 'Political liberalism', *Political Theory*, 18 (1990), 339–60

Lassman, P., *Pluralism* (Cambridge: Polity, 2011)

Leopold, D. and Stears, M. (eds), *Political Theory – Methods and Approaches* (Oxford: Oxford University Press, 2008)

Levy, J. T., *The Multiculturalism of Fear* (Oxford: Oxford University Press, 2000)

Long, G., *Relativism and the Foundations of Liberalism* (Exeter: Imprint Academic, 2004)

Macedo, S., 'Transformative constitutionalism and the case of religion: Defending the moderate hegemony of liberalism', *Political Theory*, 26:1 (1998), 56–80

Macedo, S., *Liberal Virtues: Citizenship, Virtue and Community in Liberal Constitutionalism* (Oxford: Clarendon Press, 1991)

Macedo, S., 'The politics of justification', *Political Theory*, 18:2 (1990), 280–304

MacIntyre, A., *After Virtue* (London: Duckworth Press, 2004)

Manin, B., 'On legitimacy and political deliberation', *Political Theory*, 15 (1987), 338–69

Margalit, A., *On Compromise and Rotten Compromises* (Oxford: Princeton University Press, 2010)

Mason, A., 'Rawlsian theory and the circumstances of politics', *Political Theory*, 3:5 (2010), 658–83

Mason, A., 'Just constraints', *British Journal of Political Science*, 34:2 (2004), 251–68

McCabe, D., *Modus Vivendi Liberalism* (Cambridge: Cambridge University Press, 2010)

McCormick, J. P., *Carl Schmitt's Critique of Liberalism* (Cambridge: Cambridge University Press, 1999)

McKinnon, C. and Castiglione, D. (eds), *The Culture of Toleration in Diverse Societies* (Manchester: Manchester University Press, 2003)

Mill, J. S., *On Liberty and Other Writings*, ed. S. Collini (Cambridge: Cambridge University Press, 1989)

Morgenthau, H. J., *Politics among Nations – The Struggle for Power and Peace*, 4th ed. (New York: Alfred A. Knopf, 1967)

Morgenthau, H. J., *Scientific Man vs. Power Politics* (Chicago: Chicago University Press, 1946)

Mouffe, C., *On the Political* (London: Routledge, 2005)

Mouffe, C., *The Return of the Political* (London: Verso, 2005)

Nagel, T., *Equality and Partiality* (Oxford: Oxford University Press, 1991)

Nagel, T., 'Moral conflict and political legitimacy', *Philosophy and Public Affairs*, 16:3 (1987), 215–40

Neal, P., *Liberalism and its Discontents* (New York: New York University Press, 1997)

Newey, G., 'Two dogmas of liberalism', *European Journal of Political Theory*, 9:4 (2010), 449–65

Newey, G., *Hobbes and Leviathan* (Oxon: Routledge, 2007)

Newey, G., *After Politics – The Rejection of Politics in Contemporary Liberal Philosophy* (Basingstoke: Palgrave, 2001)

Niebuhr, R., *The Children of Light and the Children of Darkness* (London: University of Chicago Press, 2011)

Niebuhr, R., *Moral Man and Immoral Society* (London: Continuum, 2005)

Nussbaum, M. C., 'Perfectionist liberalism and political liberalism', *Philosophy & Public Affairs*, 39:1 (2011), 3–45

Ortega y Gasset, J., *The Revolt of the Masses* (London: Unwin Books, 1969)

Philp, M., 'What is to be done? Political theory and political realism', *European Journal of Political Theory*, 9:4 (2010), 466–84

Philp, M., *Political Conduct* (London: Harvard University Press, 2007)

Quong, J., *Liberalism without Perfection* (Oxford: Oxford University Press, 2010)

Quong, J., 'Disagreement, asymmetry, and liberal legitimacy', *Politics, Philosophy & Economics*, 4:3 (2005), 301–30

Rawls, J., *Lectures on the History of Political Philosophy*, ed. S. Freeman (London: Harvard University Press, 2007)

Rawls, J., *A Theory of Justice – Revised Edition* (Oxford: Oxford University Press, 1999)

Rawls, J., *Collected Papers*, ed. S. Freeman (London: Harvard University Press, 1999)

Rawls, J., *Political Liberalism* (New York: Columbia University Press, 1996)

Raz, J., *The Morality of Freedom* (Oxford: Oxford University Press, 1986)

Rorty, R., *Contingency, Irony, and Solidarity* (Cambridge: Cambridge University Press, 1989)

Rossi, E., 'Modus vivendi, consensus, and (realist) liberal legitimacy', *Public Reason*, 2:2, 21–39

Rousseau, J. J., *The Social Contract and Other Later Political Writings*, ed. Victor Gourevitch (Cambridge: Cambridge University Press, 1997)

Runciman, D., 'What is realistic political philosophy?', *Metaphilosophy*, 43:1-2 (2012), 58–70

Schmitt, C., *Political Theology* (USA: University of Chicago Press, 2005)

Schmitt, C., *The Concept of the Political* (London: University of Chicago Press, 1996)

Schmitt, C., *The Crisis of Parliamentary Democracy* (Cambridge: MIT Press, 1985)

Shklar, J. N., *Political Thought and Political Thinkers*, ed. S. Hoffman (London: University of Chicago Press, 1998)

Simmons, A. J., 'Ideal and nonideal theory', *Philosophy and Public Affairs*, 38:1 (2010), 3–36

Simmons, A. J., 'Justification and legitimacy', *Ethics*, 109:4 (1999), 739–71

Sleat, M., 'Coercing non-liberal persons: Considerations on a more realistic liberalism', *European Journal of Political Theory*, forthcoming

Sleat, M., 'Legitimacy in a non-ideal key', *Political Theory*, 40:5 (2012), 650–6

Sleat, M., 'Bernard Williams and the possibility of a realist political theory', *European Journal of Political Theory*, 9:4 (2010), 485–503

Sleat, M., 'Liberalism, fundamentalism and truth', *Journal of Applied Philosophy*, 23:4 (2006), 405–17

Sorel, G., *Reflections on Violence*, ed. J. Jennings (Cambridge: Cambridge University Press, 1999)

Stears, M., 'Liberalism and the politics of compulsion', *British Journal of Political Science*, 37 (2007), 533–53

Stemplowska, Z., 'What's ideal and ideal theory?', *Social Theory and Practice*, 34 (2008), 331–40

Swift, A., 'The value of philosophy in non-ideal circumstances', *Social Theory and Practice*, 34 (2008), 363–87

Tamir, Y., 'The land of the fearful and the free', *Constellations*, 3:3 (1997), 296–314

Tully, J., *Public Philosophy in a New Key – Volume I: Democracy and Civic Freedom* (Cambridge: Cambridge University Press, 2008)

Tully, J., *Public Philosophy in a New Key – Volume II: Imperialism and Civic Freedom* (Cambridge: Cambridge University Press, 2008)

Valentini, L., 'On the apparent paradox of ideal theory', *Journal of Political Philosophy*, 17:3 (2009), 332–55

Waldron, J., *Law and Disagreement* (Oxford: Oxford University Press, 1999)

Waldron, J., *The Dignity of Legislation* (Cambridge: Cambridge University Press, 1999)

Waldron, J., 'Theoretical foundations of liberalism', *The Philosophical Quarterly*, 37 (1987), 127–50

Weber, M., *The Vocation Lectures*, eds D. Owen and T. B. Strong (Cambridge: Hackett, 2004)

Weber, M., *Political Writings*, eds P. Lassman and R. Speirs (Cambridge: Cambridge University Press, 1994)

Whelan, F. G., *Hume and Machiavelli: Political Realism and Liberal Thought* (Oxford: Lexington Books, 2004)

Williams, B., *In the Beginning was the Deed* (Oxford: Princeton University Press, 2005)

Williams, B., *Truth and Truthfulness* (Oxford: Princeton University Press, 2002)

Williams, B., *Ethics and the Limits of Philosophy* (London: Fontana, 1985)

Williams, M. C. (ed.), *Realism Reconsidered: The Legacy of Hans J. Morgenthau* (Oxford: Oxford University Press, 2007)

Williams, M. C., *The Realist Tradition and the Limits of International Relations* (Cambridge: Cambridge University Press, 2005)

Wolfe, C., *Natural Law Liberalism* (Cambridge: Cambridge University Press, 2006)

Wolff, R. P., *In Defence of Anarchism* (London: University of California Press, 1998)

Wolin, S., 'The liberal/democratic divide. On Rawls' political liberalism', *Political Theory*, 24:1 (1996), 97–119

Young, S. P. (ed.), *Reflections on Rawls – An Assessment of his Legacy* (Surrey: Ashgate, 2009)

Index

Lightning Source UK Ltd.
Milton Keynes UK
UKOW01f1510241017
311556UK00003B/211/P